BOULDER MONUMENTS OF SASKATCHEWAN

G. Ian Brace
(Wapiskisew Mikisew)

Saskatchewan Archaeological Society
Saskatoon, Saskatchewan

2005

Saskatchewan Archaeological Society
#1 – 1730 Quebec Avenue
Saskatoon, Saskatchewan S7K 1V9
Tel.: (306) 664-4124
Fax: (306) 665-1928
E-mail: saskarchsoc@sasktel.net
Web Site: saskarchaeologicalsociety.ca

Library and Archives Canada Cataloguing in Publication

Brace, Geoffrey Ian, 1942-
Boulder Monuments of Saskatchewan / G. Ian Brace (Wapiskisew Mikisew).

Includes bibliographical references.
ISBN: 0-9691420-5-6

1. Indians of North America—Saskatchewan—Antiquities.
2. Boulders—Saskatchewan.
3. Sacred space—Saskatchewan.
4. Excavations (Archaeology)—Saskatchewan.
5. Saskatchewan—Antiquities.
I. Saskatchewan Archaeological Society
II. Title.

E78.S2B72 2005   971.24'01
C2005-902539-5

Front cover photo by Saskatchewan Archaeological Society, of the Cabri Lake Human Effigy (1988). Back cover: top photo by George Tosh, of Moose Mountain Medicine Wheel (1987), bottom photo by George Tosh and Ted Douglas, of Roy Rivers ceremonial circle (1990). Drawing of Big Beaver bison effigy by Royal Saskatchewan Museum.

Cover design by Tim Jones and Arlene Karpan.

Printed and bound in Canada by Houghton Boston, Saskatoon

To my grandmothers,
Gertrude White Sears and Kokum Marie Major,
for instilling a love for resolving the unknown

CONTENTS

FIGURES

TABLES

FOREWORD

This is a comprehensive book on the boulder monuments of Saskatchewan suitable for a wide readership. Humanity benefits from an understanding of the human past and the diverse modes of expression that ancient cultures practiced. These archaeological features are particularly fragile, and should be considered to be under permanent threat of disturbance or destruction either from inadvertence through agricultural and other activities that alter the surface of the landscape, or from vandalism.

The Saskatchewan Archaeological Society advocates for the protection and documentation of all archaeological sites. We believe that this book offers better knowledge of these sites' existence and their significance. This will help to promote respect and protection for these wonderful and awe-inspiring remnants of past human endeavour.

Ian Brace presents a well-documented and precise look at many important boulder configurations both in Saskatchewan and beyond, and proposes a number of hypotheses aimed at understanding the age and authorship of these sites. There remain many theories and speculations on the meanings, ages and functions of Saskatchewan's boulder monuments, making it difficult for any one scholar to deal with such a wide range of prehistoric phenomena. Still, this book is a major contribution to our understanding of these monuments, in Saskatchewan and across the Great Plains.

The author has noted that a great deal more research needs to be done on all aspects of this subject, from the development of better techniques for dating the sites, to carrying out more ethnological and ethnohistorical research, to simply recording more detailed information at sites where monuments may have been cursorily described. A photo boom, developed by Montana archaeologist John Brumley, that records the features by taking vertical photographs, has removed much of the subjectivity involved in other forms of mapping, yet has had the benefit of no contact or impact with the features or monuments. Using this boom, the Saskatchewan Archaeological Society will continue its long–term program of accurately recording boulder monuments and other boulder configurations such as tipi rings and vision quest site pits.

We wish to sincerely thank all the donors and sponsors who have financially supported this publication. Our intent is to get the book directly into the hands of landowners and lessees, as well as various government offices, to ensure that everyone fully comprehends the importance of these features on our landscape. This is a responsibility we all as individuals, agencies, organizations and governments share as stewards of these archaeological sites.

Norma Fraser, President
Saskatchewan Archaeological Society
April, 2005

PREFACE

The purpose of this publication is to present information on, and an appreciation for, one of the most striking aspects of the cultural landscape of the Saskatchewan portion of the Great Plains of North America. Some of the more spectacular of these Saskatchewan sites are, by any measure, important as a part of the world's cultural heritage. By so doing, I fervently hope that we will not lose any more of these precious sites.

This book is based mostly on research done as part of the requirements for my Master of Arts degree in anthropology at the University of Alberta in Edmonton, completed in 1987. A few words on this fact are necessary. First, it must be acknowledged that other archaeologists have carried out research and have published on Northern Plains boulder monuments since 1980, notably John Brumley (1988) and Rod Vickers (2003) but little detailed recording or publication has been done on Saskatchewan sites in the past 25 years. An additional goal of this book is to challenge others to re-study the sites discussed herein, and to carry out recording for archival purposes of the many sites incompletely recorded or cursorily studied.

It must be emphasized that any visitation to these sites must be predicated on the premise that these are sacred sites, and deserve the same kind of respect most people practise when they enter a church, synagogue or mosque. To that end, the *Guidelines for Visiting Archaeological Sites* developed by the Saskatchewan Archaeological Society are a good guide.

The exact site locations are not given in this book as many of the boulder monuments are on private land or relatively inaccessible (or both). A few, though, are well-known and may be visited; contact the provincial agency in charge of archaeological heritage management for such information. All boulder monuments in Saskatchewan have the automatic designation of "Sites of a Special Nature" under *The Saskatchewan Heritage Property Act*, and there are severe penalties for anyone who harms such a site. Further, anyone wishing to carry out intensive research at any such site must do so under a permit, and must be qualified.

This study has the limitation of being not comprehensive, in that it does not deal with many "new" sites found in the years intervening between the completion of the thesis and 2005. However, the book discusses a body of sites that may fairly be characterized as the major monuments in Saskatchewan. Further, it proposes a classification scheme and a number of hypotheses, both suitable for debate and testing, which together should provide a good context for new studies which may advance our understanding in the future. One approach which I hope will have promise is the dating of individual monuments and associated features through the technique of lichenometry. With the publication of this book I therefore "pass the torch" to others who desire to better understand the cultural underpinnings of these rare and fascinating features; there is abundant room for new and different research approaches.

This book is not simply a reprint of my thesis. I have modified or discarded some of my speculations and initial interpretations as my continuing research has proceeded. The text has been edited and re-arranged, and this book benefits from the inclusion of both colour and black and white photographs from a number of people. I especially thank George Tosh and Ted Douglas for their contributions in this regard.

The issue of "tribal" names – and indeed the very word tribe – needs to be discussed. "Tribe" is more or less an anthropological construct, meaning a group of people who share a territory, language, way of life and common identity. In fact, it is common for one or more of these factors to be absent, or for them to be apparent in aggregate only to an outside observer (such as an anthropologist). In short, what are called tribes in the historical and ethnological literature should be considered abstractions and not having a fixed reality or being the same in all cases; nevertheless, the term should be considered as a convenient, approximate way to deal with the diversity of ethnic entities which have lived in this region or "passed through" in a relatively brief period of time, during the past 600 to 700 years or so. Two complicating factors for the uninitiated reader are the variety of names used to refer to particular groups during the historic period, and the fact that many Canadian First Nations and Native Americans have adopted names that they now use for themselves in their own aboriginal languages (for example, Tsu T'ina for Sarcee, and Anishinabeg for Ojibwa). I have followed the usage embodied in the authoritative modern ethnological series, *Handbook of North American Indians* (DeMallie 2001).

Also concerning terminology: the alert reader will note that a number of site names (e.g. Roy Rivers Medicine Wheel) given to sites when they were first recorded, and used in the literature, assume a certain "function" or categorization of the site. The reader will also note that some of these monuments have been reinterpreted as ceremonial circles in the present study; however, we are obligated to use those original, official names.

I have endeavoured, through what I have learned from my teachers, the Elders, to follow proper protocol and respect in visiting sites, seeking information on the sites, and in my motivation in telling the wider world about these things. These things have been done in the spirit of seeking genuine understanding, which is the first step in fostering inter-connectedness between all cultures. I urge everyone to seek such knowledge in the same spirit: this is what the Elders ask.

AUTHOR'S ACKNOWLEDGEMENTS

I gratefully acknowledge the assistance, co-operation, and guidance generously bestowed by many individuals and institutions. The field work was funded by the Archaeological Section of the Royal Saskatchewan Museum (formerly called Saskatchewan Museum of Natural History). Tim Jones of the Saskatchewan Archaeological Society was responsible for locating the requisite finances, and managing the development of the manuscript into this publication. I thank the Saskatchewan Archaeological Society for initiating the idea of turning my thesis into book form, and for its efforts in achieving this reality. Tim Jones and Kim Wutzke of the Society carried out all the production work.

I especially thank my thesis advisor at the University of Alberta in Edmonton, Dr. Ruth Gruhn, formerly of the Department of Anthropology. She took on the colossal task of supervising a thesis written 690 kilometers southeast of Edmonton, with continuous and well-timed correspondences, and was a constant inspiration with well-directed instruction toward my perception of learning succinct expression.

I express appreciation to Dr. Charles Schweger, Dr. Bill Byrne, and Dr. G. Freeman, the other members of my examining committee, for their recommendations of chapter content and organization. Particular gratitude is acknowledged to Dr. John Sheard of the Department of Biology at the University of Saskatchewan in Saskatoon who identified the lichens on the numerous boulders I transported to Saskatoon, gave instruction on the recognition characteristics of *Dimelaena oreina*, and provided me with many English translations of lichenometry publications and source references. Dr. I. M. Brodo of the National Museum of Natural Sciences in Ottawa provided information to additional lichenometric analysis and published sources. I express appreciation to Dr. I. G. Dyck, Dr. Gerald T. Conaty and Dr. Margaret G. Hanna of the Royal Saskatchewan Museum for their many contributions and instruction; their patient guidance and constant availability to act as adjudicators to my multitude of theories, proposals, and occasional delinquent conceptions.

Appreciation is expressed to the numerous individuals who supplied reference or research publications from their institutions' libraries: Dr. Thomas J. Green, State Archaeologist, Idaho State Historical Society; Ray D. Lyons, Staff Archaeologist, Colorado Historical Society; Dr. Larry J. Zimmerman and Dr. Linea Sundstrom, Archaeological Laboratory, University of South Dakota; Dr. Les B. Davis, Montana State University; Dr. Ken Deaver, Professional Analyst, Oregon; Gayle F. Carlson, Curator of Anthropology, Nebraska State Historical Society; Dr. Leigh Syms, Manitoba Museum of Man and Nature; Gary Dickson, Assistant Archaeologist, Manitoba Historic Resources Branch; Dr. Richard Forbis, University of Calgary (deceased); Dr. Tom Lennon, Western Cultural Resource Management Incorporation, Boulder, Colorado; and Mrs. J. Hallworth, Department of Biology, University of Calgary.

Gratitude for unpublished data on boulder monuments is extended to the Archaeological Survey of Alberta in Edmonton. Additionally, Chris Rutkowski of Winnipeg, Dr. Bev Nicholson of Brandon University, Dr. Leigh Syms of the Manitoba Museum of Man and Nature, and Dr.

Morgan J. Tamplin of the University of Toronto, all gave permission to include their Manitoba unpublished boulder monument researches in this thesis.

Gratitude is expressed (posthumously) to Jim Ryder (Nakota Elder) formerly of the Saskatchewan Indian Federated College, University of Regina (now First Nations University of Canada), for his insight and his identification of the badger feature (formerly identified by Euro-Canadian archaeologists as a turtle outline). Isadore Pelletier (Saulteaux Elder), Dexter Asapace (Cree Elder), Velma Goodfeather (Lakota Elder), Howard Cameron (Willow Cree Elder), and the Wanuskewin Elders Council all extended permission to publish the data within this thesis, providing that no sacred ceremonies are described. Don Pinay of the Yorkton Tribal Council provided invaluable insight into First Nations' philosophy and ideology.

Keith (deceased) and Nora Arnold and Bob and Donna Grandy and their families provided me with the initial site record for DgMn-3, the largest and most impressive boulder site known to me; they have all extended friendship and room and board during my many excursions – words cannot express my true feelings toward these friends. My gratitude is extended to Ken Reischke of Glen Ewen for flying me over DgMn-3 so that I might appreciate the complete site extent. Special appreciation is extended posthumously to Russel Lawrence of Maple Creek; Russel was a good friend and a very enjoyable old cowboy who gave insight to depictions of both prehistoric and historic vintage. Ralph (deceased) and Karen Berg at Cabri, R.C.M.P. Sgt. Chuck Appelton (formerly at Cabri, now at Kamloops), Doug Richards of Plenty, and Marvel Houston (deceased) of Ruthilda were all excellent tour guides, provided room and board and much-needed access to bathing facilities during my field research, which lasted weeks at a time.

Additional gratitude is extended to all others who assisted my numerous research forays at a great variety of university, public and private libraries. And to the many family and friends who provided editorial and emotional support during the many long days, months and years when I was unavailable for their needs, I express my eternal gratitude for your understanding.

PUBLISHER'S ACKNOWLEDGEMENTS

The publication of this book has been made possible with the generous support of the following institutions and individuals:

The EJLB Foundation, Montréal, Québec
Arsenal Energy Ltd., Calgary, Alberta (Michael Vandale)
Historical Resource Management Ltd., Calgary, Alberta (Jim Light)
Western Heritage Services Ltd., Saskatoon, Saskatchewan
Keystone Energy Corp., Regina, Saskatchewan (E. Craig Lothian)
FMA Heritage Resources Consultants Inc., Calgary, Alberta
True Energy, Calgary, Alberta
Bison Historical Services Ltd., Calgary, Alberta

Phillips & Co. Barristers & Solicitors, Regina, Saskatchewan (Mervin C. Phillips)
Standing Buffalo Dakota Nation Chief and Council, Fort Qu'Appelle, Saskatchewan
Tatanka Najin School (Standing Buffalo School), Fort Qu'Appelle, Saskatchewan
Leslie J. Amundson, Wakaw, Saskatchewan
Jeff Baldwin, North Battleford, Saskatchewan
Ron and Mary Ann Barnett, Oyen, Alberta
Ray Cooper, Laporte, Saskatchewan
Ted and Allene Douglas, Eatonia, Saskatchewan
Ian Dyck, Orleans, Ontario
Orly Felton, Saskatoon, Saskatchewan
Chris and Laura Foley, Saskatoon, Saskatchewan
Stella Fowler, Surrey, British Columbia
Fulton and Ruth Heron, Cabri, Saskatchewan
Sandra Hill, Swift Current, Saskatchewan
Jerry Iverson, Meota, Saskatchewan
Kim Johnson, Victoria, British Columbia
Tim and Louise Jones, Saskatoon, Saskatchewan
Leith Knight, Moose Jaw, Saskatchewan
Elmer Lahti, Rosetown, Saskatchewan
Catherine Laratte, Saskatoon, Saskatchewan
Anna and Ted Leighton, Saskatoon, Saskatchewan
Doug Melton, Miles City, Montana
Wilda O'Brien, North Battleford, Saskatchewan
Adrian Paton, Arcola, Saskatchewan
Norma Fraser and George Rogers, Regina, Saskatchewan
Alan Schroedl, Salt Lake City, Utah
Barry Singer, Saskatoon, Saskatchewan
Doug Smith, Dagmar, Montana
Eleanor and Ove Smith, Kindersley, Saskatchewan
Wendy Unfreed, Calgary, Alberta
Gil Watson, Regina, Saskatchewan
White Eagle, Regina, Saskatchewan

The S.A.S. is a Provincial Cultural Organization
member of SaskCulture Inc. and receives funding from

1 - INTRODUCTION

Definition and Classification

A boulder monument, like other Aboriginal boulder configurations, is a human construction made by laying boulders on (or perhaps shallowly dug into) the prairie surface, to a purpose. Thousands upon thousands of configurations made by people were once found across the Great Plains of North America, and beyond, made for a variety of reasons (Figs. 1, 2, 119). By "monument" I mean two things: a configuration made for a putative extraordinary purpose, such as commemorating an important event in the life of an individual or tribe, or as a remnant or reminder of a religious ceremony, to mention only two possibilities; and secondarily, a construction often of large size. The outlines and figures created by this process consist of circles, straight and curved lines, anthropomorphic and animal figures, geometric designs and line, circle and cairn combinations.

On the Great Plains, boulder monuments are scattered from central Saskatchewan and Alberta to northern Wyoming and central Nebraska (Fig. 3). They are observed from the Rocky Mountain eastern foothills and mountain areas of Idaho and Montana to the mixed forests of Manitoba, Ontario and Minnesota. One feature found near most of these monument sites is stone circles (tipi rings), evidencing habitation (Kehoe 1954; Finnigan 1982; Graspointner 1980) (Fig. 4). This conjunction may indicate a communal involvement or intent in the creation of such features. Significance to an individual may be surmised where the monument is the single observed feature. In all instances, the majority of the available boulders have been re-arranged to construct the various monuments and related features, indicating clear purpose and intent – even if we cannot always discern what the purpose and intentions of the builders were.

The recorded boulder monument sites represent a fraction of what once existed. Oral and early historic accounts report numerous alignments that were destroyed because of lack of recognition or purposeful destruction of a previous culture's symbolism some Euro-Canadians/ Americans considered "heathen". As well, untold numbers have fallen accidental victim to agricultural and industrial activities that have drastically modified the land's surface (Fig. 120).

What do boulder monuments represent? Are they ceremonial remnants, border/trail markers similar to the rock constructions used by early hunters and as taught among groups

Figure 1: Probable bison drive lines in the Cabri Lake Hills, in the snow.
Note the stone circles, and telephone poles for scale

Figure 2: The Saskatchewan short grass Prairie Ecozone holds a wide variety and number of boulder configurations.
Some, like this boulder-lined "pit" feature near Cabri Lake, may have been vision-questing places

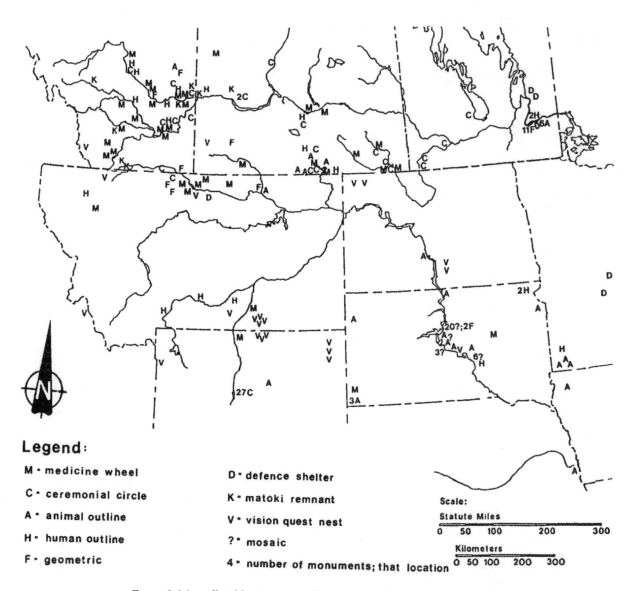

Legend:

M - medicine wheel
C - ceremonial circle
A - animal outline
H - human outline
F - geometric

D - defence shelter
K - matoki remnant
V - vision quest nest
? - mosaic
4 - number of monuments; that location

Scale:
Statute Miles
0   50   100   200   300

Kilometers
0 50 100   200   300

Figure 3: Map of boulder monument locations on the northern Great Plains

such as the Boy Scouts; or are they remnants of children's games? And finally, can their purpose or function be identified by reviewing ethno-historical accounts, surveyor's records and Native American oral histories?

Figure 4: Drawing of the Wild Man Butte effigy and associated stone circle

Previous investigators have defined some of the boulder monuments as "medicine wheels" (Dempsey 1956, Grey 1963, Kehoe 1973), "stone monuments" (Lewis 1889, 1890), "boulder mosaics" (Todd 1886) and "vision quest structures" (Fredlund 1969, Carmichael 1979). Others (Eddy 1975; Kehoe and Kehoe 1976) view some of them as being astroarchaeological or calendrical observation recording systems. The diversity of definitions, also noted by Eddy (1979:153) has been a motivation for this author to devise a classification scheme whereby these monuments might be described better and analyzed by reference to the cultural phenomena to which they seem to pertain. In addition to reviewing written sources, personal consultations with Elders (Cree, Saulteaux, Blackfoot, Dakota, Nakota, Cheyenne, Atsina and Ojibwa) have been conducted. Some different Tribal Elders proposed diametrically opposite identifications. In those instances, the analysis by the tribal group known to be most closely associated with a specific monument was the one chosen as perhaps the most authoritative. While this analysis may be imperfect, it aims to present a beginning point toward achieving a greater understanding of the cultural connections of these sites.

Boulder monuments are constructed of glacial drift boulders and rock slabs which are readily available on the prairie surface. These boulders were found in the local environment, in some places in greater concentrations than others, in the glacial deposits that blanket most of southern Saskatchewan. For the most part these boulders are bread loaf-sized. Individual boulders range in size from approximately 0.15 to 0.50 cubic meters (m³), with an overall average size approximating 0.30 m³. The boulders are generally regular in their exterior features; and are elliptical, trianguloid, rectanguloid or cuboid in shape. The more common rock types used were metamorphic (quartzite) and igneous (granite) rock, with sedimentary rocks (limestone, dolomite, shale, sandstone) and conglomerates representing the least used varieties.

The majority of the boulder outlines consist of individual boulders laid into arrangements on the prairie surface. The rearrangement of the surface boulders into cultural-related patterns was a minor alteration of the virgin prairie. Some of the boulders appear to be deeply embedded into the soil matrix, a fact which may suggest site antiquity or local soil accumulation. All exposed areas of the boulders possess colonies of lichens.

Some boulder monuments have cairns (boulder piles) in their design patterns (Figs. 121, 122).Whether the cairns were erected over a period of time or in a single construction stage is unknown. Other stone cairns have been raised over long periods of time by adding token offerings of additional stones (Malouf 1962:3; Squier and Davis 1973:184-185). The Pueblo Indians of the Southwest piled boulders on mesas to "…get rid of fatigue or an ailment" (Parsons 1939:460). Assiniboine Indians were noted in 1858 to make pilgrimages to a rock pile (in present southern Saskatchewan) which was noted as a landmark by historic explorers (Hind 1971 I: 307).

These features have been grouped into four broad classes, to more readily compare individual monuments to those mentioned or described in recorded accounts in journals and other written sources, as well as in current Native lore and oral accounts. In turn, variations within each class are defined as sub-classes.

Class I. *Medicine Wheels* are those features which possess three or more lines radiating away from a central area (cairn, circle or unmarked point) where the difference in line angles is not less than 160 degrees between the most extreme angles. The boulder lines (or medicine wheel "spokes") are single layers of boulders, with the long axes of the individual boulders usually aligned with the axes of the lines themselves. As well, the spokes are a single boulder in width. Spoke lengths are variable both at and between medicine wheels. Additionally, medicine wheels in Saskatchewan vary from a minimum 44.8 meters (m) to a maximum 143.6 m across their longest diameter. Medicine wheels may possess a central cairn, central transected boulder circle, peripheral boulder circle, minor cairns at the ends of the radiating spokes or just lines of boulders radiating from a central area. (John Brumley [1988] also developed a useful classification system for the medicine wheels in Alberta).

Class II. *Ceremonial Circles* include boulder circles which are in excess of 15 m in diameter, although one 7 m diameter boulder circle was included in this category because of other key characteristics. In Saskatchewan the largest ceremonial circle has an average diameter of 36.1 m (the north-south diameter is 39.9 m; the east-west diameter is 32.3 m). These features may possess a central cairn, interior small cairns, a single interior line, two or three exterior lines which articulate with the feature's exterior at a definite entranceway at one point in the circle's circumference (where the difference in boulder line directional angles are not in excess of 45 degrees between the two most pointing lines) or a double encompassing boulder circle.

Class III. *Effigies* include both animal figures and anthropomorphic patterns. Animal outlines may be further subdivided into genera. Anthropomorphic outlines generally depict gender; however, sex determination is tenuous for the animals depicted.

Class IV. *Geometrics* are configurations other than any that may be assigned to the first three categories; that is, they show clear patterning, but are not figurative in the same sense as the others. The variability of these figures precludes any generalizations of construction for all the features included in this category. There are three geometric boulder configurations in Saskatchewan. Two of these figures have circle and line boulder patterns, while the third has three boulder lines together with an earth and boulder arc. Two sets of geometrics are considered in this study: (a) those observed and mapped in Saskatchewan, which by their design attributes may encapsulize cultural phenomena; and (b) those outside Saskatchewan which were not observed, have never been mapped (or the illustrations have not been published) or have not been described by researchers beyond a "mosaic" or "effigy" classification.

The State of Our Understanding

In Saskatchewan, to 1985, the year in which the bulk of the work for this study was completed, the four classes encompassed 33 recorded boulder monuments on 30 sites across the southern third of the province (Fig. 8). By the end of 2002, an additional 78 alignment configurations and 56 possible alignments had been added to the inventory, equaling a possible 169 boulder monument sites in Saskatchewan. These new monuments are further identified as 11 additional medicine wheels (plus 9 possible medicine wheels), 15 effigies (plus 47 possible effigies) and 55 alignment/configurations. Using this criterion, we can be confident that there are now known to exist an additional nine medicine wheels, fifteen ceremonial circles, eleven effigies (human or animal) and nine more geometric configurations (eight being vision quest lodges) recorded since 1985. There is an obvious need for proper archaeological recording work to be performed on these sites before more are harmed or destroyed.

Unfortunately, none of these features were mapped during those years. As the descriptive notes accompanying those reports are not sufficient to allow us to clearly understand the shapes and nature of the features, none of those reports have been used to augment the database used for the present study. An examination of the Saskatchewan Archaeological Resource Records (SARRs) revealed that only 44 of the total could be readily assigned into the existing four class scheme, based on either accurate descriptions or by accompanying feature sketches or notations. Similarly, boulder monuments have been recorded in the neighbouring provinces and states; however, those descriptions are also generally cursory. Consequently, this analysis and classification scheme is based upon 84 Canadian and 64 American features that were either illustrated or possessed sufficient descriptions to allow analysis. It should be noted that a number of the photographs included in this book show some of these incompletely recorded or incompletely documented monuments; these certainly illustrate the fact that much additional research is needed.

Unfortunately, during this same seventeen-year period, four known boulder monuments have been destroyed; three by cultivation and one ceremonial circle covered by the flood waters of the Alameda Dam, in the southeastern corner of the province. While the loss of four features from an addition of 134 new recorded features seems insignificant, the removal of even one of these features should be viewed as disastrous, because once destroyed they can never be properly replaced. While the structure might be reconfigured, the spirituality represented by the originator(s), the physical selection of materials and structural conformity, the specific cultural event complete with the prayers, blessings, sacred songs and meaning can never be reproduced.

Research Propositions

A number of propositions were considered, in an attempt to come to a reasonable understanding of the cultural motivations and purposes underlying the reasons for the construction of boulder monuments, and as methods to date those constructions.

The propositions relate to the probable or possible tribal authorship of individual monuments, possible symbolism, a revised classification scheme and the possible times of individual feature construction. A number of sub-hypotheses are presented as substantiations of these propositions.

The first proposition is that the boulder monuments observed on the North American Great Plains represent the work of different tribes. It is possible that different boulder monuments by class and subclass can be linked to specific tribes; and also tribal cultural borrowing may be reflected in some boulder monument configurations.

A second proposition is that boulder monuments located on different landscape elevations may reveal the creators' perceptions of plains environment conditions, personal achievement , commemoration, or tribe/band memorials, where:

a. personal achievement (boasting) memorials may be located prominently on the landscape in association with a single stone circle;

b. group ceremony boulder monuments may be associated prominently with many stone habitation circles; or

c. special ceremony memorials may be located prominently away from stone circles.

A basic premise of this study is that boulder monuments can be subdivided (reclassified) into classes to describe them better and ultimately to propose better explanations of their functions and uses. Ethnographic analogy and current Native accounts might be comparable with boulder monument subclasses; and additional analysis may yield different, viable hypotheses of possible boulder monument use/meaning.

Since these are configurations made on the surface of the prairie, a method attempting to date only exposed boulder surfaces was initiated: lichenometry. One important question is whether this method can be applied to such surface features, or whether environmental and human-induced conditions limit the practicality of this dating technique. This method was attempted with the expectation that, if successful in Saskatchewan, it might be utilized to date other Great Plains boulder monuments. I propose that the radial growth of lichens, as a biological manifestation on exposed boulder monument surfaces, *does* present the opportunity to date these features by lichenometry.

A variety of analytical procedures were used to consider these propositions. Saskatchewan boulder monument sites were compared with each other, within each of the classes and with all other Great Plains boulder monuments. This comparison led to the definition of individual subclasses within each of these classes (see Chapter 2). The subclasses were then used as the basis for comparisons with ethnographic and historic illustrations and narratives relating to these phenomena. Additionally, other Native North American symbols and cultural patterns were compared. Part of this analysis involved a consideration of which cultural groups were known to, or which possibly, inhabited or "migrated" through the areas where the Saskatchewan monuments have been left for us to wonder at and appreciate.

Study Methodology

The initial field examinations were conducted from May to October in 1980 and on many weekends from June to November in 1981 through 1984. Following the completion of the thesis, at least two weeks a year were used to continue the lichenology observations and measurements. Important initial Saskatchewan information came from the Royal Saskatchewan Museum's (RSM) files and from the Saskatchewan Archaeological Society's (SAS) newsletters and journals. Accompanying this research was of course the need to obtain information and illustrations from many sources across the Plains and beyond. That information was obtained from many friends and colleagues, cited in the acknowledgements.

Lengthy field research during the initial period was necessary because much of the site information in the RSM files was incomplete for my study purposes. With few exceptions, the only recorded information focussed on the central boulder feature with sparse details concerning additional site characteristics. Stone circles, for example, were noted as present but were not counted, located or measured for either size or relationship to the central feature. Descriptions for local environments were restricted to the distance and direction to permanent sources of water.

The 1980 field research was conducted in two stages. During May to July all sites were resurveyed without an assistant. This work permitted me to define the site area and draft preliminary site maps using transit and tape measurements. All associated prehistoric features were referenced by horizontal angles and distances to the central boulder monument feature, which was in turn referenced to legal designations. All boulder monument angles were recorded from a magnetic north zero line. In this manner true north and other angles could be corrected by computing true north from the National Topographic Series (NTS) 1:50,000 maps. This survey permitted the establishment of survey reference points, and tieing them in to legal benchmarks and original land survey pins. These survey points were located to establish ready datum points for the second research stage, when a rod-chain person was hired to assist with accurately measuring elevations and horizontal distances. The reference points (0.02 m x 0.05 m wooden hub stakes) were placed immediately adjacent to the central boulder monument(s) at each site. One stake was always located on the north edge of the feature, and the second on the opposite edge aligning a magnetic north-south base line.

Five newly reported boulder monuments were mapped during the 1980 summer survey. One previously reported feature was remapped in 1982 after the original notes (ca. 1965) were lost. Boulder monument mapping was performed using a square meter wooden frame strung at 0.20 m intervals, after the method employed by Bayrock (1963:1-2).

Habitation circles were measured (outside diameter), and cairns and fire hearths were similarly recorded. During the second research stage the early map was an invaluable aid for relocating those features.

Landowners were contacted prior to site examination, to learn of any previous site disturbances and to obtain the names and locations of artifact collectors who may have collected from the boulder monument site. Collections were reported from five sites; however, the one collection observed (the other four had been dispersed) was not organized by site resource location, nor could the collector positively identify the different sites' materials. Collections were made from three other sites during the 1980 research; however, the sparse recoveries did not significantly contribute to site analysis. One landowner recollected the recovery of numerous broken projectile points by early collectors at the Big Beaver bison effigy site, although he was not aware of their names or of the designs (types) of those artifacts.

Five sites showed evidence of previous scientific excavation; however, written reports exist for only three of those researches: Montgomery (1908), Kehoe (1954) and Kehoe and Kehoe (1979). Of the remaining unexcavated sites three have been completely eradicated, one so altered as to be virtually destroyed and in 1967 three others were moved to a provincial park north of Regina (the Cabri Lake Human effigy was returned following condemnation of the theft of the feature by local citizens and the two animal outlines [Mankota Salamander and Hardy Turtle] were returned to their original sites by current RSM staff in 1998). Eight other sites have been disturbed to some extent, although a sufficient amount of the original structures remain to identify the features depicted. Thirteen monuments remain in relatively pristine condition (disturbed only by grazing animals). The majority of these monuments were protected by interested landowners who consciously guarded these fragile resources; however, four of the eleven owe their preservation by having been "recognized" as large tipi rings.

Lichenometric measurements were taken at all sites where undisturbed boulders were located and where lichens were observed to be in virile conditions (some sites had been white-washed by early investigators for aerial photography identification). Lichenometry, as a relative dating technique, was employed as an empirical, potential dating technique calculated to have no site disturbance effects. With the proposition that these are sacred sites, this methodology could be employed without desecrating the sites.

Native plant specimens were collected and identified to allow comparisons between site classes or subclasses, in the event that concentrations of plant species might denote seasonality or regeneration of specific species from the seeds of ceremonially utilized plants. No such concentrations of any plants were noted at any of the sites.

The local site topography, natural resources and distances and directions to other boulder monuments were recorded for inter-site comparisons. In most instances either the topographic situation or the available local resources were common between sites.

The availability, nature and types of local rocks were noted for probable construction methodology or possible rock preferences. Most sites displayed a preference for boulders similar in size to each other, and a probable practice of clearing away all other surface rock before the particular monument was constructed. There seemed to be a preference for erosion-rounded boulders, as opposed to jagged or fractured rock. Only one boulder monument (the Bone Creek Effigy) was completely constructed of a single rock type, while the surrounding tipi rings were constructed of a variety of locally-obtained rocks, excluding the rock type used for that monument.

Boulder weights and the numbers of boulders used to construct monuments were not measured or counted, as it was assumed that the particular features would be added on to by the builder(s) until an appropriate configuration was achieved. Boulder colours were noted to ascertain whether there was any aesthetic or other selection process evident. Limestone or dolomite varied from a single boulder at one site, to nine of these boulders at another site. Feldspathic metamorphic rocks were slightly more common; however, the granites and quartzites were the predominant variety used.

Extensive correspondence was conducted to obtain the exact feature locations for the Canadian and American Great Plains area. It was assumed that distributions might reveal possible migration routes and feature type concentrations. The Canadian sites were plotted on NTS 1:50,000 maps. The American sites were plotted on the United States Department of the Interior 1:1,000,000 maps. In some cases, neither Canadian nor American legal locations were available. Consequently, those sites were plotted by county or the nearest town or landmark after which they had been named. The Canadian sites are numbered according to the nationwide Borden site numbering system, and the American site numbers are those of the Smithsonian Trinomial System. As boulder monuments are protected cultural resources in each jurisdiction, none of the exact locations have been provided within this text (at the request of all registering agencies). It is not possible to navigate one's way to the vast majority of the sites discussed herein without properly convincing each jurisdiction's archaeological resource management agency of one's ethical research purpose.

The Study Area

The study area consists of the northern Great Plains where boulder monuments have been identified. In this study the northern Plains area is bordered on the north by the North Saskatchewan River, by the Rocky Mountain foothills on the west, by the Platte River (Nebraska) to the south and by the mixed aspen forest of Minnesota and Manitoba to the east and northeast. In Canada this area includes the southern portions of Alberta, Saskatchewan and Manitoba; in the United States it consists of the eastern two-thirds of Montana, the central eastern portion of Wyoming, the northern half of Nebraska, the northwest corner of Iowa, the western third of Minnesota and all of both North Dakota and South Dakota (Fig. 5). An isolated Ontario site was included as it may indicate an eastern origin or extension of Plains phenomena.

The major Saskatchewan bedrock formations are the Cretaceous and Tertiary silts and clays. These are overlain by glacial sands and gravels which were subsequently intermixed with fluvial and alluvial silts and clays (Fig. 6). The northwestern Great Plains area is cross trenched by two major drainage systems and one minor one, and their tributaries (Fig. 5). The rivers cut through the underlying sediment and bedrock, transporting or exposing a great variety of rock materials, some of which were utilized by prehistoric itinerants for tool manufacture. The South Saskatchewan River and the Missouri River are the major systems, while the Assiniboine River and its tributaries constitute the minor source.

Numerous uplands, some timbered, are observed. Among these uplands are the Missouri Coteau in Saskatchewan and North Dakota (Coteau du Missouri, in the latter), the Black Hills of South Dakota and Wyoming, the Moose Mountain of Saskatchewan, the Cypress Hills of Saskatchewan and Alberta, the Sweetgrass Hills of Montana, and the Turtle Mountains of Manitoba and North Dakota. Other minor uplands, too numerous to cite, are found in each of the political areas listed for the Great Plains area. These uplands are interspaced among plains-plate regions, characterized by level to gently rolling (0 to 40 percent) knob and kettle topography. The predominant soils are black, dark brown and brown chernozems with scattered solonetzic and regosolic soils. The black chernozems tend to be sandy loams and the dark brown chernozems a loamy clay, while the brown chernozems are either heavily clayed or a mixed clayey loam. Solonetzic soils are characteristically saline, whereas regosols are weakly developed parent material soils (Hedlin 1978).

The Plains are characterized by a continental climate with dominant northwesterly winds and predominant southeasterly summer air masses. The average annual precipitation varies from approximately 38 centimeters (cm) in the central plains to approximately 70 cm along the eastern margins. The majority of precipitation occurs during the frost-free summer growing season, with the remaining 30 to 35 percent falling as rain or snow during the other three seasons (Fig. 7).

The southern boundary of this area is typically tall grass plains with a gradual

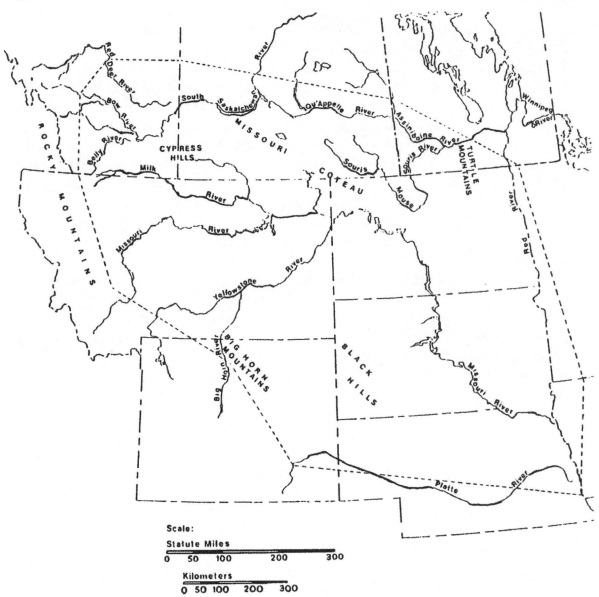

Figure 5: Map of northern Great Plains area of boulder monument occurrence and major physiographic features

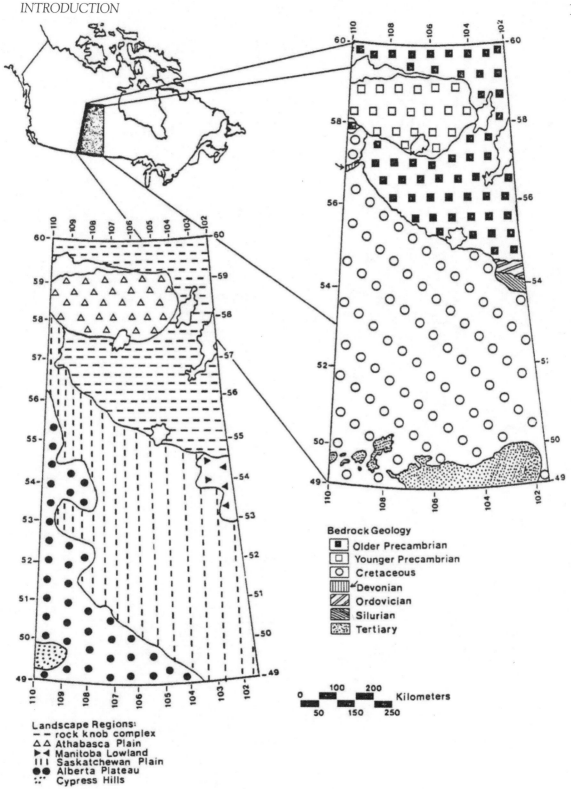

Bedrock Geology
- ■ Older Precambrian
- □ Younger Precambrian
- ○ Cretaceous
- ⦀ Devonian
- ⬗ Ordovician
- ⬖ Silurian
- ⠿ Tertiary

Landscape Regions:
- – – rock knob complex
- △ △ Athabasca Plain
- ▶◀ Manitoba Lowland
- ⦀⦀ Saskatchewan Plain
- ●● Alberta Plateau
- ∴ Cypress Hills

Figure 6: Maps of Saskatchewan bedrock geology (right) and surface landscape (left)

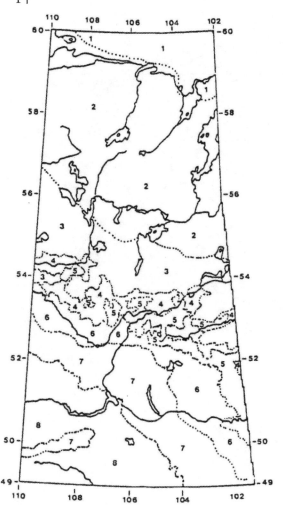

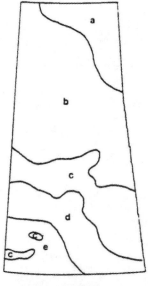

CLIMATIC REGIONS:

a - arctic transition
b - sub-arctic
c - humid continental
d - sub-humid continental
e - semi-arid

SOIL ZONES:
1 - forest-tundra, podzolic & organic; rock outcrops
2 - podzolic & organic; rock outcrops
3 - podzolic & organic
4 - gray wooded podzolic
5 - transitional (black-grey) organic & meadow
6 - black
7 - dark brown
8 - brown

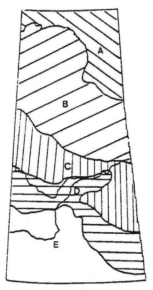

VEGETATION AREAS:
A - forest-tundra transition
B - coniferous forest
C - mixed forest
D - aspen parkland
E - mixed prairie

Figure 7: Maps of Saskatchewan soils, vegetation and climate

northwestern transition to short grass plains, corresponding with an increased east to west aridity. The major transecting rivers and most of the minor ravines and coulees support cottonwoods (*Populus deltoides*) and native shrubs and vegetable foods such as choke-cherry (*Prunus virginiana*), saskatoon (*Amelanchier alnifolia*), dewberry (*Rubus pubescens*), wild gooseberry (*Ribes oxyacanthoides*), wild onions (*Allium* spp.), and other herbs and forbs (Angier 1972). The dominant native plains grasses are spear grass (*Stipa comata*), wheatgrass (*Agropyron dasystachyum*), fescue (*Festuca scabrella*), blue grama (*Bouteloua gracilis*), and June grass (*Koeleria cristata*) (Budd and Best 1964). The eastern boundary graduates into hardwood forests, whereas the western foothills and eroded buttes have ground juniper (*Juniperus scopulorum*) and a gradual increase to softwood forests. The northern boundary's short grass prairie graduates into a mixed aspen (*Populus tremuloides*) forest and ultimately into a jack pine (*Pinus banksiana*) and black spruce (*Picea mariana*) forest.

The European fur trade and settlement, over the past three centuries, has resulted in the extinction of the buffalo wolf (*Canis lupus nubilis*), the passenger pigeon (*Ectopistes migratorius*) and the Eskimo curlew (*Numenius borealis*). Additionally, bison (*Bison bison bison*), grizzly (*Ursus horribilis*), elk/wapiti (*Cervus canadensis*), and mountain lion (*Felis concolor*) have been extirpated in all areas save marginal and divergent habitat (Maher 1969:84; Braithwaite 1975:102-103). Agriculture and urban development, in conjunction with extirpation, have induced other wildlife species to adapt to the new, altered environments (Richards and Fung 1969: 80-81).

2 – DESCRIPTION OF THE SASKATCHEWAN MONUMENTS

Introduction

Boulder monuments were first mentioned in what is now Saskatchewan in 1858 by Henry Y. Hind (1971:307). Other nineteenth century Saskatchewan observers were W. H. Clandening in 1863 (1928:246) and B. G. Hamilton in 1896 (unpublished diary, Glenbow Archives). Henry Montgomery performed the first excavation of a Saskatchewan medicine wheel in 1907 (Montgomery 1908). The Saskatchewan Museum of Natural History (SMNH) [now Royal Saskatchewan Museum - RSM] began recording boulder monument features in 1956, with the majority of the known sites being mapped between 1959 and 1975. Subsequent to that work, this research project mapped and recorded an additional eight features at five sites (including one feature that had previously only been partially recorded). Only two of the 33 Saskatchewan features (to 1987) were located by museum staff; the remainder had been located and reported by archaeologically-interested residents (Fig. 8).

The majority of the Saskatchewan boulder monuments are located on local heights of land (Fig. 124); however, not every height of land possesses these features. All are located on land which was previously too stony to cultivate. The majority of the sites are located in remote areas, away from travelled roads – a partial aid to their preservation. In Saskatchewan at least four of either the original, or newly recorded boulder monuments have been destroyed by more technically-advanced farming machinery during the last decade. These will be noted, where known.

As possible comparisons the pertinent landforms, degrees of unobstructed view, and the distance and direction to a permanent water source were detailed for each site. With the exception of two sites (Dick Giles Circle, DgNg-1; and Dewdney Avenue Human Effigy, EcNh-1), all sites were comparable as they are on local heights or secondary heights of land, afford a minimum 160 degrees of field of view of the surrounding landscape, and are within three kilometers of a permanent water source. The landforms were comparable only as to elevation (Tables 1 and 3). The heights together with the degrees of view may indicate that the occasion of each monument's construction was to present the builder(s) with the best view of their surroundings, possibly for either defence or for hunting considerations.

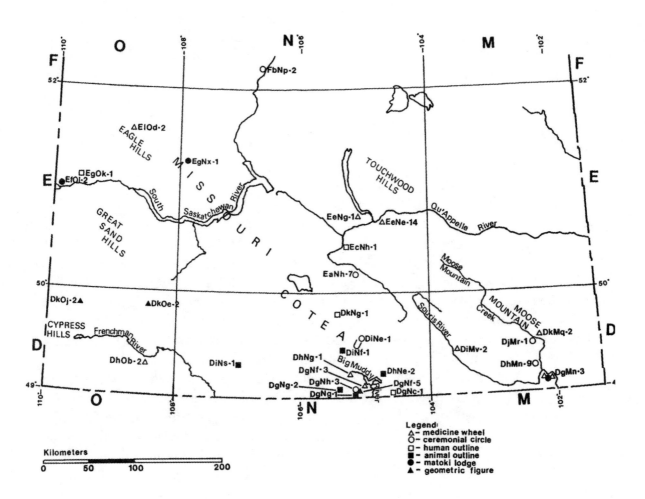

Figure 8: Map of Saskatchewan boulder monument locations and border zones

Table 1
IMPORTANT ATTRIBUTES OF SASKATCHEWAN
BOULDER MONUMENT SITES

Boulder Monument Type	Height of Land 1°	2°	Water Source Max. Distance [Average]	Number of Associated Stone Circles	Sites With Other Boulder Monument Types	Intra-Site Comparable Aspects By Type	Total Number Located
Medicine Wheels	1	9	500 m[100 m]	4-182*	1	yes	10
Ceremonial Circles	1	10	500 m[100 m]	1-182*	2	yes	11
Effigy Figures							
- Animals	5	-	300 m[100 m]	4-23	-	yes	5
- Humans	3	1	3 km	1	1	males only	4
Geometrics	1	2	1-300 m 2-3 km [2.5 km]	0.44	-	no	3

Legend: m - meters   * - same site, maximum number observed
          km - kilometers

Alternatively, it may provide a hidden or restrained art form which suggests "…the real message of tribal art is not its form or beauty, but its reminder of the gift of privacy" (Carpenter 1978:99), or as an offering between the builder(s) and the Creator. The distance from permanent water may suggest that the monuments were constructed away from the annoyance of biting or stinging insects (e.g. mosquitoes, wasps) but within sufficient proximity to the commodity.

The majority, if not all, of the boulder monuments were probably constructed during the warmer seasons of the year. The removal of the glacial outwash boulders from the prairie sod matrix is most easily accomplished during the frost-free months. The removal of boulders from the sod in late fall or early spring requires extreme force using a substantial lever, often accompanied by a heating source (burning large volumes of grass/straw) to loosen the adhering frost (personal observation). In winter boulders are visible on the plains only on the most snow-free, windswept ridges, and are virtually impossible to dislodge from the landscape.

Stone Circles

In this research all stone circles less than 10 meters in diameter are regarded as habitation circles or tipi rings, and thus they do not fall under the definition of "boulder monuments". The scope of other lodge types found at a habitation site may include death lodges, dual function lodges, sweat lodges, menstrual lodges, and birthing lodges (Graspointner 1980:64-69). Habitation circles are reported to range in size from 2.5 m to 7.4 m diameter with an average diameter of 4.6 m (Finnigan 1980:4). Bushnell described the larger stone circles as remnants of a chief's tipi, the remains of a communal dwelling or the remains of a ceremonial lodge (1922:29,62,63). However, Maximilian recorded a chief's lodge as being approximately 15 paces (12 m?) across (Thomas and Ronnefeldt 1976:101).

A Classification of the Saskatchewan Boulder Monuments

Subdividing boulder monuments into four descriptive classes permits common outline varieties to be analyzed in terms of construction attributes. By this methodology it is also possible to observe and group common site characteristics. Comparable sites from other political areas were included. By amassing a larger volume of similar sites, a larger population sample was available.

The sites in each class are grouped according to outline attributes. By this analysis some previously named structures are lumped together, while others are reassigned to different classes. Other previous types are reclassified. The subclasses are devised on the basis of similar site attributes and feature similarities.

Class I. Medicine wheels were subdivided into four subclasses:
        Subclass A: Large Central Cairn
        Subclass B: Large Central Cairn Encompassed
        Subclass C: Small/ No Central Cairn
        Subclass D: Encompassed Feature

Class II. Ceremonial circles, by their size and pattern orientation, were subdivided into four subclasses:
        Subclass A: Circle with Marked Entrance Path
        Subclass B: Large Circle, Enclosed Boulder(s)
        Subclass C: Enclosed Cairns
        Subclass D: Enclosed Boulder Line

Class III. Effigy Figure boulder monuments in Saskatchewan portray four species of animals and the two assumed sexes of human effigies:
        Subclass A: Animal Outlines
            Turtle Effigies
            Badger Effigy
            Salamander Effigy
            Bison Effigy
      Subclass B: Human Effigies
            Male Effigies
            Female Effigies

Class IV. Geometric boulder monuments, subdivided with reference to descriptions of features described by others or by site observations consist of:

Subclass A - personal tribulation

Subclass B - stealth encampment

Subclass C - subtle site indictor

Subclass D - undefined human-made configurations

Other geometrics were described in various publications for Northwestern Plains sites. As none of those sites were personally inspected, and in most cases were not completely described or illustrated, their assumed classifications in Table 9 were in reference to published accounts.

Class I: Medicine Wheels

This popular "catch-all" group originally included 12 Saskatchewan boulder monuments. Subsequent to this analysis, two have been reassigned to the ceremonial circles (Class II) definition. Of the ten remaining, one (DhOb-2) has been completely destroyed, while two others (DgNf-3 and DhNg-1) have been so drastically altered as to be almost unidentifiable when compared with the original mapped outlines. These medicine wheels represent ten different structures, of which no two are alike by size or configuration. The number of spokes at each site, the individual spoke angles (in reference to measured True North), and the numbers of boulders used in the construction of each spoke are presented in Table 2. Table 3 lists the individual sites by common names, plus data pertaining to the natural and cultural attributes noted at each site; their distributions are shown in Figure 8 along with the other Saskatchewan boulder monument locations. Figure 9 illustrates the complete lack of spoke angle conformity.

The numbers of boulders in each spoke were counted, and the spoke angles were measured (Table 2) to verify whether the builder(s) conceived a common construction plan. While the number of boulders per spoke varied at each and all sites, a slight similarity of spoke angles was observed for the southwest quadrants at most of the sites. The absence of identical construction features prompted the hypothesis that each of these structures was built to represent individual occasions, and that the outlines were added onto until a conceptualized pattern had been achieved. However, certain design motifs enabled the formulation of the four sub-groups within the medicine wheel classification. The predominance of four spokes at six of the ten medicine wheel sites (Table 2) may imply a definite pattern, as the numeral four is a sacred number and is common among many plains tribes. For example, the Cheyenne pipe ceremony (Powell 1969:17); the Blackfoot Matoki ceremony (Ewers 1958:106) and tobacco dance (McClintock 1923:44); the Cree smoking lodge and Wewahtahokan (Mandelbaum 1979:199 and 183-186, respectively); the Crow high lodge dance (Lowie 1922:436-437); the Dakota fast for visions (Hassrick 1964:271-272); and the Sun Dance among the Bungi (Howard 1977:153), Atsina (Cooper 1956:192), and Sarcee (Jenness 1938:11); all use four as the basic denominator for certain ceremonial aspects.

A number of different attributes were noted among the ten Saskatchewan medicine wheels. Each of the possible hypothesized medicine wheel subclasses will be discussed according

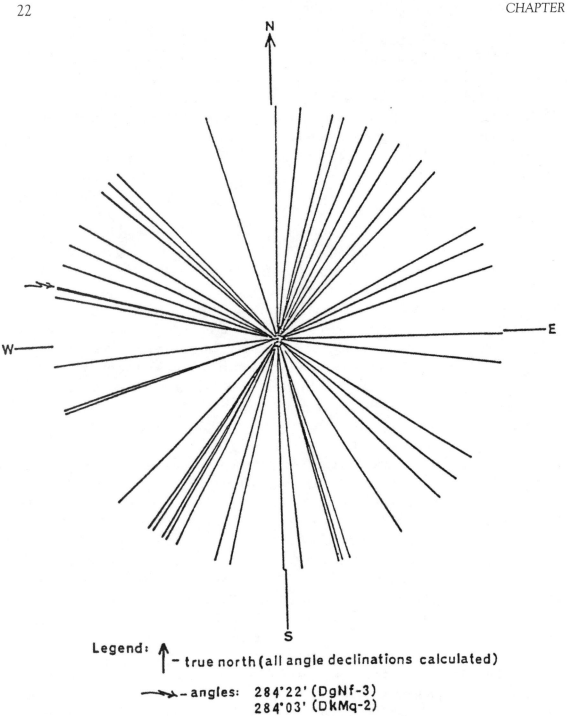

Figure 9: Saskatchewan medicine wheel spoke angles

Table 2
SASKATCHEWAN MEDICINE WHEEL SPOKE ANGLES AND NUMBERS OF BOULDERS PER SPOKE

Spoke Angles* Sites	N-O° 337°30' to 22°30'	NE-45° 22°30' to 67°30'	E-90° 67°30' to 112°30'	SE-135° 112°30' to 157°30'	S-180° 157°30' to 202°30'	SW-225° 202°30' to 247°30'	W-270° 247°30' to 292°30'	NW-315° 292°30' to 337°30'	# of Spokes	Total Boulders All Spokes
DgMn-3(1)		34°18' (316)		148°58' (288)		227°08' (301)		313°42' (208)	4	1113
DgMn-3(3)		46°11' (38)	91°52' (20)		165°26' 166°32' (191)(327)		253°44' 282°04' (232)(127)	316°39' (169)	7	1331
DiMv-2	18°58' (88)			123°04' (104)		209°35' (121)		300°37' (116)	4	429
DkMq-2	7°48' (39**)(+152)	63°13' (47**)(+90)			176°03' (40**)(+123)	216°18' (294)	284°03' (34***)(+151)		5	970
DgNf3	15°52' (129)			129°47' (184)	194°52' (133)		284°22' (175)		4	621
DhNg-1***		24°56' (?)			180°31' (?)	213°26' (?)	253°06' (?)		Destroyed	Destroyed
DhOb-2		29°36' (31)	67°51' 98°16' (34)(17)			217°26' (17)	264°46' (44)	310°46' (31)	6	174
EeNe-14****	1°17' (113)			155°02' (61)	198°47' (66)		290°02' (82)		4	332
EeNg-1	342°53' (64)		73°58' (62)		163°33' (42)				3	168
ElOd-2		41°34' (63)		135°48' (242)		212°21' (39)		295°08' (66)	4	410
Total Spokes/ direction	5	6	4	5	7	6	7	5	45	

Legend: Number of boulders per spoke under angle in parenthesis, where two spokes are located in the same quadrant, the number of boulders in the first parentheses refers to the top angle.

* All Angles with declination accounted for, are in relation to 00° as being True North.

** Number of boulders within the stone ring surrounding the central cairn.

*** Never mapped, destroyed after basic angles were noted, angles measured from interior spoke alignment.

**** No central point of spoke intersection, spoke angles measured from an assumed interior spoke alignment.

to comparable site attributes. Personal field observations and communications with landowners are added where available. As the observed Saskatchewan medicine wheels are few in number (see Tables 2 and 3), the other recorded Great Plains medicine wheels have been individually assigned within the four subclasses with reference to the observed Saskatchewan classes, regardless of their previous named definitions elsewhere (see Table 4 and appropriate Figures). Each subclass will be described with reference to attributes additional to spoke angles, individual boulder orientations, and spoke sizes.

Medicine Wheel Subclass A

The four Saskatchewan medicine wheels: DgMn-3(1) Oxbow (Figs. 10, 125), DiMv-2 Halbrite (Fig. 11), DhOb-2 Canuck (Fig. 12), and EeNg-1 Jelly Ranch (Figs. 13, 126) possess large central cairns with three to six relatively straight radiating spokes, although one Alberta example has nine spokes. When originally described DiMv-2 was noted to possess three spokes (Montgomery 1908:39). When Tom Kehoe mapped the site in 1965 he included a fourth spoke; however, only three were evident in 1980. The questionable spoke is that which extends to the northwest angle. DiMv-2 is located on a gravelly hill in a knob and kettle morainic landscape approximately one kilometer east of a minor river valley. This medicine wheel originally had five habitation circles associated with it (all were destroyed subsequent to 1960s oil well drilling). The entire site area is now slightly less than a square hectare.

DgMn-3 (feature 1) possesses a large central cairn and four relatively straight spokes, one pointing to each of the four cardinal compass positions. In addition to this feature, a second medicine wheel of Subclass B, a ceremonial circle (Fig. 127), and one hundred and eighty-two habitation circles are located at this site. The site extends approximately one kilometer east-west and approximately 400 meters north-south. The majority of the site is located on an ancient island-bar between the present height of land to the south and the Oxbow River valley to the north. The ancient river drainage to the south possesses numerous flowing springs and an intermittent slough.

DhOb-2 was destroyed by farming operations in the 1960s. The medicine wheel had a large central cairn and six spoke lines. The one hectare site is on rolling uplands plains topography, approximately two kilometers south of the Frenchman River. No habitation circles were noted during the initial site mapping (G. Watson, personal communication).

EeNg-1 has a large central cairn and three spoke lines. The spokes extend toward compass magnetic north, south and east. The medicine wheel is within fifteen meters of a minor valley rim. In addition to the forty-four associated habitation circles, an alignment of twenty-four cairns extends from the eastern side of the feature to the top of a small hill approximately three hundred meters to the south. This site (not including the cairn alignment) occupies approximately ten hectares.

Figures 14 and 15 show similar features found in Alberta.

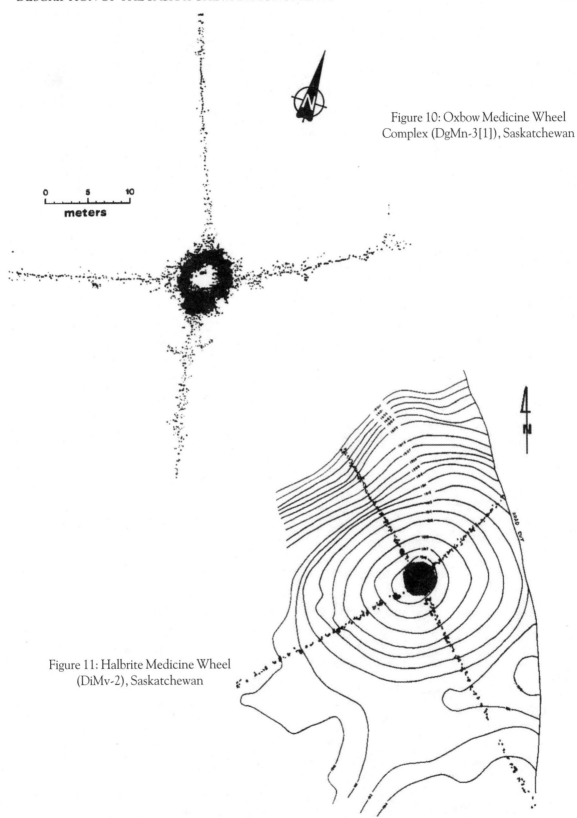

Figure 10: Oxbow Medicine Wheel
Complex (DgMn-3[1]), Saskatchewan

Figure 11: Halbrite Medicine Wheel
(DiMv-2), Saskatchewan

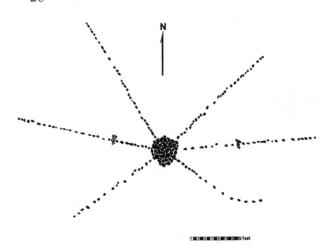

Figure 12: Canuck Medicine Wheel
(DhOb-2), Saskatchewan

Figure 13: Jelly Ranch Medicine Wheel
(EeNg-1), Saskatchewan

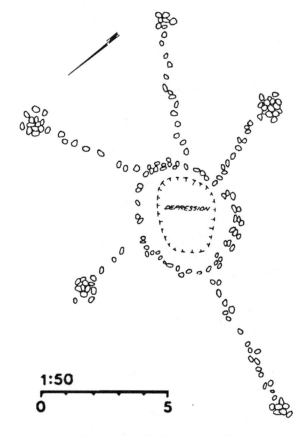

Figure 14: Suffield Medicine Wheel
(EaOs-2), Alberta

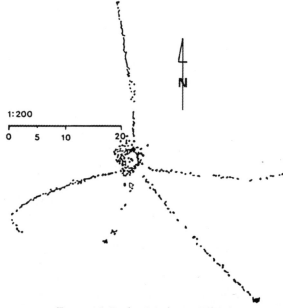

Figure 15: Rinker Medicine Wheel
(EfOp-58), Alberta

Table 3

SASKATCHEWAN MEDICINE WHEEL NATURAL AND CULTURAL ATTRIBUTES

Site Borden Reference	Common Name	(n) Stone Circles Observed	(n) Cairns Observed	Site Location Landform	Water Source stream	Water Source spring	Year Mapped by	Author Year Published
DgMn-3(1)	Oxbow	182	2	Vr/Pbi	500 m		1980	*
DgMn-3(3)	Oxbow	182		Vr/Pbi		300 m	1980	*
DiMv-2	Halbrite	5		Vr	1 km		1965 K-w	k-k: 1976
DkMq-2	Moose Mountain	30	1	Hr/Hm		350 m	1962 k-k	K: 1965
DgNf-3	Doug Wade	3		Vr	3 km		1961 K	k-k:1976
DhNg-1	Bird Foot	?	in alignment	Vr/Hm		1 km	1956 m	*
DhOb-2	Canuck	?		Hm/Tp	3 km		1967 w	w: 1974
EeNe-14	Wilson Russell	23	2	Vr		350 m	1980	*
EeNg-1	Jelly Ranch	45		Vr	1 km		1960 K	w:1972
ElOd-2	Plenty	28	3	Vr/T		500 m	1965 K-w	k-k: 1976

Legend:

Hm - hummocky moraine
Tp - till plain
Vr - valley rim
Hr - highland rim

T - terrace
Pbi - point bar island (glacial stream formation)
* - this research

w - G. Watson
k-k - T. Kehoe & A. Kehoe
m - B. McCorquodale
K - T. Kehoe

Table 4
NON-SASKATCHEWAN MEDICINE WHEELS

Recorded Designation	# of Spokes	Variety	Associated Features	References	Text Figure
Eagle Child	4	C	-	Dempsey 1956	-
Steel	4	C	-	Dempsey 1956	30
DiPi-2	6	C	-	ASA 1976	31
DkPf-1	4	C	-	Quigg/ASA 1984	35
DlOv-2	6	B	1a	ASA 1976	18
EaOs-2	5	A	-	ASA 1976	14
EbOm-1	6	C	s?, c?, a?	Quigg/ASA 1984	36
EcOp-4	11	B	14s, 3a	ASA 1976	19
EdPc-1	26-28	D	s?	Calder 1977	40
EePl-2	4	D	15s	ASA 1976	39
EfOo-10(1)	9	B	1s, 7c	ASA 1976	23
EfOp-58	4	A	5s, 3c	ASA 1976	15
EgOx-1	8	B	2a, 1c	ASA 1976	20
EgOx-29(1)	16	B	10s	ASA 1976	21
EgOx-29(2)	7	B	9s, 4a, 2c	ASA 1976	22
EgOx-46	17	C	c?	Quigg/ASA 1984	37
EkPe-3	5	C	2s, 1a, 8c	ASA 1976	32
24BH220	6	C	-	Brown 1963	33
24BH747	4	C	s?	Quigg/ASA 1984	34
24BL331	5	-	5s	Deaver 1980	-
24HL81	-	-	201s, 18a, 18c	Deaver 1980	-
24HL87	13	-	38s, 11a	Deaver 1980	-
24HL169	9	-	97s, 17a, 25c	Deaver 1980	-
24TT67	10	B	s?	Kehoe 1973; Newcomb 1967	24
48BH302	28	D	8s	Grinnell 1922; Wilson 1981	41
39HD22	4	D	-	Rood and Rood 1983	38
Custer	5	B	s?	Over 1941	25

Legend: s – habitation circle   - - Information not available
            a – alignment   ASA – Archaeological Survey of Alberta
            c – cairn
            ? – number not reported

Medicine Wheel Subclass B

These two Saskatchewan medicine wheels DgMn-3(3) Oxbow Medicine Wheel (Fig. 16) and DkMq-2 Moose Mountain (Figs. 17, 121) each possess a boulder circle encompassing the central cairn. In both cases the boulder circle is transected by the radiating spokes. DgMn-3 (3) has one cairn and one small stone ring at the end of two of its seven spokes, whereas DkMq-2 possesses cairns or small boulder rings at the outer ends of each of its five spokes. This distribution may suggest that this figure is somewhat of a transitional type between this and the following subclass.

The spoke angles at DgMn-3(3) were measured by E. Krupp of the Griffith Observatory in California during July 1982 to test the astronomical postulations. No astronomical comparisons, such as noted for DkMq-2, were deduced from his research (T. Kehoe, personal communication).

The diameters of the two sites' central cairns were noted to be different, and the cairn heights had been previously disturbed. The landowner at DgMn-3(3) admitted to "pulling the central cairn apart as a boy" (personal communication). The height of this cairn is presently one boulder tier (10 centimeters) high. The Moose Mountain central cairn measured 0.85 meters in height in 1980 (personal observation), but when it was first recorded the cairn was "eight feet (2.4 meters) high…and…fourteen (4.27 meters) in diameter" (Hamilton 1896).

The radiocarbon date of central cairn construction at Moose Mountain was reported to be 440 B.C. (Kehoe and Kehoe 1979:42). It should be noted that this date corresponds to the central cairn only. John A. Eddy (1979:165-168) acknowledged that this date is problematic in dating the entire feature, and postulated that some alignments at this site might represent continuous use of the monument from the date of construction through to historic contact. Such reuse was noted in 1982, as local Assiniboine and Saulteaux people have been reconstructing portions of the Moose Mountain outline. Presumably many tribes used previous monuments to conform to their ideology through rearrangements of existing outline patterns (Howard 1972:300). Figures 18 to 25, all outside Saskatchewan's borders, are categorized as Subclass IB features.

Medicine Wheel Subclass C

The four Saskatchewan medicine wheels in this subclass lack a central cairn, or cairns at the end of the radiating spokes, although each possesses four spokes, and each feature is located at or near the rim of a valley complex. The Doug Wade Medicine Wheel at DgNf-3 (disturbed between 1965 and 1980) formerly had two habitation-sized stone circles within the spoke alignment (Fig. 26). Until the late 1980s, there were forty-four habitation circles 100 meters to the northwest of ElOd-2, the Plenty Medicine Wheel (Fig. 27), but these were destroyed by cultivation. Fortunately the landowner has preserved the central feature. The Big Muddy Bird Foot Effigy (medicine wheel DhNg-1) and the accompanying stone circles were destroyed by oil well construction in the early 1970s (Fig. 28). EeNe-14, the Wilson Russell medicine wheel (Fig. 29), has 26 stone circles to the north and west of the medicine

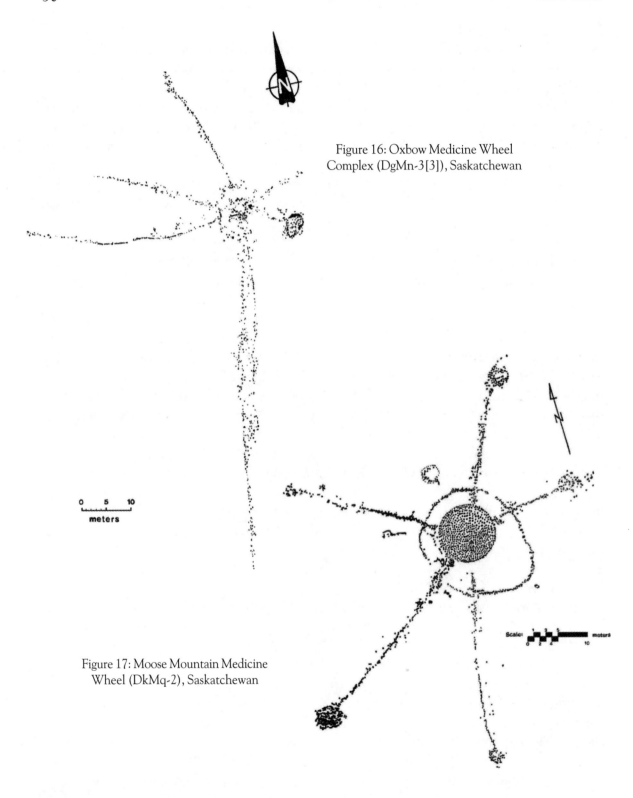

Figure 16: Oxbow Medicine Wheel
Complex (DgMn-3[3]), Saskatchewan

Figure 17: Moose Mountain Medicine
Wheel (DkMq-2), Saskatchewan

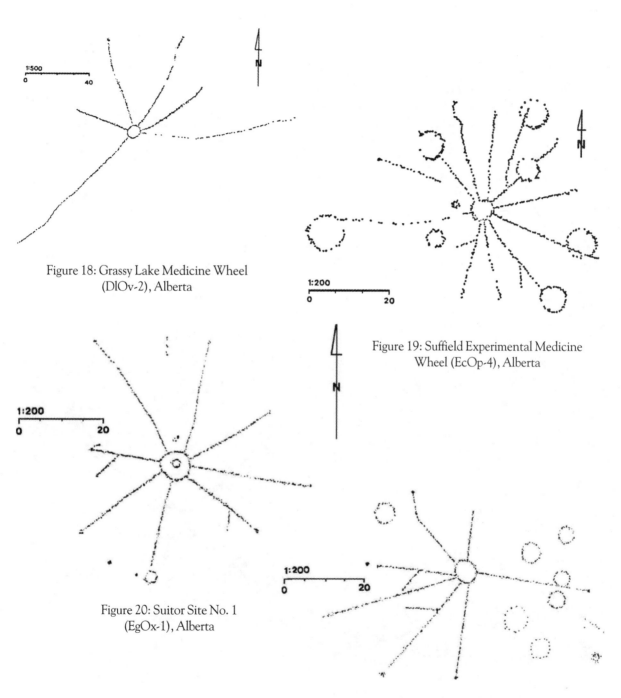

Figure 18: Grassy Lake Medicine Wheel
(DlOv-2), Alberta

Figure 19: Suffield Experimental Medicine
Wheel (EcOp-4), Alberta

Figure 20: Suitor Site No. 1
(EgOx-1), Alberta

Figure 21: Suitor Site No. 2, Wheel No. 1
(EgOx-29[1]), Alberta

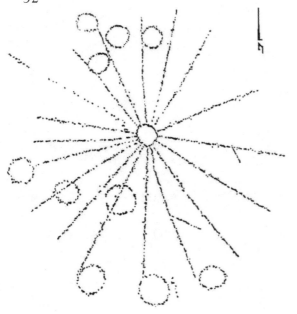

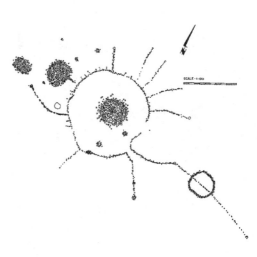

Figure 23: Miner No. 1 Medicine Wheel
(EfOo-10), Alberta

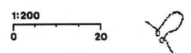

Figure 22: Suitor Site No. 2, Wheel No. 2
(EgOx-29[2]), Alberta

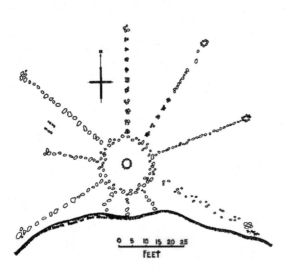

Figure 24: Sun River Medicine Wheel
(24TT67), Montana

Figure 25: Custer County Boulder
Outline, South Dakota

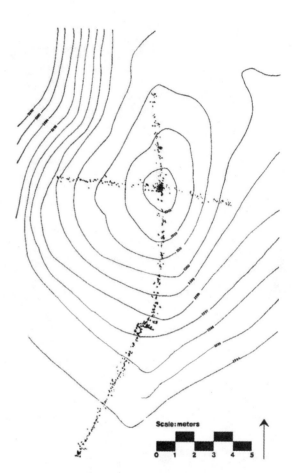

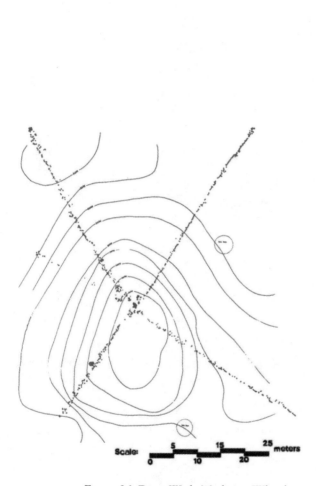

Figure 26: Doug Wade Medicine Wheel
(DgNf-3), Saskatchewan

Figure 27: Plenty Medicine Wheel
(ElOd-2), Saskatchewan

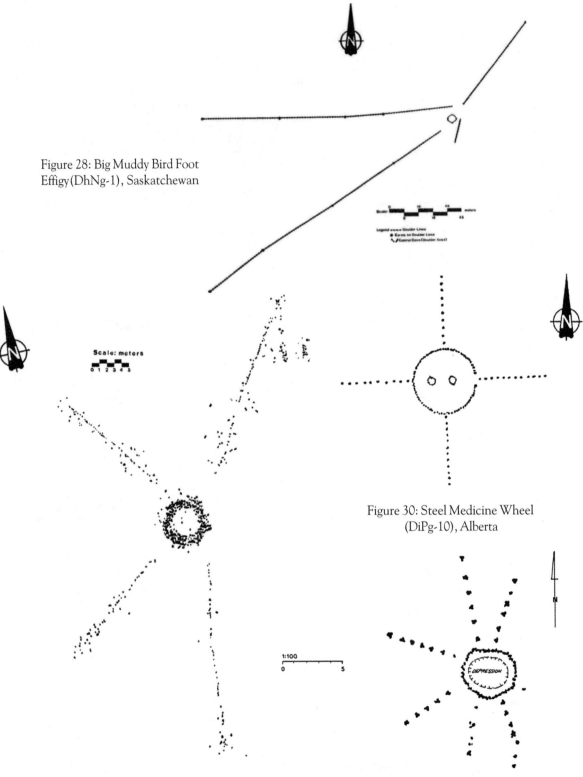

Figure 28: Big Muddy Bird Foot
Effigy(DhNg-1), Saskatchewan

Figure 30: Steel Medicine Wheel
(DiPg-10), Alberta

Figure 29: Wilson Russell Medicine Wheel
(EeNe-14), Saskatchewan

Figure 31: Wolf Child Medicine Wheel
(DiPi-2), Alberta

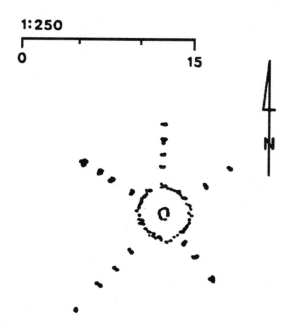

Figure 32: Ziegenbein Medicine Wheel
(EkPe-3), Alberta

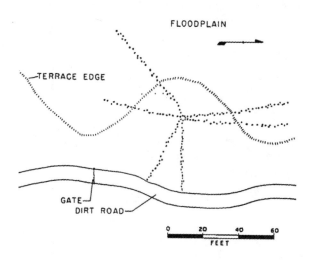

Figure 33: Fort Smith Medicine Wheel
(24BH220), Montana

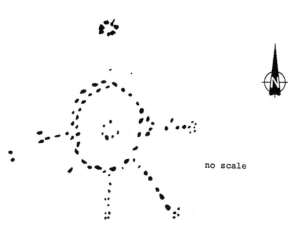

Figure 34: Grassy Knoll Site
(24BH747), Montana

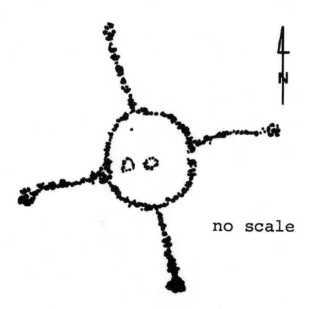

Figure 35: Many Spotted Horses Medicine
Wheel (DkPf-1), Alberta

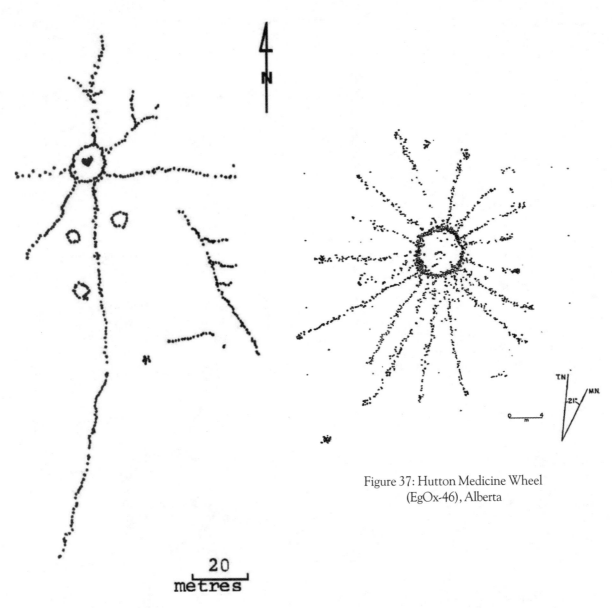

Figure 37: Hutton Medicine Wheel
(EgOx-46), Alberta

20
metres

Figure 36: Many Island Lake Medicine
Wheel (EbOm-1), Alberta

wheel, and had numerous other stone circles in the adjacent east field. The central areas where spokes intersect at DgNf-3 and ElOd-2 are at the apex of a low knoll, whereas the spoke articulation areas at DhNg-1 and EeNe-14 appear to be on a slight prehistoric man-made topographic rise. Figures 30 to 37 illustrate features in this category which lie outside Saskatchewan.

Medicine Wheel Subclass D

Among the 27 medicine wheels located beyond Saskatchewan (see Table 4), four didn't fit into the previous three-variety system. EePi-2, Figure 39 (Jamieson's Place Medicine Wheel) and EdPc-1, Figure 40 (Majorville Cairn and Medicine Wheel) are in Alberta; 48BH302, Figure 41 (Big Horn Medicine Wheel) is in Wyoming and 39HD22, Figure 38 (Jennings Site) is in South Dakota. Rather than omit them, a fourth subclass was devised. This variety is regarded as tentative, as none of these sites were visited and all site information was derived from other sources. This interpretation is presented so that all known medicine wheels might be represented in an overall scheme.

All Subclass D medicine wheels are represented by spokes radiating from a central cairn (or intersection) and terminate at the inner edge of an encompassing boulder circle. In all cases associated stone circles are lacking, few in number, or not mentioned in the research report. Both the Majorville Cairn and the Big Horn Medicine Wheel are located prominently, and afford a commanding view of the surrounding topography. Both features have been excavated and dated according to materials retrieved from their cairns. The disparity of dates obtained for their constructions may be attributed to the fact that the Majorville radiocarbon date was from bone in a disturbed buried level in the central cairn (Calder 1977:42), whereas the Big Horn dendrochronological date was obtained from a wood sample in the original construction level of the west cairn (Grey 1963:36). Support for the Big Horn date was confirmed by the retrieval of a side-notched projectile point immediately beneath a stone on the northwest encompassing rim (Wilson 1981:364).

Medicine Wheels outside Saskatchewan

Seventeen of the 27 medicine wheels beyond Saskatchewan's borders are in Alberta, seven in Montana, one in Wyoming, and two in South Dakota (see Table 4). Where possible the out-of-Saskatchewan medicine wheels were classified into the preceding four subclasses. The absence of additional site information from most sources restricted further comparisons. Illustrations of these monuments are presented. The references quoted in Table 4 are published reports together with some secondary sources. Information on four Montana medicine wheel sites was included in Table 4 because the site records contained sufficient information, without the illustrations, to adequately classify those medicine wheels.

Class II: Ceremonial Circles

Previously, enlarged boulder circles were not differentiated from smaller stone circles

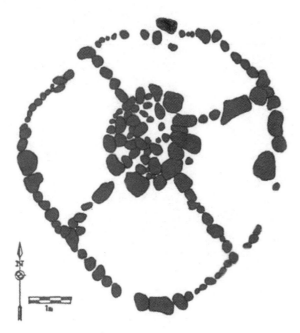

Figure 38: Jennings Site
(39HD22), South Dakota

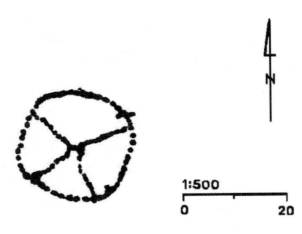

Figure 39: Jamieson's Place Medicine
Wheel (EePl-2), Alberta

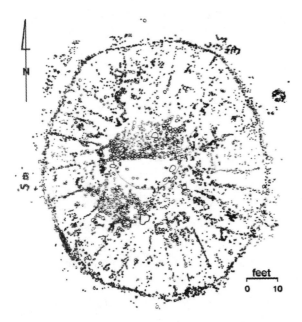

Figure 40: Majorville Cairn and Medicine
Wheel (EdPc-1), Alberta

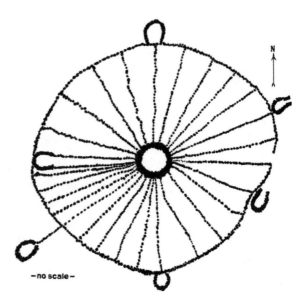

Figure 41: Big Horn Medicine Wheel
(48BH302), Wyoming

as separate functional entities. The term "ceremonial circle" was devised by Thomas F. Kehoe and Gil C. Watson (both former employees of the Saskatchewan Museum of Natural History) in 1964 to define stone circles larger than those which are presumed to represent habitational circles (G. Watson, personal communication). The term incorporates all stone circles in excess of ten meters diameter, or of a size larger than the range of habitation circles which has been assumed to be 1.2 to 9.1 meters in diameter (Kehoe 1960; Loendorf 1970; Adams 1978). Also, this classification includes boulder circles in excess of ten meters diameter with enclosed and/or peripheral boulder features. The varieties of interior and peripheral boulder features are discussed below and listed in Tables 5 and 6.

Since some of those subclasses appear to be similar, based on construction details only, some ethnographic analogies reminiscent of each subclass are presented in Chapter 5 to clarify those assumed classifications. Recent research has revealed ceremonial-related characteristics which should allow definition of a number of varieties between these large circles.

Ceremonial Circle Subclass A

The outline construction similarities at DgMn-3(2) the Oxbow Medicine Wheel Complex (Fig. 42), EgNx-1 the Hughton Medicine Wheel (Fig. 43), and at EfOl-2 the Roy Rivers Medicine Wheel (Figs. 44, 45, 128, back cover) suggest an analogous celebration event. All three possess a large boulder circle with boulder lines articulating with the periphery, suggesting a definite entrance or pathway. The scattered boulders in the interior at DgMn-3(2) suggest a small disturbed cairn. Conversations with this site's landowner revealed earlier unauthorized digging in the 1950s, by unknown persons, of the central cairns of the two medicine wheels at this site. Therefore, it may be reasonable to assume that if a cairn had existed at this feature, it too has been disturbed. The outline at EgNx-1 differs from DgMn-3(2) in the presence of a large central cairn and, beyond the boulder circle periphery, stone lines suggesting a chute or pathway. A third line, between the two chute lines, begins beyond the encompassing circle and extends to a distance equal to the ends of the two other lines (Fig. 43).

Kehoe and Kehoe (1979:15) suggest that EfOl-2was a possible summer solstice marker, using an alignment from the large central cairn through an interior "sunburst feature". When first observed in 1915, the feature was described and shown (Fig. 45) to possess only the central cairn and the northwestern periphery cairn (Begg 1915). The 1980 site examination revealed that the smaller central cairns within the encompassing circle lay high on the prairie sod, suggesting recent placement (between the time of initial observation and the 1964 mapping).

Seven out-of-province features comparable to these three structures are presented in Figures 46 to 52. When compared all reveal similar, though not exactly the same, characteristics (also see Tables 5 and 6).

Figure 42: Oxbow Medicine Wheel Complex, Feature 2 (DgMn-3), Saskatchewan

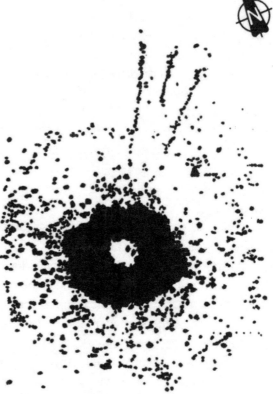

Figure 43: Hughton Medicine Wheel (EgNx-1), Saskatchewan

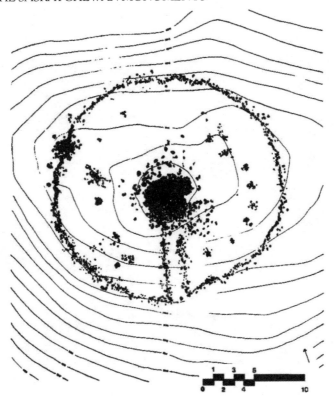

Figure 44: Roy Rivers Medicine Wheel
(EfOl-2), Saskatchewan

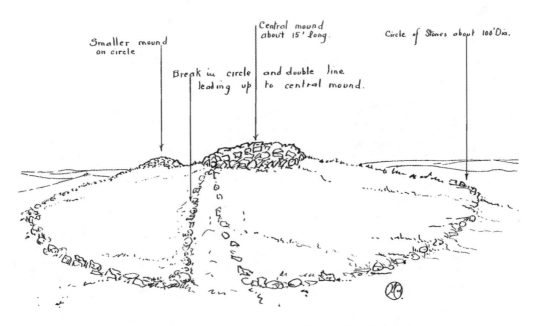

Figure 45: Drawing of Roy Rivers ceremonial circle, 1915

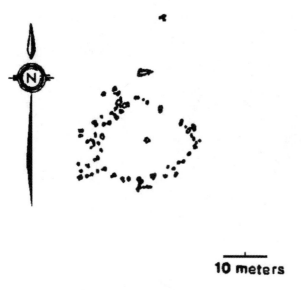

10 meters

Figure 46: Site DgOp-38, Alberta

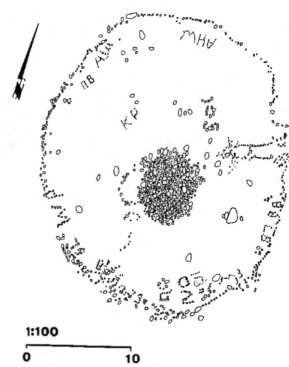

1:100

0   10

Figure 48: British Block Cairn Medicine
Wheel (EdOp-1), Alberta

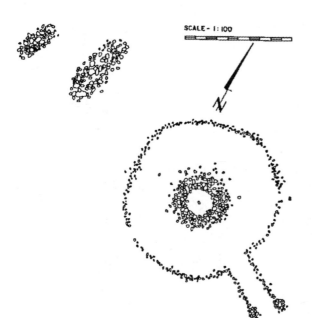

SCALE - 1:100

N

Figure 47: Antelope Hill
(DhPb-2), Alberta

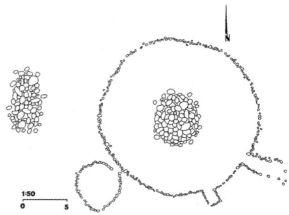

1:50

0   5

Figure 49: Anderson No. 1 Medicine
Wheel (EfOq-36), Alberta

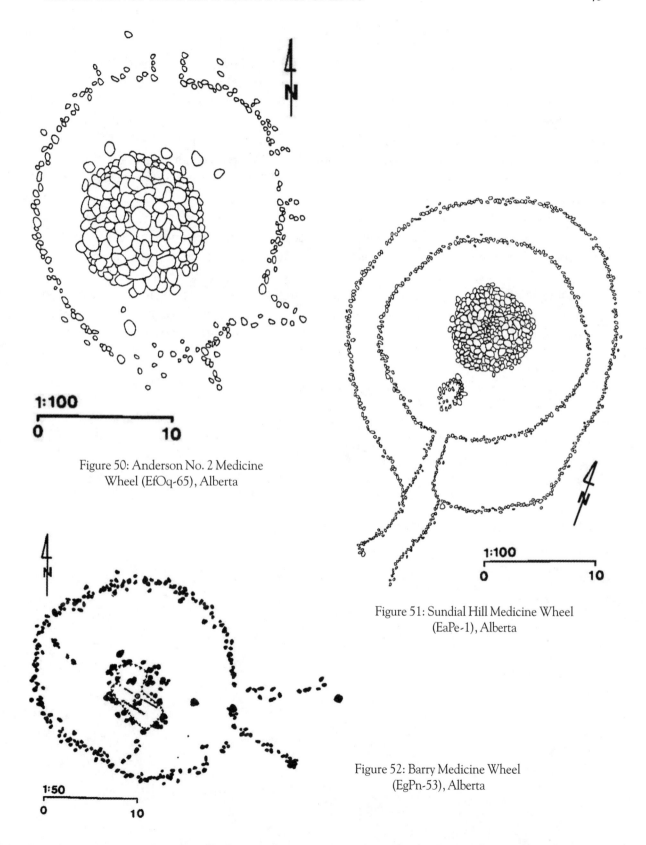

1:100
0   10

Figure 50: Anderson No. 2 Medicine
Wheel (EfOq-65), Alberta

1:100
0   10

Figure 51: Sundial Hill Medicine Wheel
(EaPe-1), Alberta

1:50
0   10

Figure 52: Barry Medicine Wheel
(EgPn-53), Alberta

Ceremonial Circle Subclass B

The Alameda circle at DhMn-9 (Fig. 53), together with the Forget circle at DjMr-1 (Fig. 54), the Claybank circle at EaNh-7 (Figs. 55, 154), and the two Perrin Ranch stone circles at EeNu-1 (Fig. 56) all possess a continuous peripheral boulder circle, and all display either a single large central boulder or an "amphitheatre"-type boulder arrangement. A reverse amphitheatre form was noted at EaNh-7, where the hill apex was 2.3 meters above the elevation of the encompassing boulder circle. The large dolomite boulder at this circle's centre may suggest a speaker's platform. Similarly, a 0.5 meter dolomite boulder in the centre of the DhMn-9 circle may have served the same function. At DjMr-1, the circle centre was recorded to be 0.4 meters below the elevation of the perimeter of the circle.

While the two circles at EeNu-1 were both relatively level across their diameters, they shared one other feature common to the other three circles – all were noted to be distant from any stone habitation circles. In each case stone circles were observed to be a minimum 275 meters from the ceremonial circle. The larger circle at EeNu-1 had a line of small cairns extending 35 meters toward the seven habitation circles. These two large circles were located on a hill apex, permitting a 360 degree view of the surrounding topography (see Table 5). Figures 57 to 60 illustrate non-Saskatchewan monuments in this category.

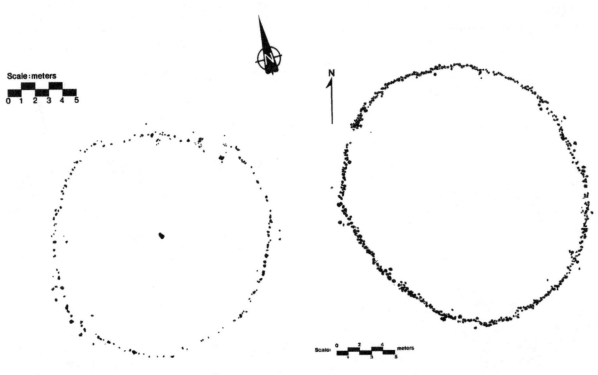

Figure 53: Alameda Ceremonial Circle (DhMn-9), Saskatchewan

Figure 54: Forget Ceremonial Circle (DjMr-1), Saskatchewan

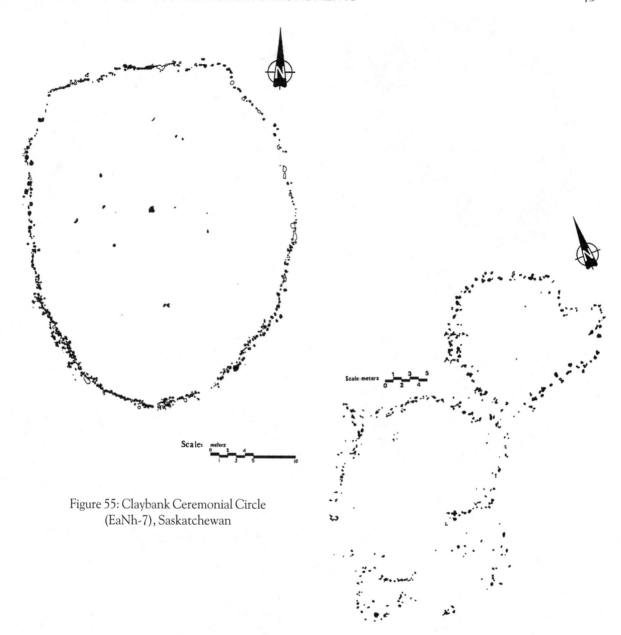

Figure 55: Claybank Ceremonial Circle
(EaNh-7), Saskatchewan

Figure 56: Perrin Ranch Stone Circles
(EeNu-1), Saskatchewan

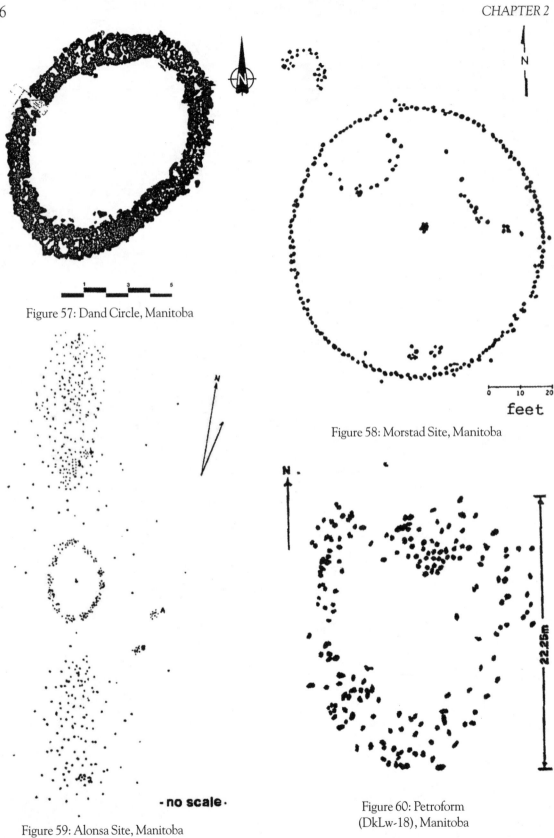

Figure 57: Dand Circle, Manitoba

Figure 58: Morstad Site, Manitoba

feet

- no scale -

Figure 59: Alonsa Site, Manitoba

Figure 60: Petroform
(DkLw-18), Manitoba

Ceremonial Circle Subclass C

The Ogema Stone Circle at DiNf-1 (Fig. 61) and Cronk's Big Circle at FbNp-2 (Figs. 62,153) are characterized as "Enclosed Cairns", as all seven (including the five sites outside of Saskatchewan) consist of a large central cairn completely surrounded by a boulder circle (also see Figs. 120 and 122). The two Saskatchewan features (see Table 5) are situated on relatively level areas at the edge of local prominent heights of land.

FbNp-2 affords a clear northerly view of the upland plains together with a southerly view toward the valley of the South Saskatchewan River. As a site marker to denote a particular coulee, it would have been evident from a variety of locations. Extensive surveys and area excavations have revealed the presence of numerous sub-surface sites, including a buffalo pound in a nearby ravine (Walker 1988). Wanuskewin Heritage Park now encompasses this feature.

DiNf-1, located on the northern edge of the Missouri Coteau, permits two 90 degree views (which may be equivalent to a single 180 degree view; see Table 5), one view to the east and one view to the west of the site. The site is located in a small depression or saddle between the southern uplands and a northern knob landform. Vision toward the north permits a maximum view of 0.5 km of the upslope; however, the knob rises abruptly within 10 meters south of the feature to an elevation of eight meters higher than the site. A natural spring, located to the northeast of the site, has never diminished its flow volume over the past 60 years (landowner, personal communication). As such, this feature might have served as a marker for a fresh water supply. Stones from the central cairn at DiNf-1 are now scattered throughout the central circle. The features in Figures 63 to 67 are outside Saskatchewan.

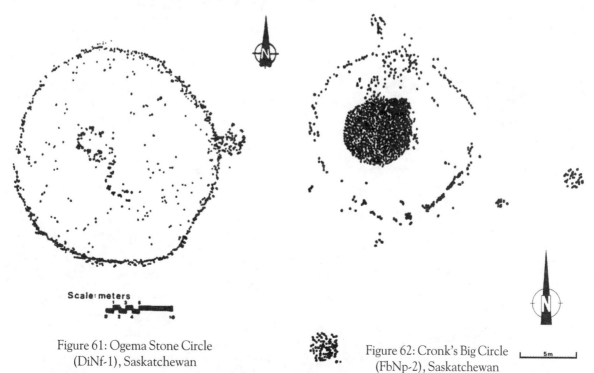

Scale: meters

Figure 61: Ogema Stone Circle (DiNf-1), Saskatchewan

Figure 62: Cronk's Big Circle (FbNp-2), Saskatchewan

5m

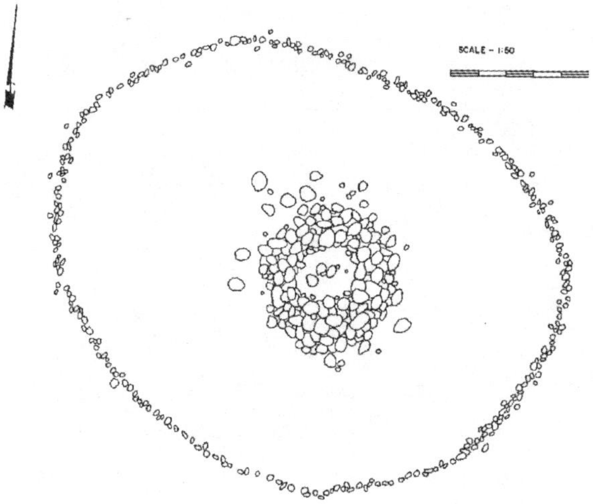

SCALE – 1:50

Figure 63: Miner No. 3 Medicine Wheel
(EfOo-24), Alberta

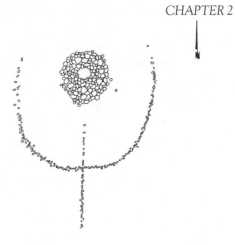

Figure 64: Buffalo Bird Medicine Wheel
(EhOp-1), Alberta

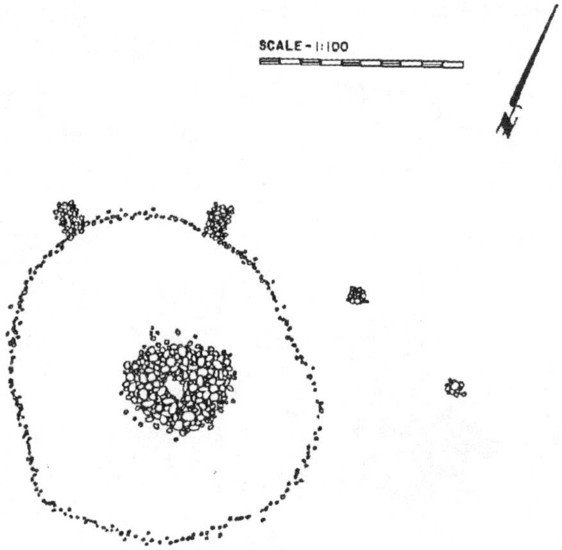

SCALE – 1:100

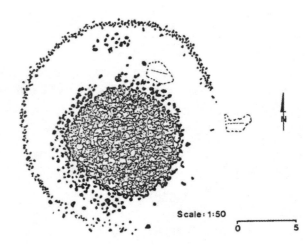

Scale: 1:50

0   5

Figure 66: Rumsey Cairn and Medicine Wheel
(EkPf-1), Alberta

Figure 65: Miner No. 2 Medicine Wheel
(EpOo-10), Alberta

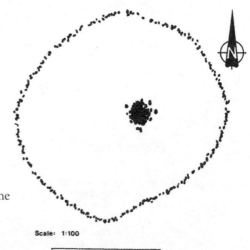

Figure 67: Byrne's M40 Medicine
Wheel (EdOq-30), Alberta

Scale: 1:100

0   10

Ceremonial Circle Subclass D

The Dick Giles Ceremonial Circle at DgNg-2 (Figs. 68, 131) does not have a known comparative form on the Great Plains. While the outline is somewhat elliptical, no other large circle possessed a central line almost dissecting the "circle" into two halves. The other contributing factor that justifies a separate variety is that this figure is within a valley complex adjacent to a stream, on one side, and nine habitation circles on the opposite side (see Table 5). In all other instances, the ceremonial circles occupied higher topographical locations. The only other ceremonial circle directly associated with habitation circles was the figure at DgMn-3. All other (large) ceremonial circles are removed from any habitation proximity.

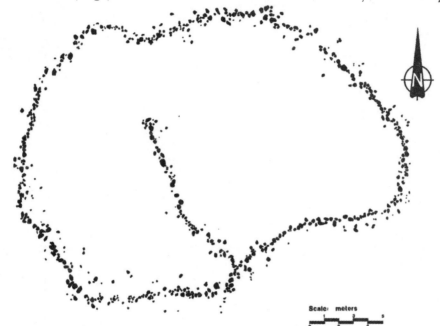

Figure 68: Dick Giles Circle (DgNg-2), Saskatchewan

Class III: Effigy Figures

These figures are divided into animal and human outlines for ease of discussion. Animal boulder outlines show various fauna in sagittal, dorsal, or ventral views. Most human figures were depicted from a ventral view, although one outline illustrates a seated figure with the head and upper torso ventrally and the lower body in sagittal section.

Effigy Subclass IIIA: Animal Outlines

In Saskatchewan animal outlines were located on local heights of land, usually at or near the edge of a valley rim. All of these outlines are/were associated with habitation circles. While habitation circles were not described for most out-of-province sites (Table 7), different types of dwelling structures might have been located in the vicinity of those sites, prehistorically.

The five Saskatchewan animal boulder outlines have been interpreted previously as

Table 5

SASKATCHEWAN CEREMONIAL CIRCLES

Borden Number (Common Name)	Circle Diameters (meters)			Other Immediate Structures	Associated Site Features	Degrees of View	Landform Topography	Water Source Distance/ Direction	Variety (Text Figure)
	N-S	E-W	avg.						
DgMn-3(2) (Oxbow)	15.2	14.2	14.7	Dc, 2el	182s, 2mw, 2c	360	PbI, Tp	river (300m-N)	A (42)
DhMn-9 (Alameda)	15.9	16.1	16.0	B	1s	270	Tp	river (500m-E)	B (53)
DjMr-1 (Forget)	22.5	21.5	22.0			360	K, Tp	spring (150m-SW)	B (54)
DgNg-2 (Dick Giles)	17.5	25.9	21.7	dl	9s	160	Fp	spring (50m-NE)	D (68)
DiNf-1 (Ogema)	32.0	30.5	31.3	De, de	3s	90(x2)	KK, Tp	spring (1km-NE)	C (61)
EaNh-7 (Claybank)	41.9	31.7	36.8	B, sb	5s	270	KK, Tp	spring (450m-SE)	B (55)
EeNu-1 (Perrin Ranch)	19.0			C, Dc,	7s, c	360	Vr, Tp	river (1km-S)	B (56)
	15.5			C, Dc,	7s, c	360	Vr, Tp		
EgNx-1 (Hughton)	7.5	7.1	7.3	Cc, 3il		270	KK, Tp	spring (500m-SW)	A (43)
EfOl-2 (Roy Rivers)	25.2	26.6	25.9	Cc, dc, 2il	1s	360	Vr, Tp	river (1.5km-S)	A (44)
FbNp-2 (Cronk's)	14.9	15.1	15.0	Cc, sb	1s	360	Vr, Tp	river (300m-S)	C (62)

Legend:

Dc	- disturbed cairn	C	- ceremonial circle	KK	- knob and kettle
cl	- exterior lines	Cc	- large central cairn	Vr	- valley rim
B	- central boulder	il	- interior boulder lines	s	- stone circle
dl	- interior disecting line	PbI	- glacial point bar island	mw	- medicine wheel
dc	- diameter cairn	Tp	- till plain	m	- meters
c	- stone cairn	sb	- scattered boulders interiorally		

km - kilometers
Fb - flood plain
K - knob

Table 6

CEREMONIAL CIRCLES OUTSIDE SASKATCHEWAN

Site Reference	Average Diameter (meters)	Variety	Site Features				Structure Features	Text Figure	Reference Source
			s	a	b	c			
DgOp-38(26)	19.0	A	19	4	4	1	scc, ep	46	Graspointner 1980
DhPb-2	13.4	A	2	2		1	lcc, ep	47	ASA
EdOp-1	27.9	A	26	2		4	lcc, ip	48	ASA
EdOq-30	19.7	C				1	scc	67	ASA
EfOo-24	17.6	C	13				lcc	63	ASA
EfOq-36	14.0	A	9	1			lcc, ep	49	ASA
EfOq-65	20.0	A					lcc, ep	50	ASA
EhOp-1	22.5	C					lcc, ep	64	ASA
EpOo-10(2)	15.4	C	20	1	1	8	lcc, 2pc	65	ASA
EaPe-1	26.0	A				4	lcc, ec, ep, ip	51	ASA
EgPn-53	10.9	A					scc, ep	52	ASA
EkPf-1	17.4	C		1		1	lcc	66	ASA
24HL160	30.0	B	402	6	24	27		-	Deaver 1980
GRC-81-2	23.0	B			1	3	scc	-	Deaver 1980
Morstad	23.9	B	6		1	2	scc, 2ea	58	Jerde 1979
Alonsa	14.5	B				2	scc	59	Rutkowski and Westcott 1979
Dand	9.75	B	1	5		1		57	Tamplin (unpublished)
	19.8	B					ea	-	Syms 1970
DkLw-18	19.3	B						60	Nicholson 1980

Legend:
s - stone circles
a - alignment
b - semicircle
c - cairn
scc - small central cairn
lcc - large central cairn

ep - external passageway
ip - internal passageway
ea - enclosed alignment
pc - peripheral circle cairn
ec - enclosed circle
ASA - Archaeological Survey of Alberta 1980

three turtles, one bison, and one salamander. In 1967, two of these monuments, the Mankota Salamander and the Hardy Turtle, were moved and reconstructed in the Condie Wildlife Refuge, a local wildlife park north of Regina. In 1998, both were returned to their original locations (Fig. 71). The ancillary site data at one of those sites had been removed by cultivation during the intervening years; however, the other site remained in pristine condition. Also, one of the three turtle outlines was redefined because of its significant difference from the two other features.

Turtle Effigies

The Pat Giles Turtle at DgNg-1 (Figs. 69, 70) and the Hardy Turtle at DiNe-1 (Figs. 71, 72) depict the animal from a dorsal view (eyes on the top of the head), and show the head wider than the neck. Both show a carapace with outlined feet protruding anterioposteriorly, and displaying claw-like appendages. The tails are depicted at both sites as short 'nubs' terminating in straight boulder lines. DgNg-1 was located within five meters of a valley rim, with the head directed away from the valley creek. Correspondingly, the effigy at DiNe-1 had the tail pointing toward a fresh water spring 400 meters to the west. The boulder line extending from the tail to the neck may indicate a direction toward a water source, an indication of a straight-flowing water source, or possibly a depiction of the carapace ridge. DgNg-1 is located 18 meters west of five habitation circles and within 1.5 kilometers of the Dick Giles ceremonial circle and 2.5 kilometers of a suspected war lodge remnant. Only the ceremonial circle is associated with habitation circles. The war lodge, being on the opposite rim of a tributary valley, is within sight of the DgNf-5 turtle effigy. DiNe-1 possesses four habitation circles approximately 200 meters east of the effigy. Figures 73 to 81 depict turtles in areas ouside of Saskatchewan.

Badger Effigy

DhNe-2 (Figs. 82, 133), originally dubbed the "Minton Turtle" (Kehoe 1965:1,6), was reinterpreted because of differences previously described for the two turtle effigies. The initial investigations presented a perplexity because of the disparity of the depiction of head, legs, tail, and internal features displayed by this effigy. To elucidate the problem, Jim Ryder, an Assiniboine Elder, was shown the field drawing. Mr. Ryder immediately identified the illustration as being the outline of a badger. Additionally he related why a badger would be depicted. In the intervening years other Elders (Velma Goodfeather, Isadore Pelletier, Dexter Asapace, and Howard Cameron) have correspondingly confirmed Mr. Ryder's identification (personal communications).

The head on this effigy was depicted with eyes, anterior nasal openings, proximal mouth and lateral ear protrusions, characteristics not observed on the turtle outlines. Subsequent investigations revealed that when a turtle is laid on its back, the mouth appears as a slit proximally, completely without eye or nostril view. Conversely, when a turtle was depicted dorsally, the eyes should have been located laterally without a mouth depiction. The legs depicted on this feature are shown as single boulder lines extending out to semi-circular boulder circles, without claws (as noted for both turtles). The large boulder cairn in the center of the figure, coupled with a boulder heart line anteriorally and straight boulder life line posteriorly, were noted as non-turtle monument characteristics. Additionally, the tail was depicted as a short stub with a boulder line crossing it and without the boulder line extending away from its end.

During mapping operations, local informants reported the presence of possible "human bones in the central cairn" (G. Watson, personal communication). Research into early SMNH archaeological daily log books revealed a conversation between the initial site reporter and Bruce McCorquodale, the museum's investigator. The diary contents reveal:

> During a conversation with Mr. Leon Uyttenhager…he stated that he had visited the turtle effigy in 1917 and had noticed a large white boulder perched upright on top of the central stone pile. This boulder had a face and numerous other marks incised in it. During the following year (1918) he visited the site and noticed that the boulder [petroglyph] was missing. Mr. Uyttenhager also informed us that during a visit to the site several years after 1918 he observed evidence of an excavation into the central pile of rocks together with the presence of human ribs in the earth removed in the excavation (McCorquodale notes, March 1, 1961).

Salamander Effigy

Constructed showing a dorsal view (lack of eye depiction), the Mankota Salamander (Fig. 83) is an anomaly on the Great Plains. Although first recorded in 1962, the effigy was not mapped until T. F. Kehoe began a project to record Saskatchewan's boulder monuments. After it was mapped in 1964, the outline was defined as that of a tiger salamander (*Ambystoma tigrinum*) by a University of Regina biologist (T. F. Kehoe, personal communication).

This feature was the other boulder effigy that had been taken to the wildlife park near Regina. During the years when the effigy was "away", the landowner had cultivated the immediate environs, destroying the adjacent habitation circles and whatever else may have been associated with this feature.

Bison Effigy

The Big Beaver Buffalo Effigy at DgNh-4 (Figs. 84, 132), located on a prominent hill, is within a habitation camp of 23 stone circles. The effigy is located 32 meters from the crest of a coulee which descends toward the south, opening into a minor valley half a kilometer from the site. The valley has a small, seasonal oxbow creek which drains to the east. The creek maintains small pools only until mid-summer. A second coulee to the west possesses a flowing spring which supplies water to a small slough in the valley, approximately two kilometers upstream from the site.

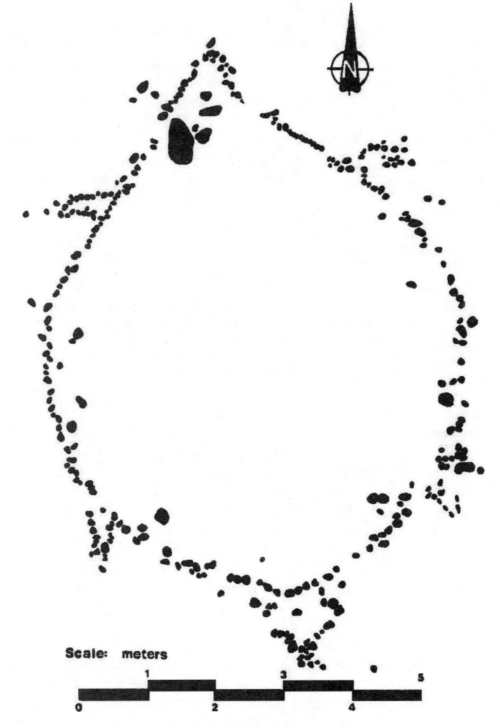

Scale: meters

Figure 69: Pat Giles Turtle
(DgNg-1), Saskatchewan

Figure 70: Photograph of the Pat Giles Turtle Effigy, enclosed in a fence. This feature
has been part of a regional tourism tour in recent decades

Figure 71: Photograph of the restored Hardy Turtle Effigy, shortly after its restoration to its original site in 1998

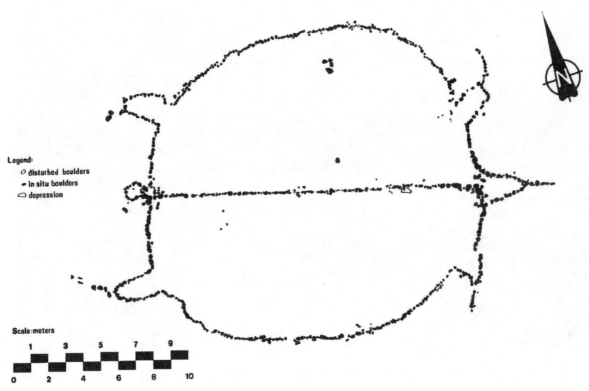

Figure 72: Hardy Turtle
(DiNe-1), Saskatchewan

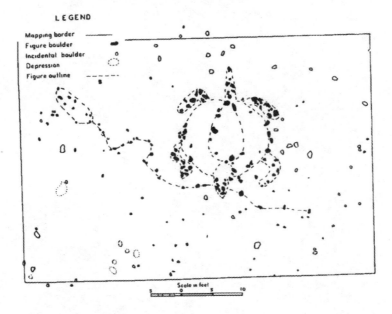

Figure 73: Consort Turtle and Snake, Alberta

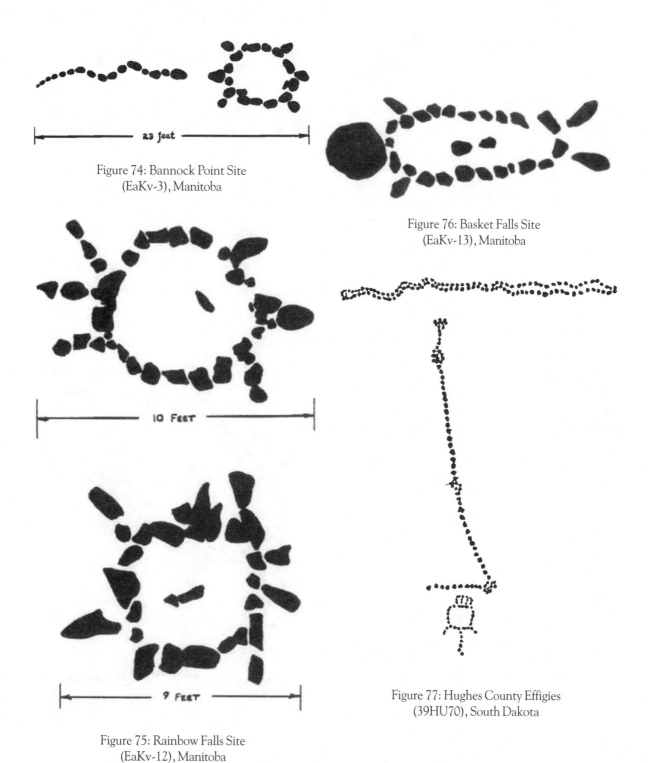

Figure 74: Bannock Point Site
(EaKv-3), Manitoba

Figure 76: Basket Falls Site
(EaKv-13), Manitoba

Figure 75: Rainbow Falls Site
(EaKv-12), Manitoba

Figure 77: Hughes County Effigies
(39HU70), South Dakota

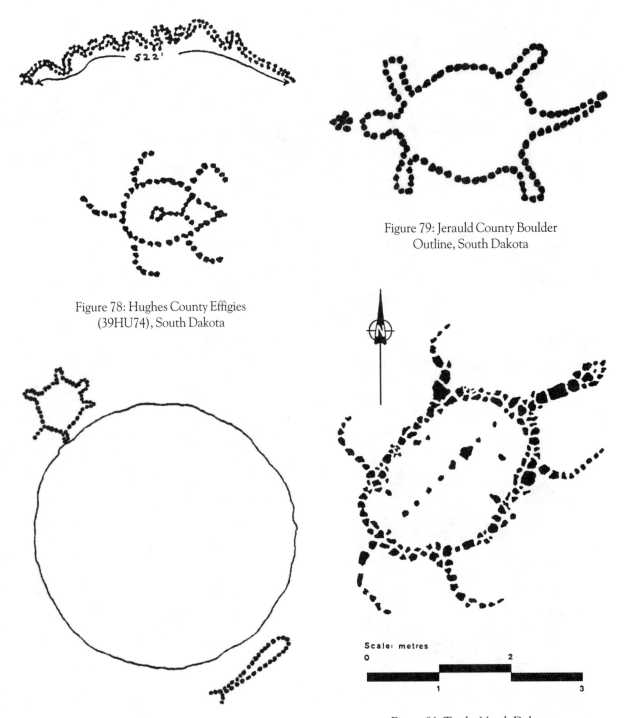

Figure 78: Hughes County Effigies
(39HU74), South Dakota

Figure 79: Jerauld County Boulder
Outline, South Dakota

Figure 80: Minnehaha County Effigies,
South Dakota

Figure 81: Turtle, North Dakota

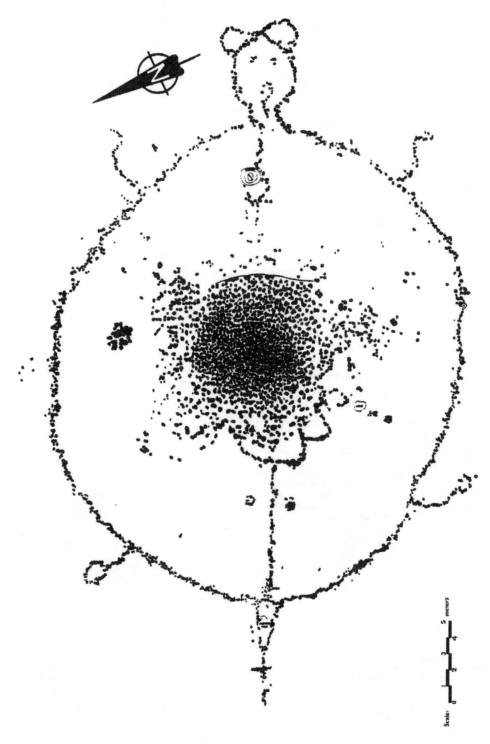

Figure 82: Minton Effigy
(DhNe-2), Saskatchewan

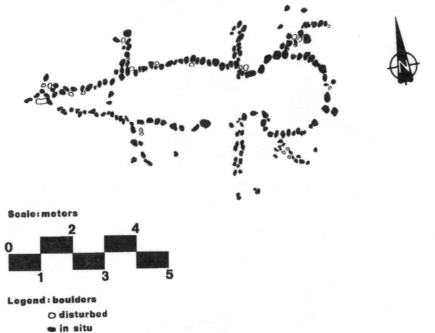

Scale: meters

Legend: boulders
○ disturbed
● in situ

Figure 83: Mankota Salamander
(DiNs-1), Saskatchewan

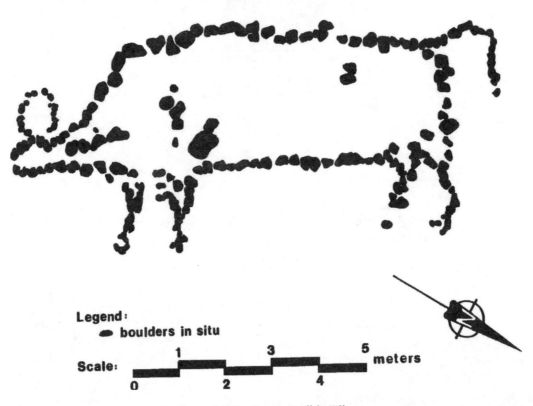

Legend:
● boulders in situ

Scale: meters

Figure 84: Big Beaver Buffalo Effigy
(DgNh-3), Saskatchewan

The effigy's head is lowered, possibly depicting a pre-charge stance. The lowered tail, however, should denote that the animal is not charging. The head points toward the valley, while the feet point east toward the first coulee. A somewhat incomplete heart-line is depicted. The presence of two large boulders ventrally to the tail may suggest the male gender, though no penis is depicted.

Animal Effigies outside Saskatchewan

An additional 13 turtle effigies (Steinbring 1980 [n=9]; Bayrock 1963 [n=2]; Will 1921 [n=2]), three snake effigies (Steinbring 1980), and a bird effigy (Over 1941) are known for the northern Great Plains. Lewis (1890:271) reported three animal effigies with the Minnesota bison, which respectively resembled "...a crane, a turtle, and a bear" (Hudak 1972:245). The lack of illustrations and comparable site information precluded inclusion of these 21 effigies in Table 7. Figures 85 to 92 show various animal effigies outside Saskatchewan (see Chapter 5).

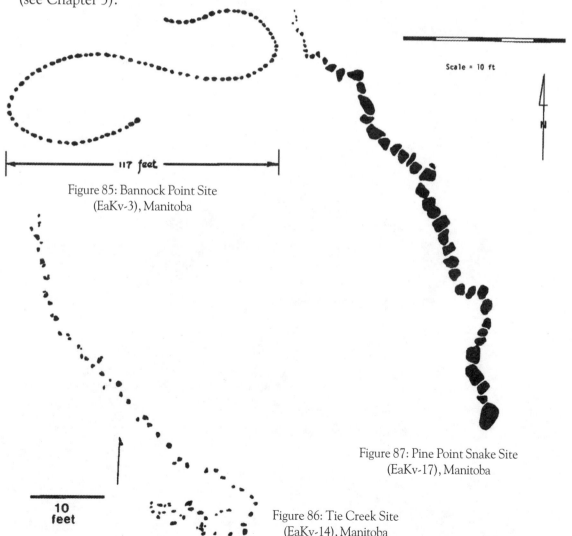

Scale = 10 ft

117 feet

Figure 85: Bannock Point Site
(EaKv-3), Manitoba

Figure 87: Pine Point Snake Site
(EaKv-17), Manitoba

10 feet

Figure 86: Tie Creek Site
(EaKv-14), Manitoba

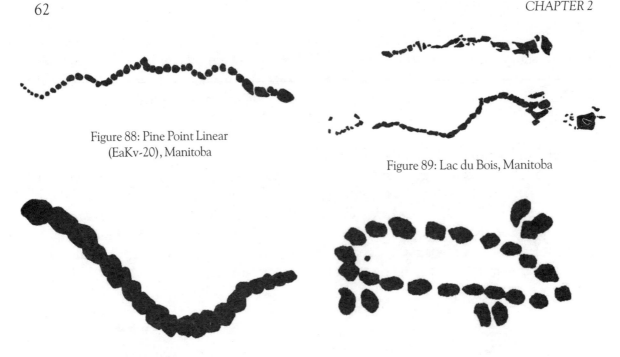

Figure 88: Pine Point Linear
(EaKv-20), Manitoba

Figure 89: Lac du Bois, Manitoba

Figure 90: Fred Sieg Farm
(EaLa-6), Manitoba

Figure 91: Custer County Boulder
Outline, South Dakota

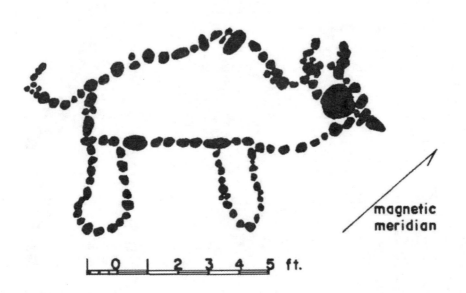

magnetic
meridian

0   1   2   3   4   5 ft.

Figure 92: Minnesota Bison Effigy, Minnesota

Table 7

ANIMAL EFFIGY BOULDER MONUMENTS ON THE NORTHERN GREAT PLAINS

Site Designation	Site Name Or Location	Animal(s) Depicted	Monument Size (Meters) Length	Width	Internal Features	Ancillary Features	Landform Topography	Water Source (Dist.)	Text Figure Number
DgNg-1	Pat Giles Turtle	Turtle	10.55	14.20	c	6sc	Vr-Tp	creek (120m)	69
DgNh-3	Big Beaver Buffalo	Bison	10.48	4.68		23sc	Vr-Tp	spring (1.5km)	84
DhNe-2	Minton Turtle	Badger*	41.98	26.07	hl, al, c	9ac	Vr-Tp	lake (3.5km)	82
DiNe-1	Hardy Turtle	Turtle	26.50	17.08	cl	?sc	KK-Tp	creek (200m)	72
DiNs-1	Mankota Salamander	Salamander	10.55	4.64		?sc	KK-Tp	creek (200m)	83
	Consort Site	Turtle	3.66	3.05					
		Snake	8.05	.57			R-Tp		73
EaKv-3	Bannock Point	Turtle	2.57	1.75					74
		Snake	3.90						
		Snake	35.66			e, gf, c	Bedrock		85
EaKv-12	Rainbow Falls	Turtle	3.05	1.96			Bedrock	river (50m)	75
EaKv-13	Basket Falls	Turtle	2.74	2.46			Bedrock	river (50m)	76
EaKv-14	Tie Creek	Turtle	12.80	3.2			Bedrock		
EaKv-17	Pine Point Snake Creek	Snake	20.66			al, c, gf, e	Bedrock		86
EaKv-20	Pine Point Linear	Snake	2.40				Bedrock	river (200m)	87
	Lac du Bois	Snake	NA	NA					
		Snake	13.01				Bedrock		88

Site	County / Location	Figure				Monument features	Topography	Dist.	Fig. #
EaKv-20		Snake	6.70	6.0			Bedrock	lake	89
EaLa-6		Snake	1.5						90
24PH1707					*	15as, 3c, al		(500m)	-
39HU70	Hughes County	Snake	14.0	5.56	al/h		Vr-Tp	river	77
39HU74	Hughes County	Turtle	82.3	1.83	hl		Vr-Tp	(120m)	78
		Turtle	10.76	3.6				river	
		Snake	2.70						
		Bird	159.11						
	Custer County	Rabbit	NA	NA		gf		river	91
	Jerauld County	Turtle	4.57	2.94				(?)	79
		Snake	47.8			h, c		river	
	Minnehaha County	Turtle	NA	NA				(?)	80
		Fish	NA	NA		mound		river	
Nebraska		Turtle	4.19	3.05	c		Vr	(200m)	92
Minnesota	Murray County	Bison	2.95	1.62	e	al, c, smsc			
North Dakota	Oliver	Turtle	4.63	3.1	cl		Vr	river	81

Legend:

c   - cairn
hl   - heart-line
al   - alignment
Smsc - small stone circles
*   - redefined this research

cl   - centre line
e   - eyes
al/h - head alignments

sc   - stone circles
gf   - geometric figures
h   - human figure
Dist. - distance from the monument to a water source
NA   - not applicable

Vr - Valley rim
Tp - Till plain
r - ridge

Effigy Subclass IIIB: Human Effigies

Human effigies are the second most common of the animalistic boulder monuments, and the best described (Table 8). The 17 recorded human boulder outline sites on the northern Great Plains account for 19 human figures, of which 11 were identified as males and six as females. The two remaining figures did not possess characteristics suitable for gender determination.

Saskatchewan Human Effigies

The four human effigy boulder outlines found in the southern part of Saskatchewan consist of two male and probably two female figures (the precise outline of one female figure was unclear, but was defined on the basis of ethnographic analogy).

The Wild Man Butte - DgNc-l (Figs. 4,93) and Cabri Lake human - EgOk-l (Figs. 95, front cover) outlines share common elements and site characteristics. Both figures have the head oriented toward a northerly direction; both figures are accompanied by a single stone circle (Dyck 1981; Gill and Hymers 1968); both are located within five kilometers southeast of an alkali lake, both are shown with the arms in an elevated position, and both possess a boulder heart-line.

The Wild Man Butte figure could be of Ojibwa origin as was suggested by Dyck (1981); however, its location in southern Saskatchewan might represent an Assiniboine figure also, as the Yanktons were noted to use pictograph symbols (Howard 1976). When first observed in 1863 the Wild Man Butte site was described as:

> ...the peak we passed yesterday... It is quite flat on the top and in the earth is the prostrate form of an elk cut in the ground by the Indians. The body is about 12 feet long, the antlers are very large, and in the place where the body is excavated is a round stone four inches in diameter painted red with some strips of red cloth beneath it. On a less elevated peak adjacent is the large figure of a man with his feet south and his toes east. Nothing but the outlines are made which are of round stones eight inches in diameter embedded in the earth. His length from head to foot is 36 feet. Across the shoulders nine feet, from hand to hand which are in an elevated position 18 feet and in his right hand is a bow and arrow (Clandening 1928:260).

While this basic description fits the Wild Man Butte human effigy, the definition of gender was omitted, possibly due to the vagueness of the penis structure location or because of Victorian modesty. The sex may have been assumed on the basis of the bow and arrow, such tools being attributed to males.

The Cabri Lake Human Effigy at EgOk-l (Fig. 95) is the other Saskatchewan male human effigy. Gender is unambiguously indicated by the boulder depiction of two testes and a penis. Other similarities between this figure and DgNc-l are an outlined trunk, feet pointing toward the figure's left, a definite heart-line, and elevated arms.

Figure 93: Vertical photograph of the Wild Man Butte Effigy. This is one
of the earliest reported boulder monuments in Saskatchewan

Both legs are outlines filled with boulders from the hips to the knees, with single boulder lines from the knees to the toes of the feet. The arms and neck are single boulder lines; however, the 1965 illustration (Kehoe 1965) appears to have fingers depicted. When first sketched by V. A. Vigfusson in 1938, the hands appeared as circular boulder rings (see Fig. 95b). Vigfusson noted that the site had been discovered in 1903 (Sewell 1944). Unfortunately, neither Vigfusson nor the original observer wrote any observations. The 1938 illustration also shows a well-formed head without a neck.

Gill and Hymers (1968:26,27) made pertinent observations when studying and recording this site in 1966 to the extent of measuring and recording six associated cairns and a stone circle (Fig. 94). None of these features had been mentioned during the 1964 site recording. The stone circle suggests a site comparison with DgNc-1, even though the compass orientations of the effigies at each site are different. The presence of cairns in 1967 (absent in 1980) confirms some of Vigfusson's 1938 observations of "...mounds of stone which had been dug into, four of them 1(one) N.E. (northeast) 3 (three) W (west) several artifacts" (Sewell June 28, 1944:1938 notes). By 1980 only the effigy survived to indicate a site.

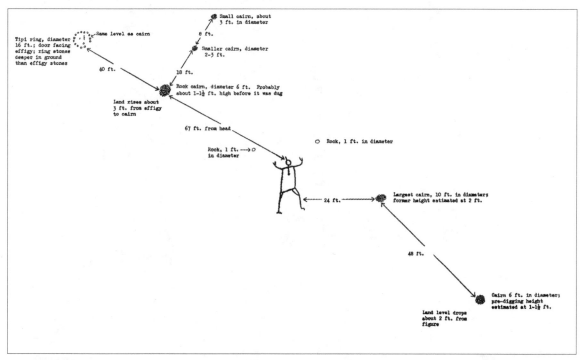

Figure 94: The Cabri Lake effigy and associated stone features as recorded by Gill and Hymers in 1966

The configuration at DkNg-2, the Kayville Human Effigy (Fig. 96), is the smallest human boulder outline recorded. The figure was completely surrounded by a boulder square. The figure was located on a high hill in a knob and kettle terrain, with water available seasonally in small sloughs located in the kettle depressions. As this feature rests on a hill apex, adjacent to a gravelling operation, no ancillary features had survived to the 1980 research

SCALE IN METERS

Figure 95: Cabri Lake Human Effigy (a: left, by Gill and Hymers 1968; b: upper right, by Vigfusson; c: lower right, by Kehoe 1965), (EgOk-1), Saskatchewan

Figure 96: Kayville Human Effigy
(DkNg-2), Saskatchewan

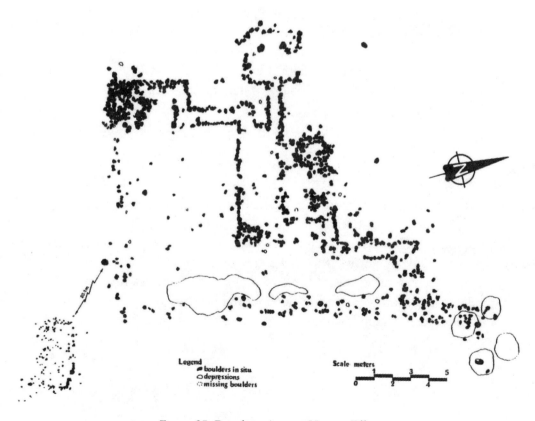

Figure 97: Dewdney Avenue Human Effigy
(EcNh-1), Saskatchewan

date. Habitation circles and stone piles (?) had been mentioned by the persons reporting the location; however, none were noted on the original site inventory. The lack of genital depiction is inferred to indicate that this is probably a female figure.

The Dewdney Avenue Human Effigy at EcNh-1 (Fig. 97), the other female figure, is the only human boulder effigy located within a valley complex. The outline seems to depict a seated female with a child upon her knee, the child's head level with the appearance of her breast. The female's face is portrayed by the presence of eyes only, whereas the child's face is complete with eyes, nose, and mouth. The female's right arm appears to be in a slightly elevated position, and may be holding some object. Beneath the hand-held object a line of boulders extends straight downward to a second line which underlies the seated female. A small rectangular boulder outline was located 23 meters southeast of the effigy. These boulder outlines lie at the eastern base of the valley slope on an old floodplain, 120 meters east of Moose Jaw River, a permanent flowing creek. A small grove of aspen (*Populus tremuloides*) and assorted native fruit shrubs are located immediately to the west of the female's head at the edge of the floodplain. Habitation circles are located on the rim of the valley east of this site.

Human Effigies beyond Saskatchewan

The 13 effigies beyond Saskatchewan's borders have been identified by the individual authors (Table 8) as pertaining to many cultural phenomena; all these are also illustrated in Figures 98 to 110. Readers are directed to the descriptions provided by the original authors (see references in Table 8), as repetition of their analyses is too voluminous to be presented here. The illustrations are provided to exhibit the variability of depiction, and are presented in Figure 3 to show their dispersal across the Plains. Figures 99, 100, and 104 were interpreted to be disturbed human effigies, contrary to the analyses presented for the second two by the article authors, based on their similarity to the other effigies presented in this category.

Class IV: Geometrics

This classification was designed to incorporate those boulder alignments which were definite products of human manufacture, but which may not illustrate distinct form patterns. In this research geometrics include those boulder monuments which may have presented a particular meaning to earlier Plains cultures, even to groups who did not create that monument. Only the Saskatchewan geometrics were personally observed.

Geometrics, representing assumed defense shelters, mosaics, vision-quest retreats, quarry locations, and war lodges are scattered throughout the northwestern Great Plains. Only one of each of the last three examples is clearly documented for Saskatchewan. Of the three,

Figure 98: Human effigy,
Consort Medicine Wheel Site, Alberta

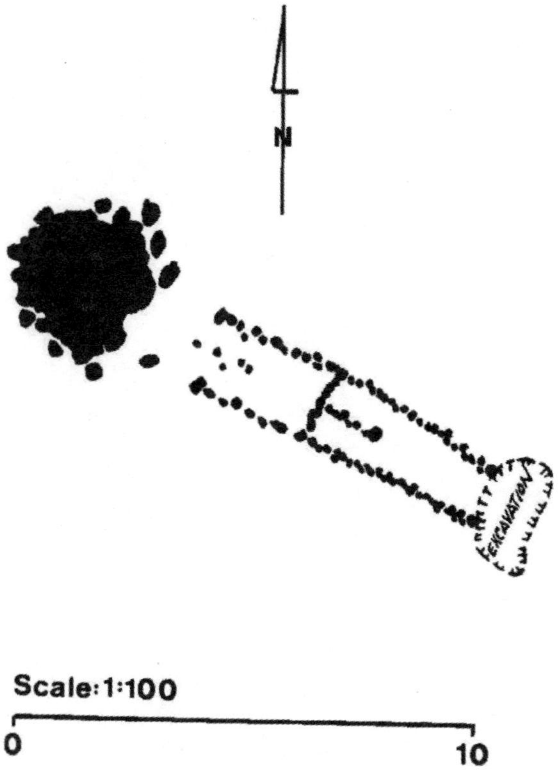

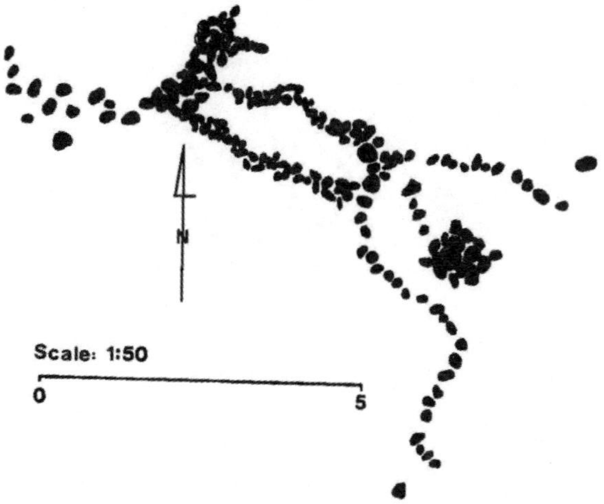

Figure 100: Rumsey Cairn and Medicine Wheel
(EkPf-1), Alberta

Figure 99: Ross Medicine Wheel
(EfOs-36), Alberta

Undisturbed boulder —
Disturbed boulder —
Edge of depression —

Figure 102: Steveville Boulder
Outline, Alberta

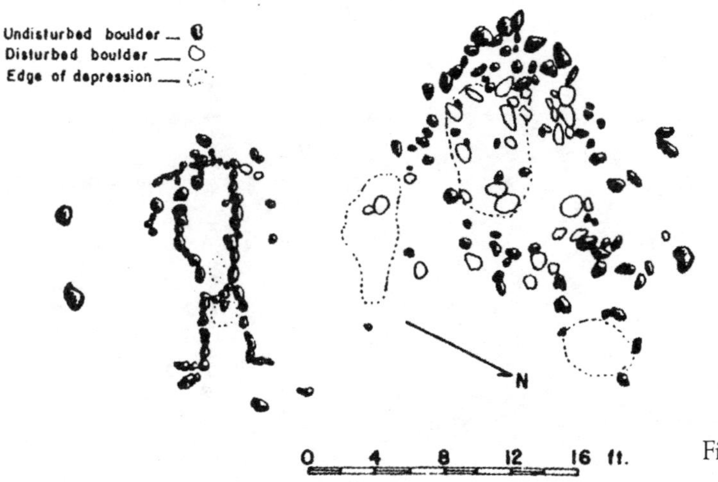

Figure 101: Cluny Human Effigy, Alberta

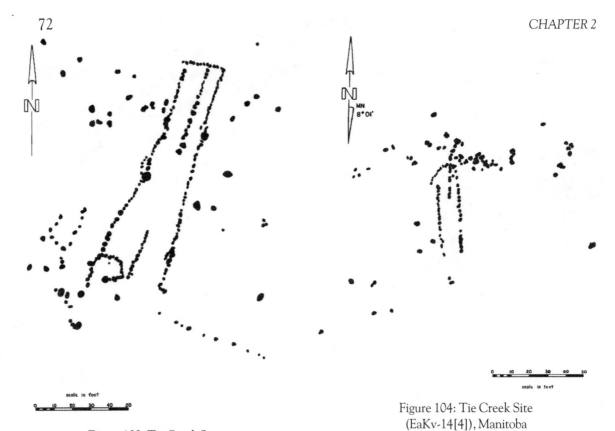

Figure 103: Tie Creek Site
(EaKv-14[1]), Manitoba

Figure 104: Tie Creek Site
(EaKv-14[4]), Manitoba

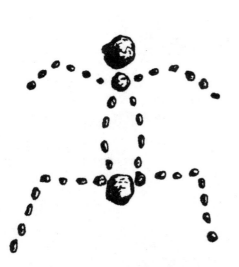

Figure 105: Pryor East Site, Wyoming

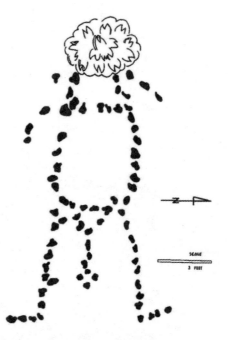

Figure 106: Bozeman Human Effigy
(24GA106), Montana

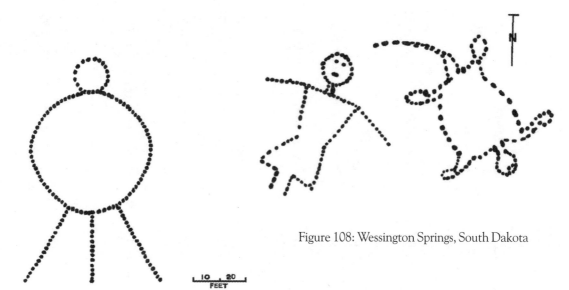

Figure 108: Wessington Springs, South Dakota

Figure 107: Landslide Butte, Montana

Figure 109: Punished Woman's Hill,
South Dakota

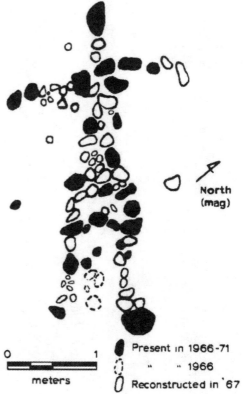

Figure 110: Tuyan-witchashta-karapi,
Minnesota

Table 8
NORTHERN GREAT PLAINS HUMAN BOULDER OUTLINES

Site Designation	Name	Gender	Head (Toward) Direction	Internal Boulders	Ancillary Features	Text Figure Number	References
DgNc-1	Wild Man Butte	M	N	Hl, ma, b	sc	4	Kehoe 1965; Clandening 1928; Dyck 1981
DkNg-2	Kayville	F	S	+	9sc	96	Watson 1975
EcNh-1	Dewdney Avenue	F & ?	W	e, br, b	r	97	This research
EgOk-1	Cabri Lake	M	ENE	Hl, k, p, +	sc, c	95	Watson 1976; Kehoe 1965
EfOs-36	Ross Medicine Wheel	M*	WNW	Hl, p, +	c, al	99	ASA
EkPf-1	Rumsey Cairn						
1965	Medicine Wheel	?	WSW	+	lsc	100	ASA
	Consort	M	WSW	Hl, p, +	sc, c	98	Wormington and Forbis
	Cluny	M	S	+	al	101	Kehoe and Kehoe 1957
	Steveville	M	SE	Hl, p, +		102	Bryan 1968; Kehoe 1965
EaKv-14(1)	Tie Creek Site	F*	SSE	Hl, br, b	al	103	Buchner 1976a; Steinbring 1970
EaKv-14(4)	Tie Creek Site	M*		Hl, +		104	Buchner 1976a; Steinbring 1970
24GA106	Bozeman	M	W	p, +		106	Malouf 1975; Kehoe and Kehoe 1957
	Pryor East	F		v, +		105	Simms 1903b
	Landslide Butte	M		p, +		107	Kehoe and Kehoe 1957
	Wessington Springs	F	NNE	e, m, +	sc	108	Todd 1886; Lewis 1891
	Punished Woman's Hill	M & F	NW	M: p, + F: br, v, +	c, al	109	Lewis 1889
	Murray County	M	NW	+		110	Hudak 1972

Legend:
M - Male   sc - stone circle   al - alignment   v - vagina   * - gender defined   b - body outline
F - Female   e - eyes   c - cairn   * - gender defined by this research   + - stick body depiction
? - sex indeterminate   p - penis   m - mouth   ASA - Archaeological Survey of Alberta
Hl - heart line   br - breast   lsc - large stone circle   r - Rectangular boulder configuration

vision-quest retreats are the most prolific type encountered, with sites identified across the western portion of the study area. While other geometrics have been identified (see Table 9 and Figure 3), only the visited Saskatchewan sites have been classified into the assumed subclasses.

Geometric Subclass IVA

The Lawrence Ranch Vision Quest retreat at DkOj-2 (Fig. 111) is located on a regional height of land within the Cypress Hills escarpment. The glaciated hills resemble mountain foothills with deep, narrow coulees, and shallow surface soils and are "…rolling areas in which ground moraine, with strong swell and swale…though there are local till and outwash plains" (Richards 1969:41).

The site consists of an inverted 'U'-shaped configuration 9.3 meters wide and 11 meters long, constructed of boulders and heaped earth half a meter in height. Two boulder lines extend out from the tips of the 'U', and a central boulder line (between the two other lines) begins halfway between the two tips and extends an equal length. A large dolomite boulder (0.93 m long x 0.79 m wide x 0.57 m high) is situated between the centre and west lines at the opening of the 'U'. A small concentration of fire-cracked rock is located 8.57

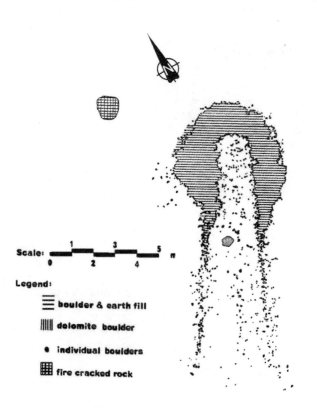

Figure 111: Lawrence Ranch Vision Quest Site
(DkOj-2), Saskatchewan

Figure 112: Burmis Boulder Paving
(DgPn-28), Alberta

meters west of the centre of the top of the 'U'. A habitation camp existed 2.5 kilometers east of the site prior to 1950 (Russel Lawrence, personal communication). The structure occupies the height of land toward the eastern edge of the escarpment. A permanent creek is located 3.2 kilometers to the west.

A similar feature is found at the Burmis Boulder Paving site in Alberta (Fig. 112).

Geometric Subclass IVB

The Marj Giles Effigy located at DgNf-5 (Fig. 113,159) is adjacent to a valley edge. The valley and some of the contributing coulees possess both aspen poplar (*Populus tremuloides*) and river (or black) poplar (*P. deltoides*) which offer an ample supply of logs, bark and brush. This site is within one kilometer of DgNg-1 and DgNg-2 (previously described as a turtle effigy and a possible dance-floor area), both of which are associated with habitation circles. As neither of these two sites is visible from DgNf-5, the chance of this feature being used during occupation of either of the two other sites is possible.

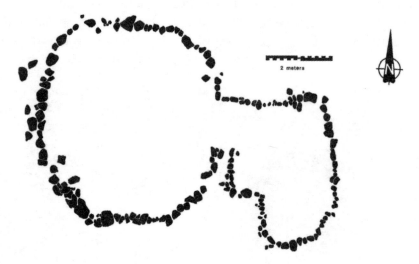

Figure 113: Marj Giles Effigy
(DgNf-5), Saskatchewan

The valley below this site possesses a permanent, spring-fed, stream producing an ample water supply which hasn't diminished its volume of flow since the land was first homesteaded in 1908 (Dick Giles, landowner, personal communication). This small stream flows south into Montana and ultimately into the Missouri River system. As such it would present a viable route toward other tribes camped along its banks.

Geometric Subclass IVC

The Bone Creek Effigy at DkOe-2 (Fig. 114) represents the only Saskatchewan boulder monument constructed solely of reddish-orange, iron-stained quartzite boulders. The boulders are elliptical and relatively uniform in size (averaging 23 centimeters logitudinally). Forty-five habitation circles are located to the north, south, and east, with the majority to the east, occurring up to 130 meters away. None of the habitation circles possess any iron-stained quartzite boulders. Immediately to the west the land slopes gently down to an old floodplain which is completely devoid of habitation circles, possibly indicating a spring occupation when that plain would be flooded by Bone Creek, 200 meters to the west of the site. This boulder monument lies within an old excavation which was dug 24 centimeters below the surrounding prairie level. A second excavation was located 14 meters south of the monument. Both excavations possessed an equal number of a common assortment of artifacts; however, only the north excavation possessed the iron-stained boulders.

Figure 114: Bone Creek Effigy
(DkOe-2), Saskatchewan

Geometrics beyond Saskatchewan

At least fifty other boulder alignments were located within the available literature (to 1986) on the Great Plains and eastern environs outside of Saskatchewan. Most publications list these features as mosaics, geometrics, or boulder pavements. As the majority of the publications do not illustrate these features, they cannot be speculated on as to form, function, or possible tribal association. The exceptions were the Thunderbird nests discussed by Carmichael (1979). As the comparable ethnographic material is somewhat conjectural, these features are discussed in Chapter 5. A number of these are illustrated below, in Figures 115 to 118 and 135 to 147.

Scale = 10 ft

Figure 116: Jessica Exit Site
(EaKu-8), Manitoba

Scale = 10 ft

Figure 115: Jessica Lake Portage Site
(EaKu-7), Manitoba

Figure 117: Molloy Lake Site
(EaKu-9), Manitoba

Figure 118: Astwood Petroforms
(EbKu-9), Manitoba

Figure 119: A constructed stone line, one of many in the Cabri Lake Hills

Figure 120: A ceremonial circle in the Cabri Lake Hills as photographed in 1988. Note the stone circles.
The rocky land surounding the ceremonial circle has since been plowed up

Figure 121: The Moose Mountain Medicine Wheel. Note the central cairn,
encompassing circle, and panoramic view

Figure 122: The Cabri Lake ceremonial circle (see Figure 120) as seen from the ground, in 1989

Figure 123: Tom Kehoe and Gil Watson recording Cronk's Big Circle (also called the "Tipperary Creek Medicine Wheel") in October, 1964

Figure 124: The hill on which the Roy Rivers ceremonial circle is located

Figure 125: The Oxbow Medicine Wheel Complex, feature 3

Figure 126: The Jelly Ranch Medicine Wheel; note the stone circle in the foreground

Figure 127: The Oxbow Medicine Wheel Complex, feature 1

Figure 128: The Roy Rivers ceremonial circle from the ground, showing the central cairn
on the right and the smaller cairn found on the encompassing circle, on the left

Figure 129: The diameter of a large, unmapped stone circle found on "Pony Butte" near Gouldtown
is indicated by the positioning of the people. The insect-like figure on the petroglyph boulder
(inset photo) 3.2 km distant from the circle was originally aligned so as to point to the circle

Figure 130: A large, unmapped, somewhat lopsided "circle" found near Forgan

Figure 131: The Dick Giles Ceremonial Circle (DgNg-2)

Figure 132: The Big Beaver Bison Effigy, seen from the ground

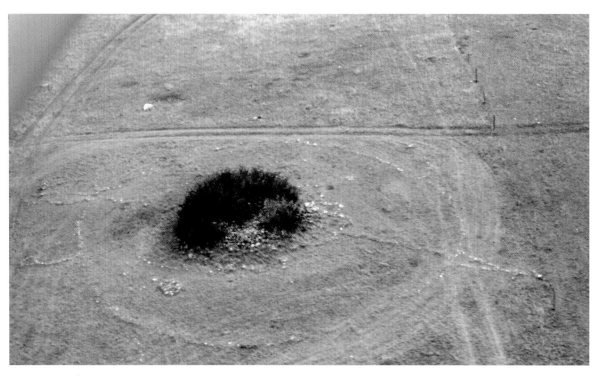

Figure 133: The Minton Effigy (DhNe-2). Note the vehicle tracks

Figure 134: Lichens growing on a boulder. *Dimelaena oreina* thalli are the light green ones (dead *D. oreina* are grey), and the orange ones are *Xanthoria* spp.

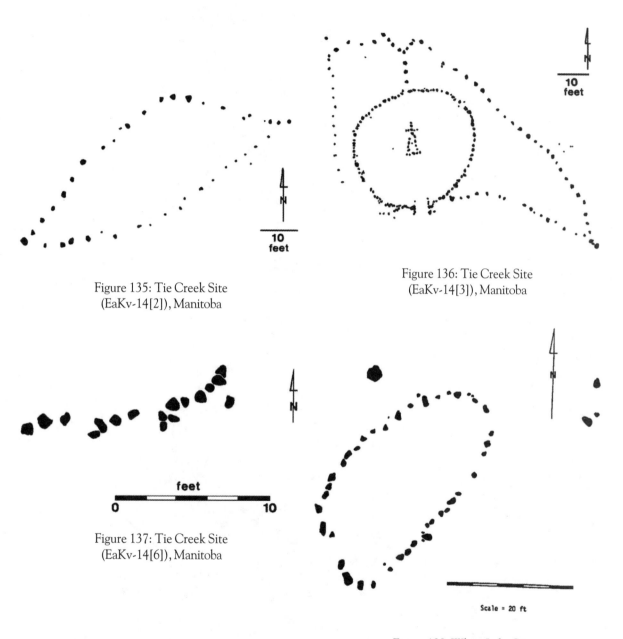

Figure 135: Tie Creek Site
(EaKv-14[2]), Manitoba

Figure 136: Tie Creek Site
(EaKv-14[3]), Manitoba

Figure 137: Tie Creek Site
(EaKv-14[6]), Manitoba

Figure 138: White Lake Site
(EaKv-21), Manitoba

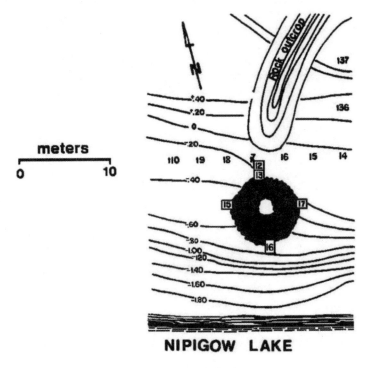

Figure139: Thunderbird Site
(EgKx-15), Manitoba

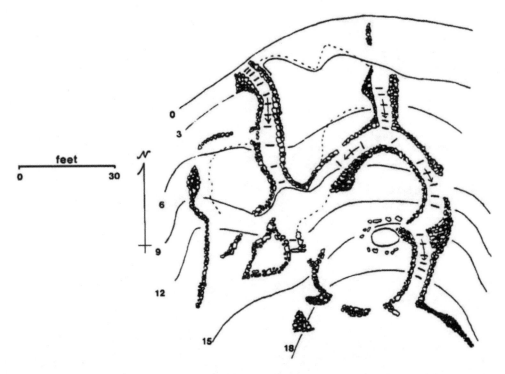

Figure 140: Palframan Sites
(CbGu-1), Ontario

Figure 141: Palframan Sites
(CbGu-2), Ontario

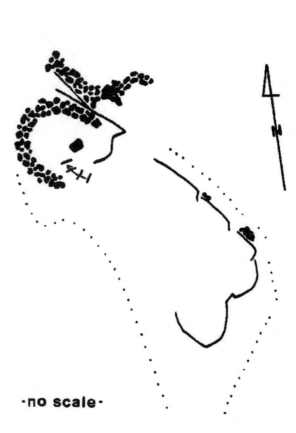

Figure 142: Talon Lake Rock Structure
(CcGs-1), Ontario

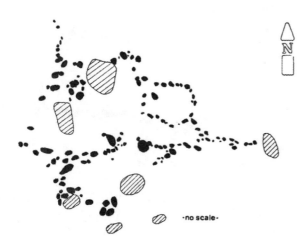

Figure 143: A. C. Marshall Site
(24PH70), Montana

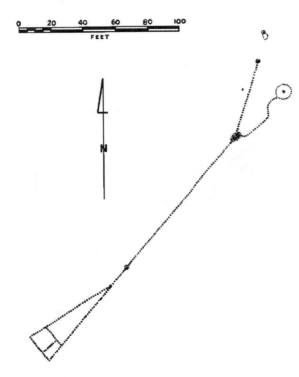

Figure 144: Hadsell Ranch Rock Figure
(48FR302), Wyoming

Figure 145: Scinger Ranch Figure,
Custer County, South Dakota

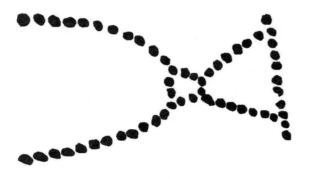

Figure 146: Boulder Outline,
Custer County, South Dakota

Figure 147: Sampson Ranch,
Custer County, South Dakota

Table 9
GEOMETRIC BOULDER MONUMENTS ON THE NORTHERN GREAT PLAINS
AND IN NEIGHBOURING AREAS

Site Designation	Geometric Type	Political Area	Reference	Text Figure
DgPn-28	G	Alberta	Carpenter 1975:38	112
DkOj-2	V. Q.	Saskatchewan	This research	111
DgNf-5	W. L.	Saskatchewan	SMNH	113
DkOe-2	G	Saskatchewan	Watson 1975:20	114
EaKu-7	G	Manitoba	Buchner 1976b:33	115
EaKu-8	G	Manitoba	Buchner 1976b:31	116
EaKu-9	G	Manitoba	Buchner 1976b:34	117
EbKu-9	G	Manitoba	Buchner & Callaghan 1980:98	118
EaKv-14(2)	G	Manitoba	Buchner 1976a:16	135
EaKv-14(3)	G	Manitoba	Buchner 1976a:17	136
EaKv-14(6)	G (?)	Manitoba	Buchner 1976a:20	137
EaKv-21	G	Manitoba	Buchner 1976b:35	138
EgKx-8	G	Manitoba	Carmichael 1979:97	N
EgKx-15	G	Manitoba	Carmichael 1979:8	139
EgKx-23	G	Manitoba	Carmichael 1979:98	N
CbGu-1	G	Ontario	Tyyska & Burns 1973:17-23	140
CbGu-2	G	Ontario	Tyyska & Burns 1973:23-27	141
CcGs-1	G	Ontario	Tyyska & Burns 1973:27	142
24CB410	V. Q.	Montana	Conner 1982:90 (Fig. 2)	N
fasting bed	V. Q.	Montana	Conner 1982:92 (Fig. 3)	N
24CB654	V. Q.	Montana	Conner 1982:94 (Fig. 4)	N
fasting place	V. Q.	Montana	Conner 1982:97 (Fig. 7)	N
24BH417	V. Q.	Montana	Conner 1982:102, 103 (Fig. 9, 10)	N
24BH665	V. Q.	Montana	Conner 1982:105 (Fig. 12)	N
24BH665IV	V. Q.	Montana	Conner 1982:106	N
24CB420	V. Q.	Montana	Conner 1982:111 (Fig. 16)	N
24PA551	V. Q.	Montana	Conner 1982:114 (Fig. 17)	N
24CB411	2-V. Q.	Montana	Conner 1982:87	N
24CB419	4-V. Q.	Montana	Conner 1982:91	N
24PH70	G	Montana	Davis 1975:32	143
24HL28	3-V. Q.	Montana	Keyser 1979:21	N
24CB750	3-V. Q.	Montana	Loendorf 1969:49	N
Pryor Mountains	5-V. Q.	Montana	Wedel 1961:266	N
Glacier Park	3-V. Q.	Montana	Kehoe 1958:431-432	N
48FR302	G	Wyoming	Rea 1966:15-21	144
Custer County	G	South Dakota	Over 1941:47	145

Custer County	G	South Dakota	Over 1941:48	146
Custer County	G	South Dakota	Over 1941:49	147
39CU46	G	South Dakota	U. S. D. (*) 1981	N
39FA150	G	South Dakota	U. S. D. (*) 1981	N
39FA168	G	South Dakota	U. S. D. (*) 1981	N
39FA186	G	South Dakota	U. S. D. (*) 1981	N
39FA341	G	South Dakota	U. S. D. (*) 1981	N
39FA369	G	South Dakota	U. S. D. (*) 1981	N
39FA383	G	South Dakota	U. S. D. (*) 1981	N
39HU227	G	South Dakota	U. S. D. (*) 1981	N
39HU352	G	South Dakota	U. S. D. (*) 1981	N
39HU353	G	South Dakota	U. S. D. (*) 1981	N
39JE4	G	South Dakota	U. S. D. (*) 1981	N
39JE6	G	South Dakota	U. S. D. (*) 1981	N
39SL85	G	South Dakota	U. S. D. (*) 1981	N
39SL92	G	South Dakota	U. S. D. (*) 1981	N
39SL136	G	South Dakota	U. S. D. (*) 1981	N
39SL143	G	South Dakota	U. S. D. (*) 1981	N
39SL146	G	South Dakota	U. S. D. (*) 1981	N
39SL147	G	South Dakota	U. S. D. (*) 1981	N
39SL149	G	South Dakota	U. S. D. (*) 1981	N
39SL158	G	South Dakota	U. S. D. (*) 1981	N
39SL162	G	South Dakota	U. S. D. (*) 1981	N
39SL163	G	South Dakota	U. S. D. (*) 1981	N
39SL168	G	South Dakota	U. S. D. (*) 1981	N
39SL175	G	South Dakota	U. S. D. (*) 1981	N
39SL177	G	South Dakota	U. S. D. (*) 1981	N
39SL179	G	South Dakota	U. S. D. (*) 1981	N
39SL186	G	South Dakota	U. S. D. (*) 1981	N
39SL213	G	South Dakota	U. S. D. (*) 1981	N
39SL229	G	South Dakota	U. S. D. (*) 1981	N
39SL230	G	South Dakota	U. S. D. (*) 1981	N
39SL232	G	South Dakota	U. S. D. (*) 1981	N
	V. Q.	South Dakota	Howard 1972:300	N
32MN40	V. Q.	North Dakota	Fox 1980:88	N
32MN41	V. Q.	North Dakota	Fox 1980:88	N

Legend: G   - geometric

V. Q. - visioning site

W. L. - war lodge

(?)   - disturbed

(*)   - computer printout, no illustrations available

N   - no illustrations available

3 – THE HISTORICAL AND ETHNO-CULTURAL CONTEXT

...the ethnohistorian has two main tasks: (1) the critical editing and presentation of historical documents relating to Indian cultures, and (2) the interpretation of data gleaned from these sources (Wedel and DeMallie 1980:118).

Introduction

The date of the initial human habitation of the southern Saskatchewan Plains region, where these people originated, and how they integrated with one another are problems remaining to be solved. The variety of projectile point forms and the introduced changes in tool and weapon technology (see Dyck 1983: 65-68) suggest continual introductions of peoples and cultures through time although there has been continuous occupation over the past 12,000 years (Dyck 1983:63-140).

Two hundred and fifty years ago Edward Umfreville (1954:91-92) noted eight major tribes (Blackfoot [Siksika, Piegan and Blood], Plains Cree, Ojibwa [Saulteaux/Bungi/Western Chippewa], Sarcee, Arapaho, Gros Ventre (Atsina), Lakota Sioux, and Assiniboine [Nakota]) occupying the Northern Plains. Similarly fifteen major tribes (Cheyenne, Crow, Mandan, Hidatsa, Shoshoni, Arikara, Comanche, Tunaxa, Pawnee, Teton [Dakota], Padouca, Gattack, Kiowa, Yankton [Nakota] and Kiowa-Apache) were noted for the American portion of this Great Plains area (Spencer and Jennings 1965:339; Malouf 1967:15; Ewers 1979:Plate 1).

To try to discover the possible identity of the original boulder monument constructors, it is necessary to review which tribes were residing on the northwestern Great Plains at first European contact (ca. 1690) and, so far as it is possible, during the preceding centuries. This review is intended as an examination not only of the residents and their possible origins, but as an examination of different tribal migrations on and across the study area as they may relate to the authorship of boulder monuments. This is particularly difficult to do, since movements of peoples and changes in their territories were common and complex in (for example) the early 19th century (DeMallie 2001: viii) and probably much earlier.

Thirty tribes, representing ten language families, occupied the North American Great Plains over the past 700 years (Spencer, Jennings, et al. 1965; Ewers 1979; Malouf 1967). Fifteen tribes, representing six language groups, are directly connected with the northern

Great Plains area as shown in Figure 148 (Wissler 1927:140-141; Skeels 1967: 23). It is feasible that many other tribes representing other language groups explored, or at least traversed this northern area. The ethnic identities of the total Great Plains occupant entourage may never be known.

As boulder monuments are surface configurations, it has been assumed that these features were constructed by people within the past 3000 years (wind borne soils and the ensuing colonization of these deposits by vegetation usually obliterate all surface disturbances within one to two hundred years). Consequently, the earlier Paleo-Indian (or Early) and Middle Periods are not discussed here.

Potential Prehistoric Antecedents

The effigy mounds of Minnesota and the Adena and Hopewell mounds of the upper Mississippi River area share some design similarities with Plains boulder monument animal outlines. However, there are significant differences in construction materials, sizes, and purposes: the earthen mounds served as burial mounds (Stoltman 1979:127).

The Hopewell Culture, 100 B.C. to A.D. 200, appears to have maintained trading networks across the Great Plains as far west as the Rocky Mountains (Prufer 1965:132). While such trade may have influenced their trading partners' style motifs, the absence of earthen effigy mounds on the Great Plains may suggest that there was little or no Hopewell burial ceremonial influence in this area. Also, boulder monuments are usually located singly, whereas earthen effigy mounds are "... more commonly found in groups of a dozen or more..." (Ritzenthaler 1963:2).

Wedel (1959:564-566) proposed that the Middle Missouri Central Plains Tradition (ca. A.D. 1000) evolved from Middle Mississippi influences (approximately A.D. 900), based on general similarities in ceramics and house styles. The earthlodge peoples are contemporaneous with Initial and Extended Middle Missouri but have dissimilarities in geographical distributions, architecture, village layouts, burial customs, and several artifact types (Lehmer 1971:107), and therefore they may possibly share only some influences of the late stage of Mississippian dispersal. The Initial and Extended Middle Missouri peoples were probably Siouan speakers, and resemble similar tribes in southern Minnesota and northern Iowa (Lehmer 1971:100, 120, 126). Additionally, the Arikara, as a Post Contact Coalescent Variant of Middle Missouri, possibly represent a late Caddoan migration and adoption of earthlodge village traditions (Lehmer 1971:136). The northern earthlodge people's burial patterns are poorly known (Lehmer 1971). Even the earliest migrants into the middle Missouri may possibly be viewed as peripheral to Mississippian traditions (Willey 1966:320, 338).

Based on 19 groups of human crania (a total of 942 individuals), Ossenberg's 1974 study illustrated that the Minnesota and Illinois Woodland samples were dissimilar to one another, although the Minnesota series "...was morphologically closer to local prehistoric groups and to historic Plains tribes than it [was] to the Hopewell series" (Buikstra 1979:228-229).

Consequently, there seems to be sufficient evidence to dispel any notion that Adena, Hopewell, or the Middle Missouri cultures were ancestral to, or the basis from which, Plains boulder monuments evolved. Even the analysis of human burials discounts any possibility of a migration of those peoples into Minnesota as possible originators of the later boulder designs. Finally, the near lack of earthen animal effigies in the vicinity of areas occupied by the late-date descendants of the Middle Missouri cultures yields them as unlikely boulder monument constructors.

The earliest radiocarbon dates (see Calder 1977:vii,41-42; Kehoe and Kehoe 1979:42) for Plains boulder monuments fall within the Late Period (2000 BC to AD 1750) as defined by Dyck and Morlan (2001:115). The Late Period in Saskatchewan is notable for the introduction of two new forms of artifacts into the traditional bison hunter's tool assemblage: clay pottery and side-notched arrow projectile points. The pottery probably represents a dispersal of population and technology from the east, whereas the arrow points may have evolved on the western Plains (Dyck 1983:110).

The major complexes attributed to the Late Period are Pelican Lake, Besant, Avonlea, and various Phases and Complexes within the last millenium. Besant ceramic styles are known best from North Dakota, South Dakota and eastern Montana (Dyck 1983:115). Additionally, the emphasis in these tool kits toward the use of Knife River Flint from western North Dakota also reflects the "hallmark of the Illinois Hopewell complex which thrust its far flung trading relationships and cultural influences into the Missouri River area between 2050 B.P. and 1750 B.P." (Willey 1966:273, 280). Several theories exist concerning the fate of the Besant Complex. Some see it developing into Prairie Side-notched forms, developing into the later Avonlea Complex, or developing into a separate entity and displacing Avonlea. Byrne (1973:470) contends that the selection of the most appropriate analysis requires future comparisons of all complexes present in the northern Plains in this time period.

Avonlea Complex sites seem concentrated in the southern portions of Alberta and Saskatchewan and in northern Montana, with isolated sites in southern portions of Manitoba and northern Wyoming (Dyck 1983:123; Davis 1988). Reeves (1983:163-166) regards Avonlea as a transformation of the earlier Pelican Lake Complex. Avonlea people may have absorbed the earlier Besant Complex and evolved into the later complexes, or they may have been displaced by these later complexes (Dyck 1983:125). The final analysis is yet to be done.

Currently, more is known about the Plains villages of North and South Dakota than any other late prehistoric northern Plains group (Dyck 1983:126). When Prairie Side-notched complexes first appeared in Saskatchewan approximately 1100 years ago, the Late Woodland Blackduck Complex ceramics also began to appear in southern Manitoba and northern Minnesota. Blackduck was characterized as using Prairie Side-notched projectile points similar to those of the buffalo plains and larger Middle Woodland side-notched and corner-notched forms characteristic of the Great Lakes region (Dyck 1983:126).

While the archaeological record substantiates a continuous ten to twelve thousand year occupation, the Natives that the Europeans encountered may evidence only the most recent migrants. Beginning approximately 1100 years ago, the occurrence of the Blackduck ceramic phase in Manitoba denotes a cultural intrusion (possibly early Algonkians) from eastern woodlands (Syms 1977). A population surge from the Middle Missouri agricultural peoples (Johnson 1969:13) corresponding with a warmer and more moist climate (Bryson and Wendland 1967:294) may indicate the beginning of new western migrations. Following a two-hundred year drought, ending at 500 B.P. (Lehmer 1971:128), there may also have been another surge of Algonkian and Siouan peoples westward from the eastern woodlands onto the Great Plains (Ewers 1968:173). While some ethno-archaeological identifications, based on ceramic analysis (Byrne 1973) or projectile point forms (Dickson 1977), are possible, the identification of all cultures by technological analysis may be questionable.

"Recent" Inhabitants and Migrants

Historical journals indicate great influxes of peoples onto the northern Great Plains in the protohistoric and early historic periods (James 1830; Cocking 1909; Hind 1971). Many historic and late prehistoric tribes laid tentative claims to portions of this area (Lewis 1942; Malouf 1967; Mooney 1907), each with varying degrees of success. The tribal entities discussed below are those whose claims or presence are recorded in many of the early written records. Figure 148 illustrates the presumed general tribal locations during the periods A.D. 1600 to 1690, 1690 to 1730, 1730 to 1840, and 1840 to 1870. These four periods define the assumed late prehistoric migrant areas, migrations initiated by the fur trade onto the prairies, the period of unrest caused by fur trade rivalry and the latest migrations up to the era of the treaties with the Indians. As the tribes occupying this area are believed to have constantly engaged in inter- and intra-tribal warfare, all named areas delineate tentative locations. Additionally, these migrations were probably by small homogeneous ethnic groups, representing bands or autonomous kin factions of a tribal unit (Syms 1982:2-3). The remaining tribe portions may have followed later, amalgamated with other tribes, or ultimately formed their own *in situ* separate and distinct units.

As earlier residents may have been displaced, or are not readily definable in ethnographic terms, this review of recent migrants onto the Plains begins with the Algonkians. Their possible arrival 1100 years ago, as denoted by Blackduck ceramics and an assemblage comparable to both the Plains and Woodland projectile points, suggests that they are the possible earliest recent migrants onto the Northern Plains.

Linguistically, the earliest recorded migrants were possibly Algonkians (Blackfoot and Arapaho) from the eastern woodlands and Dene moving south from northern Canada. Kootenayans may have entered from southwestern intermontane areas, Siouan bands from the southeast, and Caddoans from the south.

The traditional impression of an empty Plains region awaiting peripheral occupants (Kroeber 1952:257) is no longer accepted, as the archaeological record clearly indicates considerable antiquity (Dyck 1983). While former travel and technological modes may have been abandoned, migrants must change culturally in a new environment. This change might involve cultural blending among migrants emerging from different directions toward what is sometimes referred to as a "Plains Identity". In this model the later Plains Indians might all adopt certain features from each other's cultures and blend them into more homogeneous cultures. Mandelbaum (1979:24) notes that the Cree traded with "Slaves and Eskimo"; and that the Assiniboine, Monsoni, Ojibwa, eastern Algonkians, Dakota, Athapaskans, and Blackfoot "occasionally camped with and married into the bands of the Cree" (1979:34). In these exchanges, men and women might be viewed as the vehicle for both genetic exchange and the movement of styles, ceremonies, and language alterations (adoption of idiomatic expression and new words) between tribes.

Algonkian Linguistic Family
Blackfoot

The Blackfoot confederacy is comprised of the Blood (Kainai), Piegan (Pikunis), and the Blackfoot (Siksikas) (Schultz 1980:311). During historic times the Blackfoot occupied southern Alberta and northern Montana. The Piegan, the most populous segment (Malouf 1967:8), occupied the Eagle Hills in Saskatchewan prior to 1730 (Lewis 1942:14-15; Thompson 1916:348). By approximately 1730 the Piegan had moved to southern Alberta (Wormington and Forbis 1965: 238). In 1789 the Blood were located north of the Piegan, along the South Saskatchewan River; and the Blackfoot were reported north of the Blood (Lamb 1970:116). While the original Blackfoot "heartland" has not been established, their linguistic affiliation as Algonkian assumes an ultimate eastern origin (Barbeau 1974:37). Their earlier territory probably extended from the North Saskatchewan to the Missouri River (Coues 1897:532-533; Barbeau 1974:37) and from the Rocky Mountains into southeastern Saskatchewan, "… the eastern edge of the plains near the transition region between the forests and the plains…" (Lewis 1942:5).

The Saulteaux at Crooked Lake in southeastern Saskatchewan indicated that before 1700 the area belonged to the Blackfoot (Tarasoff 1980:8).

Plains Cree

The earliest records identify the Cree as the Keskachewan or Christinaux. The latter term was applied to these people by the French, whereas the Hudson's Bay Company and the Northwest Company men referred to them in the west as Cree (Russell 1991:121). When selling their furs at York Factory in the early 1700s, the Hudson's Bay Company recorded 19 distinct Cree Bands (Russell 1991:123). As an originally woodland people, their southern movement south of the North Saskatchewan River into the central parklands followed the smallpox epidemics of 1781-1782. Prior to 1840 the Cree occupied the mixed poplar forest area of Saskatchewan (Burpee 1927:25); however, during the 1690s they were making seasonal raids against the Crow and Mandan on the Missouri River (Russell 1991:216). This sporadic warring, as opposed to residency, may be evidenced by their attempts to sell Crow and Mandan

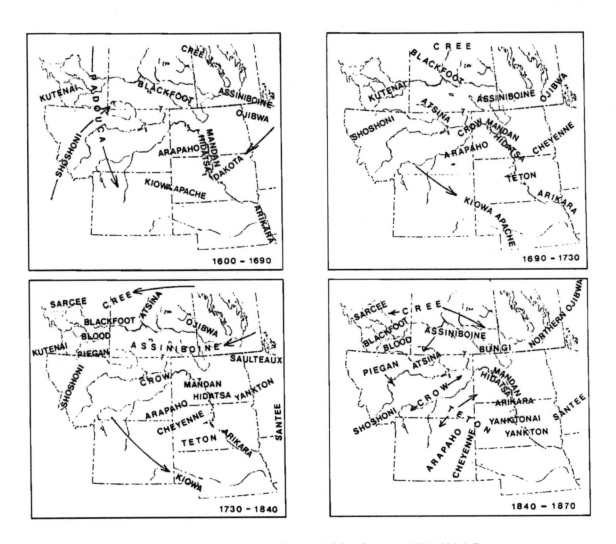

Figure 148: Northern Great Plains tribal distributions, 1600-1870 A.D.

captives at York Factory between 1697 to 1714 (Russell 1991:216).

Plains Ojibwa

The Plains Ojibwa (Bungi) and Saulteaux (Northern Chippewa) were divisions of the Minnesota Chippewa (Hickerson 1962:2; Howard 1977:5-6) who migrated out of Minnesota about 1740 (Hallowell 1936: 34). As early as 1790 they were plying the fur trade along the Assiniboine River in western Manitoba and eastern Saskatchewan (James 1830:30, 37).

The Ojibwa-Cree alliance of 1737 was promoted by the Ojibwa desire to obtain firearms as a defence against their traditional Sioux enemies (Grant 1960:346). Following this alliance, the Ojibwa were noted to have attacked and defeated the Blackfoot both in Alberta and Montana (Skinner 1914:491-492).

Cheyenne

Prior to 1680 the Cheyenne may have occupied the forested area of central Canada (Mooney 1907:363). Weist (1977:11) indicates that the probable Cheyenne homeland may have been central-northern Ontario. Joliet's map of 1673 located the "Chaiena" above the mouth of the Wisconsin River, while La Salle records a group of "Chaa Indiens" near Fort Crevecoeur on the Illinois River in 1680 (Berthrong 1972:4). By 1684 the Cheyenne were located along the western Minnesota River, and by 1700 they had become sedentary farmers to the northwest of Traverse Lake in North Dakota (Berthrong 1972:5-6). By the late 1770s or early 1780s, war with the Chippewa forced the Cheyenne west to the Missouri River (Thompson 1916:261-263). As they had obtained horses from western and southern sources prior to 1750 (Berthrong 1972:9), their removal gave them "...free range from the Saskatchewan to the Rio Grande..." (Mooney 1907: 421).

By 1796 they were allied with the Arapaho in the Black Hills. When they left the Black Hills in the 1830s they divided into the Northern and Southern Cheyenne (Malouf 1967:10).The Northern Cheyenne maintained territory in South Dakota, northern Wyoming, and in southeastern Montana (Powell 1969:124). Besides the Arapaho, Berthrong notes that the Cheyenne allied themselves with the Sioux (1972:45), the Atsina and Blackfoot (1972:77), and eventually with the Kiowa, Comanche, and Kiowa-Apaches (1972:73). Their ability to traverse the entire Great Plains is confirmed by their knowledge of 46 tribal names of "importance" (Mooney 1907: 421).

Arapaho

The Arapaho were western neighbours of the Cheyenne on the Minnesota and Sheyenne Rivers (Berthrong 1972:17). Attacked by the Assiniboine and the Chippewa, as had been the Cheyenne (Swanton 1952:384-386), the Arapaho eventually allied themselves with the Cheyenne; and together they effectively drove the Kiowa and Kiowa-Apache out of the Black Hills (Berthrong 1972: 17). As there was friction between the Teton Dakota and the Cheyenne (Berthrong 1972: 19), the latter alliance would have provided greater security against any foe. Since the Cheyenne were acting as middlemen between the Arapaho and the eastern Missouri Indians, the alliance would have assured the Arapaho of a continuous supply of goods.

Hudson's Bay Company explorer and trader Peter Fidler traded with the "Tattooed Indians" at Chesterfield House, at the junction of the South Saskatchewan and Red Deer rivers in 1800 (Johnson 1967). These are most likely Arapaho.

Linguistically the Arapaho are closer to the Atsina, and both once may have been a common tribe (Malouf 1963:13). This linguistic affiliation may have been the means for later unification among the Arapaho, Cheyenne, Atsina and Blackfoot.

Gros Ventre (Atsina)

The Gros Ventre are also known as the Fall Indians, Rapid Indians, Gros Ventres of the Plains, Gros Ventres of the Prairies and Atsina. The second last two names distinguish them from the Hidatsa (Minnetari or Minetaree), who were known as the Gros Ventres of the Missouri (Swanton 1952:389; Kroeber 1908:146). The term "Gros Ventres" was applied to the Atsina by French traders' [mis?]interpretation of the hand sign the Atsina used for identification: "…a gesture of the hand over the stomach indicating always hungry…" (Morton 1939: 16). Atsina is derived from the Blackfoot term "Atsena", meaning "Gut People" (Morton 1939:16; Kroeber 1908:145).

Originally the Atsina were separated from the Arapaho by the Crow (Swanton 1952:385). The Arapaho moved to the southwest into southeastern Montana and South Dakota, while the Atsina were forced into Saskatchewan (Swanton 1952:385) and into southern Manitoba (Lamb 1970:112). Where they entered Saskatchewan is unknown; however, their presence was known later near Prince Albert, as: "…the old South Branch House was destroyed by the Fall Indians in the summer of 1794" (Johnson 1967:253).

They are noted along the South Saskatchewan River, as it was recorded by Masson as "La Fourche de Gros Ventres" (Masson 1960:map). That map also indicates an Alberta occupation, as the Belly River is referenced as "Rivière des Gros Ventres".

The Atsina became Blackfoot allies possibly when the latter resided in or near Saskatchewan's Eagle Hills. About 1867 the Atsina became Crow allies and were later heavily decimated during a conflict with the Piegan (Kroeber 1908: 146).

Siouan Linguistic Family
Dakota

Commonly known collectively as Sioux, the Dakota are subdivided into seven bands: 1) Mdewakantwan (Spirit Lake People), 2) Wahpekute (Shooters Among the Leaves), 3) Sisitonwan (Sisseton), 4) Wahpetonwan (Wahpeton), 5) Ihanktonwan (Yankton), 6) Ihanktonwana (Yanktonai), and 7) Titonwan (Teton)… (Howard 1966:3).

The first four are collectively known as the "Santee or Eastern Dakota" (Swanton

1952:282), whose dialect is "Dakota" (Howard 1966:4). Bands 5 and 6 are the "Middle Dakota", whose dialect is "Nakota" (Howard 1966:3-4). Band 7 is the "Western Dakota", whose dialect is "Lakota" (Howard 1966:3-4).

The Dakota are first mentioned in the Jesuit Relations at or near Lake Nipigon or the Lake-of-the-Woods region (Swanton 1952:283,388). These Dakota were not specified either by band or dialect, but may have been Middle or Western Dakota, as both these groups were noted, in 1683, in northern Minnesota (Howard 1966:11,20). Shortly after, both groups migrated toward the southwest. The Yankton moved into southeastern South Dakota, the Yanktonai settled to the north of them in southern North Dakota and eastern South Dakota, while the Western Dakota moved toward the Black Hills.

By 1700 to 1750 the Western Dakota, or Teton, migrated to the high Plains along the Missouri River. Ultimately, their numbers increased until their band became larger than the six other Dakota bands combined (Howard 1966:20). As their populations multiplied: "...the Tetons ranged southward into Nebraska, westward into Colorado and Wyoming, and northward into western North Dakota and Montana, with occasional forays into Manitoba and Saskatchewan..." (Howard 1966:21).

Assiniboine (Nakota)

Originally a portion of the Yanktonai Dakota Hunkpatina sub-band, the Nakota separated from them when the Hunkpatina occupied the Lake-of-the-Woods district of Ontario (Swanton 1952:282, 388). By approximately 1661 they had become Cree allies, who were expanding northwest and west out of Ontario. This alliance was to obtain firearms and other trade goods which the Cree were receiving from British fur trade companies (Mandelbaum 1979:17-22).

The Nakota are commonly referred to in the historical literature as Assiniboine and are called Stoneys in Alberta because of their original method of cooking food with hot stones (Bryan 1968:289). They speak the 'N' dialect of Dakota. The Dakota refer to them as: "Rebels, an appellation earned [by] joining the Plains Ojibwa and Plains Cree..."(Howard 1966:19).

Kennedy (1961:XXV) suggests that the Assiniboine movements after 1650 were toward northern Ontario and Manitoba, around the northern end of Lakes Winnipeg and Winnipegosis, and onto the Saskatchewan Plains (District of Assiniboia) by 1750. James (1830) suggests that Assiniboine movement was south of those two lakes, with the occupation along the Assiniboine River, and ultimately (1780s) onto the Plains. Undoubtedly, both routes are feasible. The same routes were probably followed by the Assiniboine as recent Cree allies (Swanton 1952:388).

By 1807, Alexander Henry could account for eleven Assiniboine bands in the Saskatchewan region (Rodnick 1937:410-411). Eventually, they spread to the Milk River districts of Alberta and Montana, and some to the northern Missouri River in Montana (Swanton 1952: 87).

During the 170 year period of 1690 to 1860, Assiniboine territory fluctuated. Their eastern exploitation border was reduced to the extreme southwestern corner of Manitoba, while their northwestern border shifted toward the Edmonton district, gradually decreasing to southwestern Saskatchewan (Ray 1974:5-22). Between 1821 and 1860 they extended south into northeastern Montana and northwestern North Dakota (Ray 1974:96-101,184).

Hidatsa

Also known as Minnetarees or Gros Ventres of the Missouri, the Hidatsa claim their origin near Devil's Lake in North Dakota (Swanton 1952:276). They eventually migrated to the Missouri River area and allied with the Mandan, who introduced them to a horticultural mode of life (Bowers 1965:15). Originally composed of three sub-tribes (Awaxawi, Awatixa, Hidatsa-proper), they eventually redivided into the Hidatsa-proper (commonly referred to as Hidatsa), the Crow and the Mountain Crow (Bowers 1965:14-15).

The Hidatsa extended their villages along the Knife River in western North Dakota as well as maintaining villages among the Mandan (Wedel 1961:202-208). They may originally have lived in Canada "…on the north side of the international boundary", prior to their settlement on the Heart River of western North Dakota (Swanton 1952:573).

Mandan

La Vérendrye noted Mandan villages along the Heart River (a tributary of the Missouri in North Dakota) in 1793 (Burpee 1927:335-337). Their oral history suggests a southwesterly migration from an eastern sea coast (Thomas and Ronnefeldt 1976:241). The Mandan maintained two villages on the Missouri River between the Heart and Little Missouri Rivers (Swanton 1952:276). The summer residence was near their gardens on the Heart River; the winter village was in a wooded area downstream from Fort Clark on the Missouri (Thomas and Ronnefeldt 1976:224). As sedentary semi-agriculturalists, the Mandan enjoyed the advantages of their crops and the bison which frequented the Missouri River Valley (Thomas and Ronnefeldt 1976:174,241).

Crow

The Crow separated from a sedentary, agricultural mode of life about 1776 (Denig 1953:17-19). Following their separation from the Hidatsa, they further divided into the Mountain Crow occupying the Powder, Wind and Big Horn Rivers of southern Montana and northern Wyoming, and into the River Crow occupying the Yellowstone River from the Montana highlands to its confluence with the Missouri River (Lowie 1956:4; Swanton 1952:391). As instigators of the Atsina-Arapaho separation (Swanton 1952:386), the Crow may have pursued the Atsina north into Saskatchewan, thereby explaining the Atsina's displacement toward Saskatchewan's geographical centre (Johnson 1967).

Caddoan Linguistic Family
Arikara

Sometime before 1714 the Arikara split from the Skidi-Pawnee in southern Nebraska (Swanton 1952:274; Wedel 1961:162,200). These semi-sedentary earth lodge dwellers ate fish and freshwater clams from the Missouri River. Also tool types found in their village remnants and middens suggest their utilization of a variety of Plains birds and mammals (Wedel 1961:161-176). The majority of their villages existed from the Missouri River at its confluence with the Grand and Musselshell Rivers in North Dakota south to the central portion of South Dakota's Missouri drainage system (Thomas and Ronnefeldt 1976).

Numic Linguistic Stock
Shoshone (or Shoshoni)

Plains Shoshone were former residents of the southwestern Great Basin and intermontane areas of Utah and Nevada. Their northward migration may have been to search for more bountiful territories. The Wyoming Comanche separated from them during the migration; the remainder of the tribe continued north into Idaho and Montana and possibly into Alberta and Saskatchewan (Swanton 1952:403-404; Lowie 1909:169-173). Following their defeat by the Blackfoot, the Shoshone were expelled from the Canadian Plains by the end of the eighteenth century (Malouf 1967:13). A variety of other Plains tribes further harassed them, eventually displacing them into the intermontane areas of Montana and Idaho (Lowie 1909:171-173).

The Shoshone have also been referenced as the "Snake Indians" (Turney-High 1941:14). Previously this "Snake"-Shoshoni link has been used to qualify the Shoshoni in Thompson's 1730 reference to a Piegan-Cree alliance to "Drive the Snake out of Blackfoot territory" (after Glover 1962:240-241). However, the term "Snake" also was an appellation used by both early chroniclers and other tribes to indicate a general reference to an enemy or to a different tribe (Byrne 1973; Forbis 1963; McGee 1897).

Byrne (1973:515-538) contends that there never was a Shoshone occupation of the Alberta plains, based on known ceramic analyses. However, the absence of definite Shoshone ceramics from the known Alberta ceramic sites (recorded up to 1973), may not be sufficient evidence to deny their possible seasonal or sporadic forays onto the Alberta and Saskatchewan plains.

Kootenayan Linguistic Stock
Kootenay (Kutenai)

The Kutenai, a division of the Tunaha (or Tunaxa) (Swanton 1952:392), were located along the Belly River in southern Alberta (Lewis 1942:15). The Piegan also displaced the Kutenai along the Bow River during the mid-eighteenth century, and drove them back into their former intermontane homelands in Idaho and British Columbia (Lewis 1942:11).

Na Dene (Athabaskan or Athapascan) Linguistic Family
Sarcee (or Sarsi)

The Sarcee were first mentioned by Cocking (1909:iii) in 1772. Umfreville (1954:198) later located the Sarcee in 1790 near "Stoney Mountain". Alexander Henry (the Younger) described their early nineteenth century location as

> ...formerly on the north side of the Saskatchewan, but they removed to the south side, and now dwell commonly south of the Beaver Hills near the Blackfoot with whom they are at peace (Coues 1897:531).

Also, Henry mentioned that the Sarcee "have a smattering of the Cree language" (Coues 1897:532). This ability to communicate may indicate an earlier contact with the Cree, possibly occurring when the Cree first migrated into the northern [Alberta] woodlands.

Apacheans

Sieur de La Salle first recorded Apacheans west of the Mississippi River in 1692 (Terrell 1975:13). Recorded as Gattackas and Padoucas, these bands were later identified as the Kiowa-Apache (Terrell 1975:18) and the Padouca Apache (Terrell 1975:14), respectively. Linguistically affiliated with Alaskan and Canadian Dene speakers, the Apachean bands were estimated to have arrived on the northwestern Plains between 1000 and 1500 A.D. (Basso 1971:12). At that time the Navajo shared a common language and culture with the Apache (Welsch et al. 1984:9). Additionally, the Gattackas were assumed to be closely related to the Sarcee (Terrell 1975:25-26). The Kiowa-Apache estimate their origin as:

> ...in the "hot-water country" along and north of the Yellowstone (river). About 1690, they began to drift eastward toward the Black Hills settling near Devil's Tower in Wyoming (Nye 1962:vii).

Separate migrations must have occurred as Dene also were noted on the Oregon coast and into northern California (Basso 1971:12). The Apache bands, however:

> ...moved southward from the immense Mackenzie River Basin, their route transecting the high open plains of Alberta, Saskatchewan, Montana, Wyoming, Nebraska, Colorado, Kansas, New Mexico, and the panhandles of Oklahoma and Texas...in the end all of them moved on, seeping southward...for no tribes speaking the Athapascan tongue [other than the Sarcee {my note}] settled permanently between northern Canada and Nebraska (Terrell 1975:13).

Other Tribes

The Pend d'Oreille, Flathead and Comanche tribes occupied various intermontane areas of the western portions of the northern Great Plains (Swanton 1952:239,394,386 – respectively). These tribes are not discussed, as their presence on the Plains probably represented seasonal Plains margin forays. Similarly, tribes bordering to the east, north, and south were omitted because of their likely intermittent and tenuous use of the Plains habitat.

Discussion

The late prehistoric and early historic northern Great Plains occupants varied culturally and linguistically. The Blackfoot and the Arapaho were probably among the earliest Algonkian protohistoric migrants onto the Plains:

> ...these groups are both Algonkian, but of speech highly diversified, as well from each other as from the great body of Algonkian...Differentiations of such strength does not generally occur in languages that remain in geographical contiguity and intercommunication with the parent stock. It does often proceed with rapidity in languages that are subjected to contacts principally with alien idioms. If the Arapaho and Blackfoot drifted to the base of the Rockies a fairly long time ago, we should have them fulfilling all the geographical and historical conditions which in theory would be needed to account for their set-off linguistic status. Moving them into their recent habitat since the introduction of the horse, or even a century or so before, would not allow time for the existing degree of diversity, according to all authentic precedent on the rate of alteration of speech. We may therefore regard these two groups of tribes as ancient occupants of the northern true plains, or rather foothills of the Rockies and the plains tributary thereto...it cannot be asserted that the Blackfoot and Arapaho were the only ones formerly in the northern plains. They are the only ones we can be reasonably sure were there (Kroeber 1939:81-82).

The Algonkians were the most expansive in their migrations and exploits, ranging as far west as the Rocky Mountains and from Hudson Bay to the Rio Grande. The Siouan speakers tended to congregate centrally, toward the southern area. Groups speaking other languages than these were either repulsed early after their arrival; or, as in the case of the Sarcee and the Arikara, allied themselves with well-established area residents. The success or failure of most of the migrants in the historic period was reflective of their ability to interact peacefully with the fur trade companies.

The Blackfoot had been acknowledged as "Archithinue Indians" by Anthony Henday in 1772 (Burpee 1907:316). The Cree designation of Blackfoot as "strangers" (Swanton 1952:395) may indicate an inability to communicate or an acknowledgement that the Blackfoot were simply not of their tribe.

The Apache are presumed to have begun their southward migrations "...as small bands of patrilocally-related kinsmen...sometime around 1300 A.D." (Welsch et al. 1984:9); and may have been cut off from a northern homeland by confrontations with Blackfoot Plains residents. Thus, the Sarcee Plains occupation may represent a mediation and ultimate confederation with the Blackfoot.

In comparison, the Cheyenne must have been later migrants, as the Cree term for these people was: "...<u>kanchiew</u> <u>estcik</u>, Cree speakers, from the fact that the Cree could recognize some of the Cheyenne words" (Mandelbaum 1979:9). The Atsina, as former Arapaho tribesmen and precursor migrants of the Cheyenne, also must have been sufficiently early to effect an alliance with some Piegan bands, possibly through linguistic affiliation. The Blackfoot-Atsina alliance, in conjunction with the later Blackfoot-Arapaho-Cheyenne-Teton peaceful relationships, should have provided an avenue for intra-tribal exchange of physical goods and ceremonies toward the establishment of a Plains Indian identity.

Another example is that of the Cree, certainly in the historic period. They maintained alliances with the Assiniboine and Ojibwa; the Assiniboine attracted by the firearms available to the Cree, while the Ojibwa were attracted by both firearms and a means of protection against the Dakota. Similarly, Crow access to horses, firearms, and ceremonies would have been achieved through raids on neighbouring tribes. Besides capturing the first two commodities, Plains raiders also captured women, the vehicle for adoption of ceremonies, customs, and design and clothing manufacturing motifs.

Short-term peaceful relations did exist between hostile tribes. Mandelbaum cites a Cree-Blackfoot truce (1979:41), a Cree-Mandan exchange of goods (1979:38), and a Cree-Dakota ceremony exchange (1979:19-20). Additionally, Dakota, Dene, and Blackfoot all camped with the Cree at one time or another and often intermarried with Cree bands (Mandelbaum 1979:198).

Such contacts which were numerous and frequent, were sufficient to contribute to a ceremonial blending and a certain outward appearance of a common Plains identity. This amassing of tribal populations and inter-cultural contact permitted reallocations of individuals among separate bands, and the interchange of new ideas, new materials, and ceremonies.

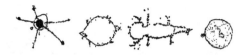

4 - DATING

Introduction

One of the key interests of archaeology when any past cultural phenomena are studied is, of course, dating those phenomena. The greater portion of North American archaeological relative dating is based upon projectile point seriation. It is assumed that the earliest populations traveled north into a formerly glaciated landscape following migratory big-game animals. The direction is probably correct for the earliest entries, but may be incorrect for later traditions represented by different point styles.

The contemporaneity of boulder monuments with the most recent Plains prehistoric occupants, or within the past 1500 years, is proposed. While other researchers have presented radiocarbon dates or artifact dates for boulder monuments in excess of this time range (see Table 10), analyses of some of their researches has shown that some of these dates may represent materials which were present prior to the construction of the overlying features. An Alberta site excavation revealed a buried habitation circle assumed to date to the Oxbow phase, usually dating to 3500 B.C. (Adams 1978:58-60), which lay under a surface habitation circle with "…side-notched projectile points…assigned to the Old Women's phase which dated between A.D. 750 and A.D. 1800" (Adams 1978:45,58).

The thirteen dated sites listed in Table 10 were dated primarily by artifact associations, historic reference, radiocarbon analysis, and dendrochronology. As no buried boulder monuments have been located on the northwestern Great Plains, the more recent construction times are reasonable since all known boulder monuments are only partially enclosed in the soil matrix, possibly denoting less antiquity than other buried components.

By 1980, only three medicine wheel sites (at Moose Mountain, Saskatchewan; Majorville Cairn, Alberta; and the Big Horn Medicine Wheel, Wyoming) had been dated by either radiocarbon or dendrochronology technology. No dates exist for the large circles, human or animal effigies or for geometric configurations. At present some medicine wheel sites in Alberta have been dated by projectile point associations; however, no dates yet exist for the other boulder monument types (B. Byrne, personal communication).

Montgomery's 1907 excavation of medicine wheel DiMv-2 in Saskatchewan's Halbrite district represents the first recorded boulder monument excavation on the northern Great Plains. His excavations were an attempt to categorize the western mounds in terms of those encountered in the Mississippi River Valley. The possibility of contemporaneity was suggested

Table 10
BOULDER MONUMENTS DATED BY ARTIFACT ASSOCIATION,
RADIOCARBON, OR HISTORIC REFERENCE

Borden Reference	Common Site Name	Site Type*	Date (Source)	Reference
DkMq-2	Moose Mountain Medicine Wheel	M.W.	B.C. 800 (radiocarbon)	Kehoe and Kehoe 1979
**	Steel Medicine Wheel	M.W.	1938 A.D. (historic reference)	Dempsey 1956
DiPi-2	Wolf Child Medicine Wheel	M.W.	Historic (glass beads)	ASA
DkPf-1	Many Spotted Horses Medicine Wheel	M.W.	1884 A.D. (historic reference)	ASA
DlOv-2	Grassy Lake Medicine Wheel	M.W.	200 A.D. (? chert point ?)	ASA
EbOm-1	Many Island Lake Medicine Wheel	M.W.	B.C. 1000-1000 A.D. (Pelican Lake - side notched)	ASA
EaPe-1	Sundial Hill Medicine Wheel	C.C.	200 A.D. (comparable to DlOv-2)	ASA
EdPc-1	Majorville Cairn and Medicine Wheel	M.W.	B.C. 1895 (radiocarbon)	Calder 1977
EgNx-1	Hughton Medicine Wheel	C.C.	900 A.D. – 1850 A.D. (late plains pottery)	SMNH
EdOp-1	British Block Cairn	M.W.	B.C. 3500-1850 A.D. (Oxbow-late historic pottery	Wormington and Forbis 1965
EhOp-1	Buffalo Bird Medicine Wheel	C.C.	B.C. 1000-750 A.D. (corner-notched point)	ASA
EkPf-1	Rumsey Cairn and Medicine Wheel	M.W.	200 A.D. - 1800 A.D. (associated artifacts)	ASA
48BH1302	Big Horn Medicine Wheel	M.W.	1760 A.D. (dendrochronology)	Grey 1963

Legend: *   - classification by this research   SMNH - Saskatchewan Museum of Natural
     M.W. - medicine wheel   History, excavated materials
     C.C.   - ceremonial circle   **   - no Borden number noted in
     ASA   - Archaeological Survey   Archaeological Survey of Alberta
           of Alberta   files

on the basis of the excavated human skeletons. The remains prompted his decision that the mound builders preceded "Siouan movements to the Plains Region" (Montgomery 1908:39-40). Unfortunately, those skeletal remains, together with any other excavated materials have been misplaced or entirely lost in the intervening years, preventing any re-examination and better analyses.

While other boulder monuments have been excavated in Saskatchewan, Manitoba and Alberta (Wormington and Forbis 1965; Calder 1977; Kehoe and Kehoe 1979; Carmichael 1979), only Calder and the Kehoes have published dates derived from radiocarbon analysis. Other sites have been excavated, but only a few estimated radiocarbon dates have been published.

Calder reported a radiocarbon date of 3845 +/- 160 B.P. (1895 B.C.) at Majorville Cairn from bone samples from the central cairn (1977:42, Figure 6). Based on the radiocarbon dates, obsidian hydration dating, and the styles of the projectile points excavated, Calder proposes a date of 3200 BC for the beginning of the cairn construction. At Moose Mountain, the Kehoes obtained a radiocarbon date of 2650 +/- 245 B.P. (440 B.C.) from small fragments of charcoal "16 cm below the rocks" (Kehoe and Kehoe 1979) which extended 1.06 m below surface. While Calder does not specify the bone species utilized for his date, his faunal analysis for that layer included only rodent, Richardson's ground squirrel and undetermined bone materials (1977:197-199, Table 27). He admits that

> An estimated minimum of 50 Richardson ground squirrels were represented in the faunal remains... (and)...rodent activity and burrows were noted in all layers, with a significant increase in such activities...similar activity was also intense beneath the cairn(Calder 1977:29).

Similarly, the Kehoes discovered pencils that gophers and rodents had stolen during their 1961 medicine wheel mapping. These rodents had deposited the pencil remnants "gnawed at sweat-stained areas" among the upper rocks (Kehoe and Kehoe 1979:54). Consequently, Calder's bone and the Kehoes' charcoal may represent rodents' removal of debris from underground burrows, particularly if the remains represented cannibalization of deceased rodents or possibly "shrub taproot" (Kehoe and Kehoe 1979:42).

Personal observations when conducting field surveys revealed that rodent den openings often possess cultural objects indicating sub-surface cultural horizons, the skeletons of former den occupants and/or scats removed from the burrow. Those back-dirt pile observations were readily available on both cultivated and non-cultivated surfaces. Therefore, the previous published radiocarbon dates may be inaccurate time estimates for the era of central cairn construction because of the rodent re-assortments.

Similarly, the use of projectile points as a dating mechanism is problematic. The use of these artifacts found in stratified sites may have little or no bearing on site age at surface sites without known stratigraphy. Certainly, early projectile points may evidence the origin era of a boulder monument; or, alternatively, they might represent numerous individuals' offerings at the monument over extended periods of time. Coupled with the problem of stratigraphy is the dating by projectile point association. For each projectile point type there is usually a range of time occurrence. Does one select the earliest time, the most recent time, or an average of the two? Additionally, what is the spatial distance between the projectile point type site and the boulder monument site? Is there a more local correlative dated site? And, to reiterate, how can one be certain that an early point wasn't used as an offering at one of these shallow-stratigraphy sites?

In the absence of excavation, seldom are dateable materials available at many of those sites. Gil Watson and Tom Kehoe, who mapped most of the Saskatchewan boulder monument sites, both reported that they had not located any diagnostic projectile points which they could use for relative dating. Additionally, most of the artifacts that they did recover originated from rodent burrow back-dirt piles, probably evidencing earlier buried occupations. Similarly, a 1972 medicine wheel excavation on the Suffield Military base in Alberta yielded a single undiagnostic lithic flake and absolutely no radiocarbon-datable material (personal observation).

The dating of these on- and above-surface sites by artifact association is the most problematic or the most questionable method. This problem was first stated by Wormington and Forbis (1965:122-123) when they noted an admixture of Oxbow and McKean projectile points together with pottery occurring throughout a deposit (artifacts indicating a wide time range – from about 4700 years to 2000 or less years ago). Similarly, pottery and Avonlea points were noted in the shallow deposits at the Hughton Medicine Wheel Site, suggesting an age of approximately 1800 to 1000 years ago (Saskatchewan Museum of Natural History, unpublished 1968 field notes). Archaeological observations of excavated sites usually evidence the most recent artifacts in the upper soil layers and the older artifacts toward the bottom of the excavation. When an unsorted assemblage of projectile points occurs a number of possibilities may be considered: 1) the site is as old as the earliest projectile point located; 2) the mixture of artifacts represents many peoples' offerings of many types collected and deposited over a relatively short period of time (Wormington and Forbis 1965:124-125); or 3) the artifacts represent mixings by burrowing rodents.

Most of the cairn configurations had possibly been disturbed prehistorically by devotees. Also, during the historic era, early archaeologists and treasure-seeking pot hunters had added their personal disturbances.

Dendrochronology is usually accurate; however, Wilson (1981: 342-344) points out that the tree fragments used by Grey (1963) may record late "treasure hunting vandalism" that occurred at the Big Horn site in the 1890s (Wilson 1981: 344).

Lichenometry: A Potential Dating Method

As the research time and finances were limited for this study, excavations for possible dateable materials (bone, carbon materials or projectile points) were beyond the scope for possible research analysis. As the scope of this research was to examine all types of boulder monuments, a dating method applicable to monuments needed to be devised. Benedict's (1967) paper describing the application of lichenometry to rock structure dating suggested a possible applicable method to date Saskatchewan's boulder monuments. As lichenometry had worked well to date prehistoric rock walls in Colorado, the application to prairie boulder monuments was an attempt toward discovering a viable dating method for surface stone configurations. In other locations lichenometry has been used to date stone buildings (Follman 1961, cited in Webber and Andrews 1973:295). Andrews and Webber (1969) found lichenometric dating valuable in tundra areas where historic records and radiocarbon materials were unavailable.

Lichens are composed of microscopic green or blue-green algae in symbiosis with colourless fungal mycelia. This symbiosis results in the formation of a thallus plant body. Lichens occur in three forms: crustose lichens forming spreading encrustrations, foliose lichens showing horizontal leafy or ruffled expansions, and fruticose lichens which are upright stalked or strap-shaped fronds (Bland 1971:1314).

In 1950 Roland Beschel developed the technique of using lichens to date morainic debris. He assumed that the lichen thallus of greatest diameter indicated the age of first surface exposure of the rocks (Beschel 1961). His preference for crustose lichens, notably *Rhizocarpon geographicum*, was based on its "constant growth rate of 1.0 cm over centuries "[that is, 1.0 cm growth in ca. 200 years] (Hale 1974:78). At the best lichen dates will provide a relative surface-exposure age, though when the growth rates have been observed over a significant period of time, absolute ages may be delineated (Webber and Andrews 1973:295). To date the retreat of glaciers, Beschel (1950, 1961) used lichen growth rates established for graveyard headstones. When the date of the growth surface is known: "…it is possible to plot the size of the thallus against its calculated age, and so determine the rate of growth" (Richardson 1975:45).

The lichen growth rate studies are mainly concerned with measurements pertaining to the radial or areal growth of a thallus over an extended period of time. Armstrong (1976) further illustrated that when using large thalli, the radial growth was comparatively constant, even if the centre of the thallus fragmented. This fragmentation suggests that the radial growth occurs independent of the thallus centre. Since radial growth is independent, thallus averaging (two directional north-south and east-west measurements) should produce a valid measurement of consistent peripheral growth of the thallus through time.

The thallus diameter, as an estimate of surface exposure age, is dependent on the radial growth rate (Armstrong 1976:314). The radial growth rate is dependent on the micro-climatic environment (Beschel 1957:11,15). Therefore, without specific knowledge of regional climatology the best dates obtainable over a short period of time (less than 10 to 20 years) must be viewed only as relative. In this study thallus measurements observed in 1980 were equal to those taken in 1981, 1985, 1990 and 2000.

Climatic environment, notably moisture and light, are the primary factors influencing growth rates:

> Lichens are capable of assimilating and growing only when in a thoroughly saturated condition…they spend the greater part of their life either in a state of xeric rest or else in a cold influenced torpor. Snowmelt, dew, and above all, rain provide lichens with

the possibility of growth, assuming that there is simultaneously a
sufficient supply of light (Beschel 1973:303).

All Saskatchewan boulder monuments examined possessed lichens on the upper and exposed lateral surfaces. Lichenometry was therefore considered to be a possible viable dating method. The size of the largest thalli measured at these sites was assumed to be an indication of the amount of elapsed time since the monument's construction when compared against the largest thalli on a dated source (cemetery headstones and dated rock piles) within the same environment. Additionally, as lichens may grow more rapidly on different parent material rocks, the rock types were noted so that specific lichen species growing on specific rock types would be compared only with their similar entities at the selected historic sites (cemetery headstones and dated rock piles). Because the cairns at some monument sites may have been added to over successive generations, the largest thalli encountered on basal rocks may indicate the total elapsed time only if the diameter of the cairn had not substantially increased (covering the previous cairn periphery). Correspondingly, thalli measured from the top or upper edges of a cairn may indicate only the time since the last additions to the structure.

It was presumed that when constructing a boulder monument, an attempt to illustrate the purpose was designed into the feature. Other viewers would then realize the feature represented something noteworthy, revealing a specific message. If such were the case, it is speculated that these features may have been constructed with the original boulder bases (clear surfaces) exposed representing an event rather than a coincidental alignment. Therefore, only those monuments of single tier construction should possess unmodified lichens (colonized on the original clear surfaces) suitable for dating.

It is important to understand one critical fact about lichen biology: that if rocks colonized by lichens are re-orientated in excess of 45 to 55 degrees away from their original orientation, the lichens will die and be dislodged by erosion (Jan Looman, Swift Current Prairie Farm Rehabilitation Experimental Station – personal communication). In any event, the newly formed monument might possess numerous boulders devoid of lichens soon after construction. Lichen re-colonization and succeeding growth should be evident from average large thalli diameters. This diameter average, as opposed to the largest thalli diameter, should then suggest a measure of the length of time since monument construction.

Lichenometric Methods

Positive lichen species identification, suitable for dating measurements, was achieved by selecting representative boulder rock types from all the Saskatchewan boulder monument sites. Following species identification by Dr. John Sheard (Department of Biology, University of Saskatchewan), all boulders were precisely replaced in their original positions.

The three lichens identified for dating measurements were a crustose (*Dimelaena oreina*), and two foliose umbilicates (*Rhizoplaca chrysoleuca* and *R. melanophthalma*). *D. oreina*, a gray-green or greenish yellow lichen (Figs. 134 and 149), was common at all Saskatchewan sites; however, the two umbilicates were represented better at one western provincial site. *D. oreina* is the most widespread species of the genus, and is notably abundant in the more arid regions of North America. It includes five chemotypes, of which chemotype V is the most common on the North American central Plains (Sheard 1977:103-104, 1974:133).

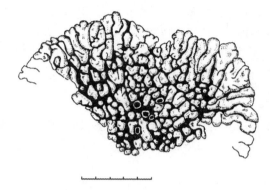

Figure 149: Thallus of *Dimelaena oreina.* Each scale unit indicates 1 mm

To obtain a representative sample from each site, the three species identified were measured at each site on single tier boulders on each side of the feature. Lichen identifications were performed by examining each boulder or headstone with a three power hand magnifying lens to determine the species and to define the lateral margins of the largest thalli. The magnifying lens was particularly useful when examining the comparative graveyard headstones, where some of the lichens were so small as to be almost invisible to normal view. Also the magnifying lens was necessary to delineate *D. oreina* from *D. radiata, D. thysanota,* and *Lecanora (sect. Aspicilia) stellata (Lynge) Sheard,* as all share similar shaped marginal lobes (Sheard 1974:137). When it was difficult to define marginal lobes, the apothecia (reproductive structures) centrally located in *D. oreina,* which are "very common with black disks" (Hale 1979:32), were first identified. Once the species was determined, the marginal lobes were traced on the rock around the thalli with a fine-tipped red felt pen so that the margins could be recognized during actual measurement under higher magnification.

A seven-power hand lens with an interior reticle calibrated in tenths of a millimeter was used to measure the lichen thalli diameters. The maximum number of clearly definable lichen thalli on each boulder was measured. In one instance it was necessary to measure all three identified species to obtain a representative sample from all portions of the feature. A minimum representative sample was considered to be ten clearly definable thalli. All thalli measured occupied the upper centre of individual boulders. The desired sample consisted of one thallus measurement on individual boulders at each of the outermost cardinal directions of the monument, one measurement each at the inter-cardinal directions representing different site elevations from the outer measurements, and two near the centre of the boulder monument at a relatively common elevation. For medicine wheels, samples were measured at the outer ends of the spokes, along the spokes, and at the centre of the feature. Because few thalli were perfectly circular, two measurements (one north to south, one east to west) were taken from which an average diameter was calculated. In some instances measurements were taken on thalli which were successfully impinging on other thalli, as it was presumed that the larger thallus would dominate and could be re-measured in future for supportive observations. In some cases the *D. oreina* sample for a single rock type was less than the ten representative samples. In those instances the thalli on both quartzite and granite boulders were independently measured for later independent comparisons.

The double direction measurement and subsequent averaging of individual lichen thalli might be questioned. Webber and Andrews (1973:295) stated a concern against the averaging of lichen dimensions; however, it is assumed that their argument was against the averaging of many thalli to obtain a maximum growth size, rather than against the method employed in this research.

Beschel's method requires comparison with lichen colony diameters on rock surface exposures of a known age. In this region there are precious few such exposures, but there are two possible candidate types: gravestones, and piles of stones created by farmers removing stones from their cultivated fields. Lichens on datable farmers' rock piles within a three kilometer radius of a site were measured, as were those on local graveyard headstones (usually graveyards were located in excess of three kilometers distance from the monument sites). Even when datable lichen thalli were available within a three kilometer radius, the separation of the monument and the datable site may introduce error in the age estimate because the environment regimens may be different at the two sites. The thalli measurements on farmers' historic rock piles (where assurances were obtained against recent pile additions) were those at the pile apex and surrounding upper boulders. Basal rocks were observed to be devoid of lichens because of shading by grasses, forbs and shrubs. The thalli measured on headstones were those colonizing the top or lateral surfaces.

A headstone memorial distributor was consulted for quarry site locations and the average term of headstone erection. Only those granite headstones quarried from Canadian Shield areas were measured, as it was assumed that these samples should possess similar chemical constituents to the surface glacially deposited granite boulders (which originated in the Shield). These similar granites should produce similar lichen establishment and growth rates, reducing the possibility of abnormal lichen diameter disparities (as between granites from many sources). As the lichens available for this dating technique do not grow on calcareous rocks, headstones and boulders composed of limestone, dolomite, marble and cement were not examined.

Of the 14 most popular types of headstone materials available to memorial dealers, only five granite types (Canadian Red, Britz Blue, Mountain Rose, Autumn Pink, and Red Diamond) are quarried from Canadian Shield locations (L. Wight, personal communication). Headstones are usually ordered and erected within two years of an individual's death. All headstones are erected at graveyards during the frost-free seasons so that the stones can be set solidly into their cement bases. Only headstones which had not been smooth cut were suitable for lichen colonization (Beschel 1973:303), because lichens require rough surfaces and crevices to establish colonies.

Problems and Concerns with Lichenometry

With any new method there are problems, and lichenometry is no exception. Early in its application in geological research, there were objections to its techniques. Some individuals assumed that lichenometry should best be researched by botanists (Jochimsen 1966). However, it was decided that a lichenometric dating technique should be attempted even by a non-specialist if a benefit possibly might be derived.

Of primary concern are the different environments of boulder monument sites and the dated comparative sites. In most instances farmers' rock piles, where available, were the best control comparisons, as most settlement (with land clearing) was during the 100 years previous to this research. Unfortunately, not all of those rock piles could be dated with absolute accuracy, as in cases when the rock pile had been constructed by a landowner who had retired elsewhere (and the current tenant was unaware of the date of construction), or when the person who could date the rock pile was deceased. In other cases rock piles had been added to, or early piles had been removed for land fill or road construction material. The headstones utilized in the absence of datable rock piles were usually located in excess of five kilometers from the monument sites. In two instances a common comparative historic site was used, as it was the only available source for each of the two boulder monument sites.

A second major concern is the lack of lichen establishment rates or growth rates for Saskatchewan. Beschel stated that lichens colonize the rock crevices and hair cracks immediately upon the rock surface exposure:

> ...at first there is a considerable period before the young lichen thallus becomes even macroscopically visible...then a relative acceleration of the growth rate occurs...to a certain diameter (the great period)...whereupon the diameter abruptly begins to grow...more slowly...at a constant rate (Beschel 1950:1).

The "great period" (Beschel 1950:1; 1957:7-8) may last only a few decades, though Webber and Andrews (1973:289-299) have shown variability in this time at different geographical locations. Therefore, a 0.57 millimeter annual growth rate observed for *D. oreina* in Connecticut will have no bearing on Great Plains sites (Hale 1974:84).

Little is known of lichen succession or of competition between lichen forms on the Great Plains. Some thalli measured had lateral margins abutted against or over adjacent thalli of either similar and different species or types. Some *D. oreina* were being colonized by *Xanthoria* spp. or *Physcia* spp.

Studies relating the absolute maximum life term of *D. oreina* seem not to exist. Most present studies concerned with this species deal with pollution control (Hale 1952) or with species identification (Sheard 1974, 1977).

Most crustose and fruticose lichens are acid chemotypes. The basal chemical constituents of the organic bases (whitewash, for example) hygroscopically remove all moisture from the lichens, enabling erosional forces to disperse the dead tissues and the complete thalli. Consequently, previous whitewashings of boulders for aerial photography identification with quicklime (calcium hydroxide [CaOH]) killed and chemically removed all lichens from the feature's boulders. This practice was curtailed in 1979. Currently, boulders are now dusted lightly with white flour if aerial photography is required, as flour is not hygroscopic and washes off in rain or is readily dispersed by prairie winds.

Similarly, lichens on the Saskatchewan sites may have been affected by wind-borne alkalies during the great 1930s drought. Those alkalies, another form of CaOH (with a hygroscopic base), may have altered regional growth rates. Atmospheres polluted with sulphur dioxide (Brodo 1964; Ferry, Baddely and Hawkesworth 1973) or fluorine (Gilbert 1971) have been observed to kill lichens. The thalli at the Alameda Ceremonial Circle, located within 1.5 kilometers of a new oil well (where the odour of sulphur dioxide was evident during the burning off of the gases) in 1980, were discoloured and were flaking off the boulders (also see Hale 1974:84). The presence of viable lichen on the boulders of the Halbrite Medicine Wheel, located directly beside a pumping well with an ignited gas vent, may signify a lack of sulphur in those emissions.

Another possible agent of lichen disturbance is predation (grazing) by invertebrates and vertebrates. Lichens are utilized as food by mollusks, mites, and insects (Gerson and Seaward 1977:74); and by mice and bats (Richardson and Young 1977:134-135). Some prairie birds utilize lichens in whole or part of their nesting materials (Richardson and Young 1977:126-127). Ants (genus *Hymenoptera*) were observed to be removing both crustose and umbilicate lichens from a number of comparative dating rock piles.

At present, there is little or no information concerning the effect of prairie fires on lichens. The destructive nature of prairie fires noted by Hind (1971:336-337,372,405), in which even buffalo dung was consumed, also may have burnt rock lichens. If the fires occurred on an annual basis, the amounts of natural fuel (grasses, dung, woody stems, etc.) might not have been in sufficiently large amounts to produce extreme ground temperatures. If the fires occurred less often, the increased amount of fuel may have produced a detrimental environment for lichen survival.

Crustose lichens were observed to be shade intolerant. Headstones shaded by surrounding trees, shrubs, forbs and grasses at cemetery sites did not bear lichens. Additionally, most cemeteries possessed some form of irrigation system. The increase in precipitation and relative humidity either by this unnatural condition or from early morning dews (many cemeteries were observed to be in valley complexes where morning dew was a regular occurrence) should have provided more optimum growing conditions. Headstones, as raised perches for both predator and prey species of birds, were noted to possess numerous bird droppings. Their dung, being primarily uric acid (Romer 1970:352), may have promoted lichen colonization and growth. For those reasons, the available dated farmers' rock piles were viewed as the better comparative dating sites, as the environmental conditions should have been more closely similar to those at the prehistoric sites.

Analysis and Discussion of the Results

Following completion of the 1980 measurements, the thallus diameters were arranged in tabular form with size observations ranging from the smallest to the largest. In almost all cases the observed sites statistically defined a normal bell curve. Theoretically all lichen thalli pertaining to a single time of construction, when measured at all site surface coordinates, should fall within one standard deviation (or 68%) of the sample mean (Thomas 1976:176-177). Larger thalli, therefore, represent the continual growth of colonies previously established, while the smaller thalli represent poorer microclimatic environments or possible surface inconsistencies to optimum growing conditions. The largest thalli within one standard deviation range at a prehistoric site was presumed to be the most viable common population, and was compared with the largest thalli meeting the same conditions of statistical analysis from the historic comparative base. The datable historic base's thallus size was translated into an assumed annual growth increment which was reapplied to the thallus size for probable number of years at the prehistoric sites.

The annual growth rate was achieved by dividing the thallus size in millimeters by the number of years since the construction of the historic comparative rock pile. The resultant numeral was an estimate of the annual growth historically. This estimated annual growth was divided into the millimetric size of the observed thallus size at the prehistoric site to yield an estimate of the number of years since that site's construction. Subtraction of the number of years from 1980 gave an estimate of the year of boulder monument construction.

With the exception of one date, all estimations were derived from the analysis of *D. oreina*. The estimates are presented by Borden designation in Table 11. Of the 18 sites where lichenometric observation was possible, four dates were based on a quartzite exposure, seven on granite, and seven on both quartzite and granite. With the exception of EcNh-1, all comparative surface-exposure dates fall within six years of one another. Of particular interest are the two close dates achieved at ElOd-2, as they were both derived from separate lichen species.

Acceptable data confidence levels range from high to questionable, based on the difference in elevation and/or the distance of the comparative dated site(s) from the individual prehistoric sites. The dates which were considered highly acceptable were those where the comparative site was within five kilometers distance and within 35 meters elevation of the prehistoric site. Fairly acceptable dates from comparative sites were those within five to ten kilometers distance of the prehistoric site, even though the elevation limitations were similar to those stated for the high confidence level sites. The poor confidence dates are those in which either the elevations or the distance between sites were more than moderately different. The extreme elevation differences observed between the prehistoric and comparative locations for the two other sites were so excessive that no confidence (due to probable environment disconformities) could be accepted.

Table 11
LICHENOMETRY DATES
(*Dimelaena oreina*)

Site Borden Number	Stratum Q	G	Type Date	Elevation Difference (m)	Distance (km)	Prehistoric Site Data Stratum & Dates Quartzite	Granite	Date Confidence Level
DgMn-3(1)	R	R	1926	+.5	1.0	1878	1881	High
DiMv-2		C	1906	0.0	5.6		1819	High
DjMr-1	R	C	1919	8.0	8.0	1885	1891	Fair
DkMq-2		C	1923	-137.0	9.6		1880	No
DgNc-1	R		1911	-14.0	.8	1851		High
DgNf-5	R	R	1926	0.0	.3	1890	1889	High
DgNg-2	R	R	1926	-15.0	.8	1861	1857	High
DgNh-3	R		1913	-34.0	4.8	1856		High
DiNf-1	R	R	1915	-30.0	.4	1830	1825	High
DkOe-2	R		1910	.5	.3	1858		High
DkOj-2	R	R	1913	+11.0	4.8	1867	1864	High
EaNh-1		C	1918	-205.0	8.2		1769	No
EcNh-1	R	R	1938	+38.0	1.6	1868	1826	Fair
EeNe-14		C	1919	-69.0	5.5		1846	Poor
EeNg-1		C	1935	+15.0	10.2		1857	Poor
EgNx-1		C	1918	-53	10.9		1834	Poor
EfOl-2	R	R	1935	-30.0	1.5	1894	1898	High
ElOd-2	R		1920	+1.8	.3	1851		High
*	R		1920	+1.8	.3	1851		High

Legend: Q - Quartzite   G - Granite
           R - Rock Pile Site   C - Cemetery Site
           m - Meters   km - Kilometers
           No - no confidence
           *   - This data based on *Rhizoplaca melanophthalma*
           +/- - Historic site x meters above or below prehistoric site elevation

(Note: undated sites, due to all boulders having been previously white-washed with quicklime,
        site destroyed, lack of comparative historic site, or lichens destroyed by enamel paint)

The high to fair confidence dates occur within the period of A.D. 1822 to A.D. 1898. The fair to low confidence dates achieved are represented by nine samples in which cases two types of surface exposures, two comparative bases, or two lichens were utilized. These dates fall between A.D. 1825 to A.D. 1898. While the poor confidence dates also might be acceptable, further research will be required to determine rates of thallus growth by site location. Five of the poor to questionable confidence level dates were those where cemetery headstones were the only datable comparative source. It is assumed that the increased distances, elevation differences, and the humidity variations at those sites are the major contributing factors which would yield such problematic dating results.

The most acceptable dates are those which utilize farmers' rock piles for the comparative bases. Those rock piles were susceptible to environmental fluctuations (prairie fires and droughts) similar to those experienced at the prehistoric sites, whereas most country cemeteries are surrounded by cultivated fields (less chance of being burned over), and most are irrigated (absence of drought conditions).

With the application of a new tool of analysis, there is often a general tendency toward acceptance of the results. In most of the other lichenometry studies examined for other geographical locations, the comparative historically dated objects displayed relatively uniform thalli diameters (Beschel 1957; Armstrong 1976). The Saskatchewan scene presents something of an enigma. Similarly dated headstones and rock piles, located regionally across the province, sometimes displayed radically different sized thalli diameters. Some of the dates computed may be correct; however, the concentration of nineteenth century dates for the entire study area seems too compact for the multitude of boulder monument types encountered, unless the dates reflect the last era of activity associated with these sites (some possibly being entirely buried, and considering the possibility that we are viewing a remnant population of these features).

To better understand the reasons for these discrepancies, the rock pile and cemetery headstone dates observed were displayed on graphs (Figures 150 and 151). Theoretically, if the two control bases produced similar thalli diameters, and therefore similar growth curves, the nineteenth century dates would be completely acceptable. Figure 150 illustrates the difference in thallus diameters and growth curves observed for *D. oreina* on two rock types. One of the major problems with these control bases is the small comparative size sample (twelve mean diameters). The growth rate for lichens on granite rocks is based on four sites, with an averaged (or balanced) growth point intersection for two observed A.D. 1926 rock piles. The growth curve for lichens on quartzite rocks, based on eight sites, was averaged toward the early end of the scale for the four close dates (A.D. 1913 and 1912 estimated size at 1912.5 years, and an estimation for two 1910 thallus size observations).

The thalli sizes observed for cemetery headstones (Figure 151), represent 20 cemeteries (mean thalli diameters). The alignment across the graph centre represents the expected growth curve based on the median of observed lichen diameters through time, as after the young lichen becomes visible:

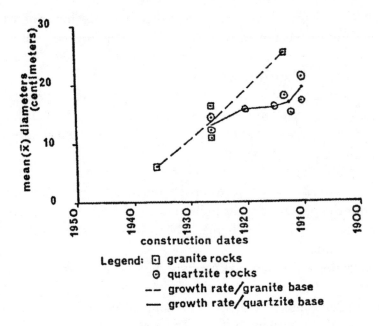

Figure 150: Rock pile dates using *Dimelaena oreina*

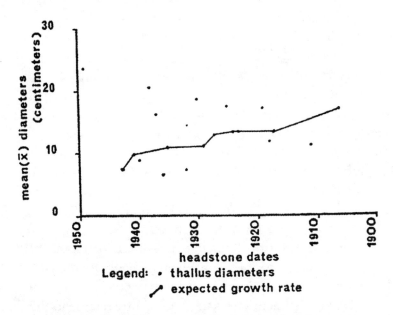

Figure 151: Dated cemetery headstones using *Dimelaena oreina*

..a relative acceleration of the growth rate occurs, which continues up to a certain diameter – whereupon the diameter abruptly begins to grow very much more slowly, yet at a constant rate...it ends within a few decades. The constant continued increase in diameter...lasts for many centuries in the case of many crustose lichens...an absolute limit has not been set for this increase (Beschel 1973:303).

In reference to the problems and concerns cited, all mean diameters above the curve alignment in Figure 151 may indicate well-cared-for cemeteries (irrigated, trimmed, and protected). For those mean diameters below the alignment it may indicate the reverse situation, insect/animal depredation or dryer micro-climates.

Re-measurements were conducted on all lichen thalli at both the prehistoric and historic comparative sites in 1981, 1985, 1990, and 2000. These latter measurements were intended to produce continued size increases, and therefore, support growth rate hypotheses and record colony succession rates and survival species identifications toward better knowledge of the species used in this study.

So much for research hypotheses based upon natural expectations! Neither thalli increases nor the expected expanding colonizations were noted during the successive three re-measurements over the twenty-year period (up to the year 2000). Additionally, three of the sites suffered permanent damage to either the feature or the entire site. A minor portion of the problem has to do with excessive alternating periods of excessive moisture years, followed by years of droughts. Also, as lichens are an indicator species of air quality, the increased air-borne pollutants and decreasing filtration provided by the atmospheric ozone layer in recent decades may have contributed to less stable growing conditions.

Regardless of the problems and erratic meteorological conditions, the technique and calculations (where thalli increases are evident) should prove the advantages of lichenometry, possibly over a longer observation term. Additionally, a greater volume of sample locations may be necessary to provide a better understanding of the many natural and induced atmospheric conditions.

Additional research into lichenometry, especially pertaining to fire effects, will be required for more reliable data concerning lichen survival for continued growth, and thus for dating purposes. Currently the best information gleaned from this research has been that it takes an average of forty-four years for *D. oreina* to become microscopically visible on headstones in this region. Also, because of pollution, no radial lichens were ever noted on cemetery headstones within the larger urban centers. The current use of this biological phenomenon may be unsuitable to date cultural or prehistoric events on a plains environment, particularly events predating the cession of the major annual or periodic prairie fires. Until more conclusive studies are published dealing with regional fire studies and precipitation measurements employing a larger lichen data base with time control measurements, lichen thalli may be useful only to separate recent historic constructions from those of prehistoric eras.

Since its acceptance as a dating tool lichenometry has been applied to dating historic and prehistoric sites where neither written records nor other datable materials are evident. The presence of lichens on boulders at prehistoric Saskatchewan sites presented an opportunity to test Beschel's methods toward the development of a viable dating tool for this Great Plains area. At present the problems and concerns outweigh the probabilities of the successful application of lichenometry in this plains situation, but this assessment is based only on a limited twenty-year term of observation. Future generations should continue to try to apply this method.

Current radiocarbon, dendrochronology and relative dating techniques will remain the more reliable dating estimation methods, but these will require the application of more effort and money to date specific sites and features than has heretofore been the case. Additionally, researchers will have to be particularly diligent and cautious, to sort out the multitude of factors that may give rise to a false sense of confidence in using these methods.

5 - ORIGINS AND FUNCTIONS

Unless anthropology is to interest itself mainly in the unique, exotic and non-recurrent particulars, it is necessary that formulations be attempted no matter how tentative they might be. It is formulations that will enable us to state new kinds of problems and to direct attention to new kinds of data which have been slighted in the past. Fact-collecting of itself is insufficient scientific procedure; facts exist only as they are related to theories, and theories are not destroyed by facts – they are replaced by new theories which better explain the facts (Steward 1955:209).

Introduction

In this chapter the boulder monuments will be compared with ethnohistoric accounts in an attempt to propose possible construction functions. While the majority of the comparisons were located from published accounts, some were obtained directly from First Nations Elders. Some of the published records were recorded by individuals who actually lived among different Plains tribes and recorded ceremonies that they actually experienced. Historians, ethnographers and early anthropologists sometimes learned their information from either second-hand sources or from dubious informants. While these are the least reliable sources, they were utilized as the only comparative material available for some feature outlines.

In some instances, notably the Kayville Human Effigy, Ceremonial Circles Subclass D, and the possible quarry site, my attempts at interpretation (admittedly) may seem to stretch speculation to the extreme. However, the speculations and hypotheses presented herein may induce other researchers to examine or re-examine other boulder monuments more intently and thus contribute toward more accurate future analyses.

Introductory Overview of Ideas Concerning the Functions of Medicine Wheels

Some investigators have hypothesized that medicine wheels pertain to astronomical alignments (Eddy 1975, 1976, 1977, 1979; Kehoe and Kehoe 1979); memorials to war chiefs (Dempsey 1956; Kehoe 1973); burials (Montgomery 1908; Ewers 1955); or sun/thirst dance lodges (Grinnell 1922; Wilson 1981). The suitability of the various theories needs to be assessed.

Some researchers avow that medicine wheels were constructed as devices to record annual solstices and stellar alignments as season harbingers. The interest in and "use" of celestial phenomena by ancient peoples is termed archaeoastronomy or astroarchaeology (Aveni 1977:XII). Though astronomy is normally believed to have been devised by cultures possessing an agricultural subsistence base with permanent settlements and designated scholars/religious leaders with leisure time (Steward 1955:193-194), it is not beyond the realm of possibility for itinerant hunting-gathering societies to have developed some basic astronomical observations.

Alice and Tom Kehoe (1979:36) postulated that the Moose Mountain boulder monument embodies a sighting system that allowed the builders to tell the summer solstice. The possible north orientation of Polaris along "Line D-O at Moose Mountain" (Kehoe and Kehoe 1979:10) is acceptable, as Polaris is termed "night clock" by the Blackfoot (Wissler 1947:8), and was a "directional North Star" for the Pawnee (Fletcher 1902:734). The Ojibwa (James 1830:322) and Cree (Mandelbaum 1979:360) use an unnamed north star for evening directions.

The use of a solstice as a calendrical system with "…an error of a couple of days"(Kehoe and Kehoe 1979:36) may be an unsupportable analysis as there is nothing recorded in Plains ethnology reports which specify solstice observations. A review of the star lore of the Blackfoot (Wissler 1947:4-26); Pawnee (Fletcher 1902:734); Arapaho (Hilger 1952:84-91); Ojibwa (James 1830:317-323); Assiniboine (Kennedy 1961:8-10); and Cree (Mandelbaum 1979:360) failed to reveal reference to native observations regarding the stars usually cited. The stars in question are Aldebaran, Sirius, Rigel, or Capella (Eddy 1974:1038; Kehoe and Kehoe 1979:7,10). Since solstices don't affect animals, nomadic hunting and gathering societies following such herds may not have had an interest or use for a longest or shortest day observation. Animal and plant cycles have been noted by Plains inhabitants as aids to their observation of annual events. For example, the Blackfoot abandoned their winter camps when they observed geese flying north and when the bison embryo had reached a certain stage of development (Ewers 1955:123-129); the Gros Ventre prepared for their Sun Dance fulfillment "about June or when the spring vegetation was well advanced" (Cooper 1956:185); and "When the Dakota saw a certain flower (*Liatris punctata*) [Dotted Blazing Star] blooming on the prairies, they knew the corn was ripe, and went to the villages of the farming Indians to trade" (Griswold 1970:83).

Alternatively, many tribes mention the use of cycles of the moon to define portions or months of the year (Ojibwa - James 1830:321-322; Assiniboine - Kennedy 1961:9). The Assiniboine used winters with noteworthy events to record an individual's age (Kennedy 1961:9; Howard 1976:2).

Finally, John A. Eddy and the Kehoes have developed the astronomical theory mainly for the Moose Mountain and Big Horn medicine wheels. As they have examined all of the known medicine wheels in Saskatchewan, Alberta, Montana and Wyoming (T. Kehoe and R. Forbis, personal communications), without discovering other comparative alignments, the inclination for the astronomical observation for most medicine wheels seems inappropriate. This is not to say that other astronomical calculations or interests by ancient monument builders are not "recorded in stone" in some boulder features, but more proof based on further researches will have to be presented by the advocates of these ideas.

The memorial and burial interpretations for medicine wheels, based on the ethnographic and interview sources (Grinnell 1922; Kehoe 1954; Dempsey 1956), are substantial arguments for the interpretation of certain medicine wheel types. Montgomery's 1907 (1908:39) excavation of the Halbrite feature (DiMv-2) revealed human skeletons and associated grave goods. The two medicine wheels at the Oxbow Medicine Wheel site (DgMn-3) and the medicine wheel at the Jelly Ranch site (EeNg-1) were reported to have possessed human bone and/or bone and bead offerings in their central cairns. Additionally, three Alberta sites (DlOv-2: Fig. 18, EdOp-1: Fig. 48, and EkPf-1: Fig. 66), were reported to possess red hematite (red ochre), sometimes used as a preparation for corpse burial (Wreschner 1980:633), in their central feature cairns (B. Byrne, personal communication). While not all Plains tribes may have used ochre, its presence at some sites may be indicative of continuity of a tribal tradition. The presence of red ochre alone might suggest a surrogate burial.

The medicine lodge hypothesis stated by Grinnell (1922:307) and elaborated on as a thirst dance use by Wilson (1981:355-358), for the Big Horn Medicine Wheel, is a viable alternative if the constructors used the boulder outline as a template for continuing ceremonialism. Elk River identified the Big Horn Medicine Wheel ground plan as "...an old time Cheyenne Medicine Lodge" (Grinnell 1922:307). Clements speculated that the Sun Dance originated with:

> ...either the Arapaho or Cheyenne at a time when they occupied a position northeast of their present habitat, but its main development came after they had reached the location they occupied when first discovered (Clements 1931: 226).

The presence of a depression in the central cairn possessing "...some fragments of rotting wood" which yielded a dendrochronology date of "1760" (Grey 1963:36), echoes Mooney's (1907:361-363) contention that the Cheyenne have acquired the majority of their ceremonies and tribal identities during the past two centuries, since their migration out of the eastern woodlands.

Karl Schlesier (2002:390-391) advances the proposition that the Big Horn Medicine Wheel resembles a Cheyenne *oxzem*, a "spirit wheel" motif, associated with the Massaum or earth-giving ceremony (Schlesier 1987:76-83). He regards the Big Horn feature as both an oxzem and a territorial marker, "commemorating the covenant between the spirits and the Cheyenne". Associated cairns were also likely used as vision quest settings near the sacred central boulder feature.

The spirits were to assist persons undertaking vision quest ceremonies. Personal communications with First Nations Elders reveal that vision quest petitioners sacrifice themselves (that is, undergo pain or great discomfort) in the belief that they will be favourably blessed with special visions and instructions.

Vision quest petitioners undoubtedly used the site, as it would have been viewed as a sacred location. The presence of wood fragments may represent the remnants of the frame from a sweat lodge, used for preliminary purification. The partial use of the site as a boundary marker (Stands in Timber and Liberty 1967:124; Schlesier 2002:390) also might suggest that the site was a neutral ground where people from neighbouring tribes might safely visit it.

Medicine Wheel Analogies (Class I)
Subclass IA

Since burials were located at DiMv-2 (Montgomery 1908:30, Capes 1963:118), it is possible that all or some of the sites of this type may have possessed burials or burial goods. The central cairn of DiMv-2 contained the remains of six individuals. In 1980 the scene of the destroyed Canuck Medicine Wheel (DhOb-2) was extensively surveyed both on the cultivated site area and at the resultant rock pile. Neither location revealed human skeletal elements, lithic materials, or suspected grave goods. As the site had been seeded to crop, permission to test-excavate could not be obtained from the landowner. The Jelly Ranch Medicine Wheel (EeNg-1) was partially disturbed by gravel testing operations in 1977. Though a thorough examination of the site failed to reveal human skeletal remains or grave goods, one of the gravel truck operators reported hearing of someone "taking some bones from the rock pile" (personal communication). Further investigation with the landowner and the gravel contractor failed to yield additional information. Feature 1 at the Oxbow Medicine Wheel site (DgMn-3) was reported by the landowner to have possessed some "bones and beads" (J. Mellom, personal communication). These materials were excavated by the landowner and his cousin in 1935. When asked if the materials could be inspected, the informant replied that they had been "taken back to the States" by his cousin.

Though the preceding information is sketchy, a description of a Blackfoot burial lodge seems to compare to this feature:

> ...the death of an important leader...was coupled with an elaborate ceremony of burial in a death lodge...under a pile of rocks...After...rocks were piled in lines extending from the death lodge in the four cardinal directions. Each pile [lines] of rocks represented one of the departed leader's coups (Ewers 1955:284).

Theoretically, if the leader was elderly or very prestigious, there might also have been many rock lines indicating a great number of coups. Important Blackfoot chiefs were buried either on the open prairie or on high buttes where their graves were marked with stones:

> Apparently the more important a chief was, the more elaborate was the arrangement of stones. The grave of Little-Medicine-Pipe is quite elaborate. Two concentric circles of stones mark the place of a tipi. Radiating out from the outer circle are seven long lines of stones at regular intervals like the spokes of a wheel. Each line is said to denote some successful expedition of this man. The line running to the east terminated in a rough square of stones, indicating the direction from which the man had originally come (Kidd 1937:62).

The design on another Blackfoot's tipi, that of Bear Chief, includes five triangles, the apex of each triangle toward the top of the lodge (Lowie 1963:110,g). The design inferred that the individual had killed five Flathead Indians. The interspaces between the triangles were shown as relatively straight lines. If upon his burial his coups were counted by the method previously discussed, Bear Chief's burial lodge may have had at least five boulder lines radiating away from his burial cairn.

Most other tribes placed their dead on scaffolds or in trees (Morgan 1959:102). The Ojibwa, Cree, and Chippewa were observed to bury their dead directly in the ground covered with "…a small dirt mound which is overlain with planks, poles, or birch bark" (Carter 1973:63). The Mandan of the Missouri River placed the putrefied skulls of the corpses in circular alignments with other human skulls, after the remaining bones had been buried (McCracken 1959:99; Thomas and Ronnefeldt 1976:210).

Subclass IB

These medicine wheels have radiating spokes which bisect a boulder circle. In both cases some or all of the spokes terminate at cairns. While other researchers rely on astroarchaeological analyses to explain these features, ethnological accounts pertaining to religious practices exist to offer alternative explanations.

A birch bark scroll brought into the SMNH in 1968 revealed a design similar to both DkMq-2 and DgMn-3(3). The scroll originated in the mixed parkland region in the vicinity of the Assiniboine River in southeastern Saskatchewan. The design (Fig. 152) shows a tipi with four radiating lines, along which animals (deer?) appear to be located. The illustration seems to indicate a divination practice where a medicine lodge has been established, and the directions leading toward game animals have been defined. Medicine lodges are documented among the Ojibwa (Howard 1977:29-30), late residents of the Assiniboine River. John Tanner related a dream where a spirit appeared in his lodge and pointed out two directions where game could be located (James 1830:180-183). Tanner further narrates that Chippewa [Ojibwa] medicine hunting consists of "…drawing an animal on its scapular bone… (and)…cast[ing] the bone…into the fire…this fulfils all those important ends" (James 1830:184).

Sub-Arctic Indians used scapula divination:

> Fixed in a cleft stick by the joint end, the shoulder blade is held to the fire, and on it brown marks appear…The interpretation of the various dots and lines…caused by the heat varies from individual to individual. A large spot in the middle usually indicates starvation, for it means "stay in camp, there are no paths to follow." Thin lines with a blob at the end indicate that there are caribou not too far away, or perhaps other Indians who will share the food they have…from the scorch marks he will divine the absence or presence of caribou and the directions in which the hunt should be made (Webber 1964:40-41).

The Saulteaux also practiced divination. The diviner would beat on an animal's scapula, and then interpret the cracks (Mandelbaum 1979:177).

The possibility of multiple uses for medicine wheels (Wilson 1981:337-338) may be reflected in these features. The Moose Mountain Wheel type, with radiating arms terminating at cairns ("blobs") might represent a double use where divination occurred at special ceremonial seasons. The bisection of the inner circle (a lodge remnant) by radiating lines (extensions from a central hearth) to exterior points (herds) is a possibility.

Figure 152: Drawing of figures on a birch bark scroll from eastern Saskatchewan

Subclass IC

All of these medicine wheels are close to stone circle sites (see Fig. 153). Possibly this peripheral placement of the feature represents some phenomenon that occurs at the habitation site or within a short time of its occupation. These medicine wheels might have been constructed to direct others' attention to something by constructing a specific pattern which could not be readily observed by viewing just the habitation camp. These particular medicine wheel features may be memorials as defined by Dempsey (1956), denoting a relationship to an important or well-respected individual.

As some Plains groups did not possess totems to indicate band or family association, some other form of affiliation, particularly to denote a deceased's memorial, could have been devised. As most Plains camps were organized by band affiliation (Arapaho - Hilger 1952:192, 230; Blackfoot - Ewers 1955:146; Teton Dakota - Howard 1966:20-22; Assiniboine -Rodnick 1937:410-411; Cree - Oliver 1962:26; Plains Ojibwa - Howard 1977:19), the location of each individual's lodge in relation to the band leaders was pre-established: "The tribal circle, each segment composed of a clan, gens, or band, make a living picture of tribal organization

Figure 153: Aerial view of Cronk's Big Circle

and responsibilities" (Hodge 1907:198). Additionally, Hilger notes for the northern Arapaho:

> ...when the people were moving and they had nearly reached
> their destination...the chiefs went ahead to the place at which
> we were to camp...Once they had decided where the entrance
> to our circle was to be, we all knew where we were to place our
> tipis. Related families always had their tipis close together
> (1952:192).

Also, Kidd (1937:118) notes for the Blackfoot: "In the Sun Dance camp, the tipis were pitched in a circle around the Sun Lodge, each band having its hereditary position with relation to all the other bands".

Kroeber (1902:8) notes that Arapaho band members always occupied one area of the camp circle. These camp alignments may have been altered slightly over the years to accommodate the loss of families through death or transfer to other bands; however, the band organization of camps would have been readily recognizable to tribal members. As a comparison, Seminole camp arrangements over a 12 year period, 1936 to 1948, remained fairly constant with reference to the central lodge and to other band locations (Capron 1953:180-181). For Plains tribes only the Crow Indians appear to have lacked individual tenting positions within the camp circle (Lowie 1912:186).

The lack of a designated central area at DgNf-3 and ElOd-2 may be similar to an illustration of an 1870 Cree encampment drawn by Fine Day, in which there were 1600 lodges representing four amalgamated bands (Mandelbaum 1979:371, Fig. 31). The four ring clusters are arranged around a central open area, with the four clusters represented by concentrations of rings only at specific locations around core areas. A description of a Blackfoot encampment supports the pattern:

> In the circle camp I counted three hundred and fifty lodges –
> thirty of them were Painted teepees with symbolic decorations.
> They belonged to the head men of different bands and were
> pitched in prominent places on the inner circles (McClintock
> 1923:259).

A camping pattern may be represented by these medicine wheels, where intersecting lines or lines articulating with a representative camp circle may suggest a band leader's or a specific tribe's camping orientation. These monuments were supposedly erected where a leader died, not where he was buried (Dempsey 1956:177); hence the lack of associated habitation rings away from the ends of the radiating spokes, but within the general proximity of the memorial.

Subclass ID

These medicine wheels all possess a boulder circle completely encompassing all of the radiating spokes. EdPc-1 and 48BH302 possess large central cairns, a feature absent at EePi-2 and 39HD22. However, EePi-2 and 39HD22 conform quite closely to a Minnesota petroglyph figure (Winchell 1911:Pl.VI#10). The two other configurations seem to be similar representations of prehistoric garden designs from Wisconsin (Riley, Moffat, and Freimuth 1981:104), Fig. 1). The garden sites in the east were "…heaps of rocks interspaced with the garden beds, which were apparently composed of materials that the prehistoric farmers had cleared from their fields" (Riley, Moffat, and Friemuth 1981:104-105).

It is possible that some medicine wheel outlines served "to insure the fertility and increase of the bison herds" (Calder 1977:208). As fertility symbols the Bighorn (48BH302) and Majorville (EdPc-1) sites somewhat resemble the ridged fields of Michigan and Wisconsin, which were: "…. associated with the Lake Winnebago Focus manifestations of the Oneota Aspect, dating to the period from about A.D. 1000 – 1300" (Peske 1966:193-195).

If the Blackfoot did arrive on the Northwestern Plains as early as suggested by the Apache displacement (Wedel 1961:100), they may have maintained this symbolism. Also, if the Blackfoot, as Algonkian speakers, had originated in the Michigan-Wisconsin-Minnesota area, their early observations or use of ridged garden fields might have promoted the outline use as a fertility symbol. This conjectural discussion does not mean to infer that the Blackfoot definitely migrated from the Michigan or Wisconsin woodlands. However:

> War and travel among foreign tribes were the two most thrilling
> adventures open to Blackfoot men. Since there could not be "many
> remarkable Warriors and Hunters", a few mix with other tribes

and learn their languages, and become acquainted with their countries and mode of hunting...This wandering off to live among other tribes had more far-reaching effects than might at first be apparent. These "students...must have been a powerful force in leveling the culture of the Plains area"; so that their permanent influence was undoubtedly of profound significance (Kidd 1937:41).

Kidd here reminds us, too, of the extensive cross-cultural sharing not only of items of material culture and economic pursuit approaches, but ideas, ceremonies and religious practices that have characterized the Plains Indian cultures for centuries.

As the hills in the vicinity of EdPc-1 are currently incapable of supporting any vegetation other than short grass and cactus (B. Byrne, personal communication), the presence of early deposited buffalo stones or *iniskim* (Peck 2002) in the central cairn (Calder 1977:208) may suggest a site use of enhancing continued buffalo fertility. The Bighorn site also could have possibly been a bison fertility symbol, as the brief summer and high altitude would have been inimical to a garden site (Simms 1903a; Wilson 1981). The lack of a central cairn at EdPi-2 and 39HD22 for buffalo stone offerings, and their smaller sizes, might suggest that these were sites known to individuals rather than being communal ceremonial sites.

Ceremonial Circle Analogies
Subclass IIA

Collectively these ceremonial circles seem to resemble miniature buffalo pounds. All have a definite entrance and central boulder cairn, and all are prominent on the landscape. Thus, they may represent the Blackfoot Woman's Buffalo Lodge:

> There was a woman's society among the Blood and Northern Blackfoot tribes which was unknown among the Piegans. Its members were wives of the most highly respected men in their tribes. Prior to the sun dance in summer, members of this Matoki Society built a ceremonial lodge which resembles a buffalo corral, and on the third day of their four-day ritual reenacted the drive of the buffalo into the corral (Ewers 1958:106).

The specific construction features of a Matoki Lodge were:

> A tipi pole is set up in the centre...A number of travois are set up in a circle around this pole and joined together by tipi poles set at the top...On the sides and over the top are stretched tipi covers. At the bottom they are weighted down with stones (Wissler 1913:430).

For the Cree style of pound a:

> ...circular area thirty to forty feet in diameter was cleared...a single tree was left standing in the centre... (from the)...entrance...a runway leading into the pound was built...The chute which guided the herds into the pound was

extended obliquely from each side of the entrance (Mandelbaum 1979:54).

This pound method of bison procurement also was used by the Northern Blackfoot, Assiniboine, and Cheyenne (Mandelbaum 1979:330; Lowie 1963:15, Figure 3).

The Saskatchewan monuments of this type, situated beside favourable camp locations and on select local secondary heights of land, suggest representations of the Blackfoot Matoki lodge. The absence of habitation circles at EgNx-1 (Fig. 43) may suggest a late nineteenth century ceremonial occurrence or a summer occupation when tipis (either leather or canvas) were held down with wooden or bone pegs. The presence of the boulder outline to hold the Matoki lodge covers in place could represent a "traditional" as opposed to a "functional" method.

The placement of a boulder cairn centrally could have been to represent the central tree or to support the central pole described by Wissler on a treeless prairie landscape. The boulder chute (deadmen) also may have been a traditional depiction in place of sticks and brush lines (two other uncommon prairie commodities). The Alberta example at EaPe-1 (Fig. 51) may represent either a variation on a theme, regarding the double encompassing boulder circles; or a second celebration at a former enactment site. The extreme disturbance at EdOp-1 (Fig. 48) is assumed to be the reason for the irregular chute depiction on the east side of the feature. The two clusters of boulders to the left and right of the peripheral surround may suggest that the "Entrance [was] to the east...where two sturdy trees [were located]" (Mandelbaum 1979:54).

Subclass IIB

Several possible functions may have been served by this class of monument. At all three of the Saskatchewan sites listed for this subclass, stone habitation circles are located within approximately two hundred meters of the enlarged circle. The location of EaNh-7, the Claybank Circle, the largest [44 m] diameter ceremonial circle, is on the northeastern upland edge of the Missouri Coteau (Fig. 154). Traditionally, this site was referred to as "ceremonial dancing grounds" (Hind 1971 I: 335). As a traditional ceremonial ground for Plains tribes composed of numerous bands, a larger diameter area would have been required to accommodate a larger audience.

As an alternative, some First Nations graves are described which match these configurations. The proximity of this feature to habitation circles may rule out this latter hypothesis, as many Plains Indians believed that graves must be placed on the opposite bank of a water source to prevent the deceased's ghosts from disturbing the living (Hall 1976:361). In all Saskatchewan circumstances, no available water source is located in the immediate vicinity. Future test excavations may be required to confirm which interpretation is the most valid.

Seven of these circles possess some form of central platform. The other four (DjMr-1, DkLw-18, and EeNu-1: a & b) may have possessed elevations which were central standing

Figure 154: The Claybank ceremonial circle seen at ground level

platforms for a speaker. The absence of habitation circles directly associated with any of these enlarged circles supports the idea that these features denoted special congregation areas set off from the common, living area.

In the absence of bush it is reasonable to assume that boulders cleared away from the central area could have been placed (left) at the edge of the meeting circle to mark the area. These assemblies were annual events where an Elder spoke of their:

> ...blessings and misfortunes since they had met the previous autumn; of the friends who had died in the interval; then he expressed his desire and hope that all present might come together again (Bushnell 1905:71).

A large feast, which was prepared a little distance from the assembly area, was brought to the gathering place following the Elder's speech (Bushnell 1905:72). The amphitheatre analysis for this subclass is reflected in the Ojibwa meeting area, where "...the ceremony [was] inside a structure cleared of bush and grass, and then a circle...some 40 feet in diameter...had been formed" (Bushnell 1905:69).

The Alonsa Ceremonial Circle (Table 6, Fig. 59) as an oval structure may suggest tribal identity, as the Crow set their lodges in an "elliptical plan" (Campbell 1927: 98; Fig. 6,f). As the lodges were elliptical, one may assume that an assembly area for a multitude would possibly follow a floor plan similar to the lodge outline, thereby permitting future observers to identify the structure and its purpose.

Subclass IIC

The central cairn aspect was the contributing factor toward devising this subclass. The great amount of scattered boulders with a remnant arc around a slight depression at DiNf-1 (Fig. 61) suggests the possible previous existence of a cairn. The original test excavations at FbNp-2 failed to reveal anything beyond the central cairn; however, there were sufficient materials within one edge of the cairn to suggest that it may have served as a burial site (T. F. Kehoe, personal communication). Similar rock piles were noted by J. N. Nicolette in Minnesota, where in 1838 he observed:

> The Sioux take advantage of these loose materials to erect signals on the most elevated spots, or to designate the place…where some exhausted hunter has died on the prairies, and desires to be buried in a more prominent situation; or they amuse themselves in shaping these into fantastic figures. They give names to these localities, which serve as landmarks in a country where there are no other geographical beacons (cited in Winchell 1911: 107).

Cree chief Payepot's 1908 grave was described thus: "…they opened a grave not more than six inches deep. In it they placed the coffin. Around the coffin and over it they placed stones. And they marked out a large circle beyond it with field stones"(Watetch 1959:22).

Additionally, the Blackfoot have been noted to cover a corpse inside a tipi with rocks prior to sealing the edge and abandoning the site (Ewers 1955:284). If the lodge edges were held in place by boulders, the present-day remnants would reveal a cairn surrounded by a ring of boulders, very similar in appearance to the monuments in this subclass.

Subclass IID

The Dick Giles Ceremonial Circle is an anomaly among the Saskatchewan boulder monuments. As well, no other large circle with similar internal features or external site attributes has been reported in any publication for any Great Plains district. As such, DgNg-2 (Fig. 68) is the most enigmatic ceremonial circle studied.

While it is an anomaly, the perimeter resembles the elliptical Atsina sun dance lodge (Kroeber 1908:262-268). The central dividing boulder line might represent a portion of an original exterior lodge wall which was partially disturbed when a second large lodge was added during the construction of a ceremonial double tipi lodge (Cooper 1956: Plate 1). While Cooper's illustration shows two lodges pegged to the ground, a different event may have used, or seasonally necessitated, boulders to hold down tent margins. Similar large, ceremonial, double lodges are cited for the Cree (Mandelbaum 1979:211-214); Crow (Denig 1953:61; Lowie 1956:317); Ojibwa (James 1830:188; Howard 1977:135); and Blackfoot, who"…used the same [type of] Sun Dance structure as the Crow" (Ewers 1973:59). The central boulder line also might represent a Dakota division of the sexes: "If a dance were given…the sexes danced in separate areas, either one on one side and the other on the other, or they formed two distinct lines…" (Hassrick 1964:136).

Animal Effigy Analogies (Class IIIA)
Turtle Effigies

The Assiniboines' western expansion may explain the turtle effigies near Consort in Alberta (Bayrock 1963:3), although these effigies could represent culture borrowing by the Blackfoot. However, as the two western Canadian turtle species, the snapping turtle (*Chelydra serpentina*) and the painted turtle (*Chrysemys picta*), occur only in the extreme south of the four western provinces (Behler and King 1979:435,450), they may have been unknown to northern Blackfoot. The absence of other known turtle effigies in southern Alberta, ultimate Blackfoot territory, adds support to the occurrence of these figures elsewhere as representing a different tribe's symbolism.

Turtles were known to be a semi-aquatic food source among the Cheyenne (Grinnell 1962:307) and Dakota (Hassrick 1964:197). Thus, their depiction on the prairie may have served a double purpose, a direction to permanent water and an indicator of a food commodity. Turtles were also a prominent part of Mandan lore: "…some think the turtle effigies were made to win favour of certain spirits. Others claim they were made to point the weary traveler to good water" (Anonymous 1950:19).

An alternative suggestion is that some turtle outlines may indicate a child's birthplace. Many tribes preserved the navel cord in small ornamental pouches: "Among the Dakota these usually took the forms of turtles and lizards, among the Blackfoot, snakes and horned toads" (Wissler 1927:95).

Similar pouches are described for the Arapaho (Hilger 1952:22-23); Cree and Saulteaux (Tarasoff 1980:20); Crow (Lowie 1956:33); and Assiniboine (Mandelbaum 1979:344). If the child born was that of an important leader, the event might have been celebrated by constructing a monument. The "turtles" at 39HU70 and 39HU74, by the length of their tails, might better depict horned toads or other reptiles not common to Manitoba, Saskatchewan, or Alberta. The difference is notable in the uniform depiction of the carapace outlines and the leg and tail portrayal of most other turtle outlines (see Table 7 and illustrations).

Badger Effigy

The Minton Effigy depiction at DhNe-2 (Figs. 82, 133), as noted in Chapter 2, has been re-interpreted as a badger. The rumoured presence of human ribs in the central cairn might denote an individual's burial at a divining [scrying] site where, for the Atsina,

> Scrying occurred in the form of peering into badger blood. When a war party had gone out on the trail, they would kill a badger, lay it on its back, slit it from throat to crotch, and leave the blood to gather in a pool around the belly…If the scryer on peering into the surface of the blood, saw himself headless or scalped, this meant he would get killed. If he saw himself reflected clearly this meant good luck (Cooper 1956:419).

A similar meaning for badger scrying occurred among the Cree (Mandelbaum 1979:176), though the Dakota interpreted scrying as a common practice with a somewhat different meaning:

> …when a man kills a badger, if he turns it on its back, cuts open
> the chest and carefully removes its insides so that no blood is
> lost, when the blood thickens, by looking in the hunter can see
> his image. Should he see himself as he is, he knows he will die
> young. But if he sees himself as an old man with white hair…Now
> he knows he can risk getting many coup and will live long to die
> with a cane in his hand (Hassrick 1964:192).

The location of numerous small cairns within the outline circumference might better describe Atsina badger scrying (Cooper 1956), as the cairns may be the locations of certain internal viscera. Alternatively, if a Dakota believed he could take many risks and inadvertently was killed during a local event, he might have been interred at his scrying site.

L. Uyttenhager's mention of a "boulder (with) a face and numerous other marks incised in it" (McCorquodale 1961, field notes) seems indicative of some form of monument marker. Indeed, Pohorecky (1979) has discussed the probable association of southern Saskatchewan boulders depicting humanoid faces with a mortuary context. The Ojibwa, late residents of this area of Saskatchewan, marked their graves with carved figures: "A small post with the tribe mark was placed at the head of a grave" (Grant 1960:364).

In the absence of trees for a post marker, a large boulder could have served the necessary purpose. As the boulder had been removed and is not available for present analysis, it is impossible to ascribe definite tribal use-identification to this feature.

Salamander Effigy

The salamander effigy at DiNs-1 might represent more than an animal's form. The two lateral neck boulder depictions (Fig. 83) suggest other possibilities. The adult land phase of a salamander is characterized by the development of lungs and the loss of its external gills, whereas an under-functioning thyroid may result in failure to develop into an amphibious individual (Stebbins 1951:46-47). The undeveloped aquatic phase (*Ambystoma tigrinum*) usually exceeds the growth size of its amphibious counterpart (G. Sutter, RSM biologist, personal communication). Short gills indicate well oxygenated water, whereas long branching gills indicate muddy or poorly oxygenated water" (Stebbins 1951:47).

As this boulder monument salamander possesses short boulder lines posterior to the head, it may indicate an exhibition alerting the viewer to a fresh water supply. (The area around this effigy has an abundance of alkaline sloughs; the proximity of this figure, pointing toward a fresh water supply, would be an invaluable sign). However, as noted earlier, the original site was cultivated while the feature was "away", so it would be difficult to reconstruct where exactly the effigy once might have "pointed".

Another alternative is that the salamander outline might have served as a monument of a child's birthplace, as was cited for ornamented naval cord preservation pouches among the Blackfoot (Wissler 1927:95) or Cree (Mandelbaum 1979:139). A third alternative might suggest the death site of a Cree, Saulteaux, or Assiniboine prevaricator, as:

...no stories founded on fiction were ever told. The Indians, with their intensely superstitious natures, believing that if any "fairy stories" were told during that season (summer) when they were supposed to use all their time to the very best advantage, the narrator would have his or her life destroyed by the lizard which would suck all his blood. The Indians, very naturally, were in terror of this little reptile, which was never actually known to have been the cause of any loss of life among them; but they assert as a reason for this that no Indian ever gave it an opportunity to put to the test its evil powers (Paget 1909:100).

As true lizards are absent in Saskatchewan, a salamander may have been depicted to represent the lizard myth.

A fourth alternative for this fascinating feature may propose that this effigy is a manifestation of a Plains water monster. Known as Unktehi among the Oglala Sioux and represented in the art of the Sioux, Blackfoot, Arapaho, Cheyenne and others, water monsters were believed to occupy certain lakes and rivers where they:

...made floods by spewing water from their mouths; they caused alkali and muddy or bad waters as well as accidents and drowning in lakes and streams. With their tails, they shot people or animals who entered the water causing their victims to cramp and sink below the surface, where the monsters ate them (Ewers 1981:39).

These powerful beings were depicted as horned snakes, serpents with horns and legs, or as a "...very large male creature with horns on its head, teeth as sharp as knives, four legs, and a long, strong tail" (James R. Walker, in Ewers 1981:39).

Similar beings have been illustrated in pictographs along the Churchill River in central northern Saskatchewan (Jones 1981:21, Figures 14 and 15) and along the Molson River in Manitoba (Dewdney 1978:118, site 241). The Saskatchewan pictographs conform to effigy depictions described by Ewers (1981:41), whereas the Manitoba depiction seems to conform to the thunderbird-monster confrontation pose depicted by Dick West (in Ewers 1981:38, Figures 1 and 44).

This salamander boulder monument might, then, depict a local source of fresh water, a birthplace, a death place, or a warning of the location of a water monster. With so many possibilities, it is impossible to attempt to suggest any individual cultural significance.

Bison Effigy

The bison effigy at DgNh-3 (Figs. 84, 132, 155) may be a *"muzzineneen"* or picture "writing" as utilized by Ojibwa Indians and mentioned by Tanner in his narrative, where he says:

..we were so reduced to hunger that it was thought necessary to have recourse to a medicine hunt...A drawing, or little image is made to represent...the animal on which the medicine is to be tried (James 1830:181).

When the figurine was completed "...the part representing the heart is punctured with a sharp instrument, if the design be to cause death" (James 1830:164). This form of sympathetic magic, also known among the Menomini, involved touching the part of the body which was to be affected and then shooting the image with an arrow (Mandelbaum 1979:315).

Local artifact collectors related that they had found a number of broken arrowheads near the heart stone or within the immediate proximity of the effigy outline. Theoretically,

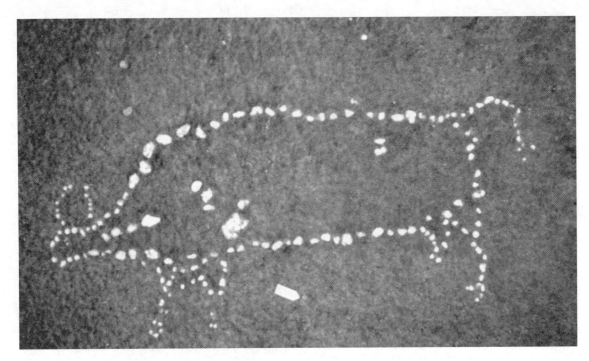

Figure 155: Vertical photograph of the Big Beaver bison effigy

those artifacts might represent those projectile points which directly struck the outline's boulders. A comparative figure (Fig. 156) and narration by Tanner give the hunter's thoughts and Tanner's interpretation:

> I am such, I am such, my friends, any animal. Any animal my
> friends, I hit him right my friends. (This boast of certain success
> in hunting, is another method by which he hopes to elevate himself
> in the estimation of his hearers. Having told them that he has
> the power to put them all to death, he goes on to speak of his
> infallible success in hunting, which will always enable him to be
> a valuable friend to such as are careful to secure his goodwill.)
> (James 1830:344).

Only one other bison effigy boulder monument was located for the northern Great Plains. This figure, recorded by T. H. Lewis (1890) in Minnesota (Fig. 92), has some similarities with the Saskatchewan example. The Minnesota figure is similarly depicted in sagittal section with its legs oriented toward the southeast, but with its head toward the northeast. The legs are shown as two outlines, one for the forelegs, and one for the hind legs. Large boulders were placed at the eye, on the hump, and forward of the hind leg outline. This latter boulder might suggest a bison cow's udder. If it is a cow, it might suggest a spring construction when the cow herds congregated prior to the rut (Arthur 1975). While it is a bit ambiguous, the Saskatchewan bison definitely has both a heart line and a heart.

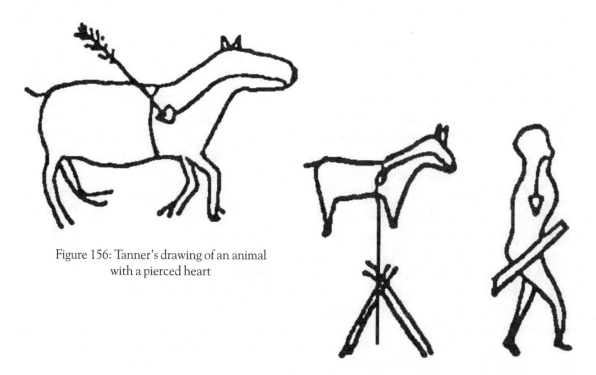

Figure 156: Tanner's drawing of an animal
with a pierced heart

Figure 157: Tanner's drawing of an animal,
man and tipi

Human Effigy Analogies (Class IIIB)
Wild Man Butte Human Effigy

Comparisons of some of the elements noted by Clandening (1928), with ethnological records, suggests the probable meaning of this site and possible tribal association. The medicine hunting, previously noted from "Tanner's Narrative", describes an Ojibwa method of obtaining game which possesses all the elements depicted at this site:

> I draw up your heart, that is what I do to you. It is intended here
> to represent a moose at a distance; and the line from his heart to
> the lodge of the Indian, indicates that he drew it, or by means of
> the power of his medicine controls the inclination of the animal,
> and brings him to a situation where he can easily be found (James

1830:372, Figure 10).

The figure depicted by Tanner (Fig. 156) was to represent a moose. In the absence of a woodland environment an elk-like figure was incised into the sod (Clandening 1928:260). Clandening's described elk was no longer evident on Wild Man Butte in 1980. The heart stone also was missing; however, a slight ridge path, enhanced by erosion, still leads from the ridge peak down to the figure's adjoining stone circle. The line in the other Tanner illustration (Fig. 157) leads from the animal's heart down to the stone circle figure, a lodge in cross-section (James 1830:372, Figure 10). The human outline was depicted in sagittal section by Tanner as compared to the ventral view at DgNc-1; however, the interesting aspect is the illustration of a long knife or spear across the waist of the human figure. The boulder line at this site, extending from the rear of the boulder figure to the front of the figure might then represent a holstered weapon rather than the speculated "…arrow or spear stuck into the figure's backside…." (Dyck 1981:56, 57).

Additionally, the Mandan were noted to depict certain effigies by cutting outlines into the sod in 1823, some of which were visible as late as 1923 (Gilmore 1929:147-151). Theoretically, the outline of an elk cut into the prairie sod may suggest elements of Mandan culture or of an Ojibwa-Mandan culture amalgamation.

A full body depiction with the limbs outlined instead of represented as stick-like appendages is common among the Plains Ojibwa Midewiwin (Dyck 1981:68). The Midewiwin ceremony, also known as the Grand Medicine Lodge and involving medicine, magic, and particular conjuring practices, was absent "…among the [other] Plains Algonkians (Blackfoot, Arapaho, Cheyenne) [which] would make it appear that the ceremony must have had its rise and spread after these people had become detached from the main stock" (Hallowell 1936:34).

Consequently, since the Midewiwin "was confined to…the central Algonkians… (and) Siouan tribes (in their) immediate contact" (Hallowell 1936:33), it would seem reasonable that such a depiction as seen in this monument could be attributed either to the Ojibwa (Dyck 1981:68) or to some Dakota tribe.

Kayville Human Effigy

The human effigy at DkNg-2 (Fig. 96) was the only effigy enclosed within a square boulder alignment. The lack of this effigy's gender depiction and its similarity to an Ojibwa pictograph (Fig. 158) may suggest a meaning resembling that which Tanner indicated in a love song:

> 'Were she on a distant island, I can make her crazy to swim over, were she on a distant island.' Here he again boasts of the power of his medicine over the inclination of females. This song seems to present a fair view of the state of passion of love among the Ojibeways (James 1830:372 [13]).

Figure 158: Tanner's drawing of a
person in a circle

As this area of Saskatchewan was known to be part of the territory, at least within the last 200 years, of the Saulteaux (Plains Ojibwa), it is possible that this figure may represent an individual Ojibwa's site for practicing his love medicine. On the prairie, devoid of birch bark (the medium employed in Tanner's narrative), this similar depiction was executed with a boulder outline.

Dewdney Avenue Human Effigy

Regrettably, this boulder monument, due to its complexity, disturbance and unusual topographic setting, is not subject to reasonable interpretation or even speculation. It is at present one of the enigmas insofar as boulder monument interpretation and analysis are concerned, and may well remain so. One possible route for unravelling at least something about its history and function might lie in archaeological investigation, to discover if there are distinctive artifacts types present here, or not, and if there are datable remains, to shed some light on when it was constructed.

Certainly, female effigy monuments are found at a few sites (e.g. Fig. 109 and probably 108), the former being connected with an incidence of elopement and subsequent punishment (Kehoe 1965:8). The possible depiction of a mother and baby in arms is unprecedented in this body of sites, and could have been created under any number of motivations.

Cabri Lake Human Effigy

This human effigy, with the arms extended over the head, is a near replica of the Wild Man Butte depiction. Tanner explains this elevation of the arms to signify an Ojibwa "look at me" pictograph depiction (James 1830:341). The very definite sex depiction together with the well-defined heart-line may be compared with Tanner's: "Look at me well, my friends; examine me, and let us understand that we are all companies" (James 1830: 341). Or, as James interprets it to mean: "The words express the boastful claim of a man, who sets himself up for the best and most skillful in the fraternity" (1830:341-342).

However, a much more convincing interpretation of the Cabri Lake monument has recently been provided by Vickers (2003), who interprets these northern Plains male effigies as *Napi* figures. In fact, Gill and Hymers first suggested this interpretation as a possible one for the Cabri Lake figure (1968:27-28). Old Man, the Trickster, was known as *Napi* among the

Blackfoot (Grinnell 1969:47), *Wesakachak* among the Cree (Beardy 1969:62), and *Nanibush* among the Ojibwa (Steinbring 1970:247). Similar beings are known as Coyote among the Kootenai and Columbia River tribes (Clark 1969:26; Underhill 1953:255), and *Iktomi* among the Sioux (Hassrick 1964:155-156). This powerful and sometimes mischievous god was seen as a benevolent deity that named all animals, created rivers, and acted as a guardian for mankind and animals threatened by malevolent deities or monsters. Trickster tales were often told around evening campfires as folklore and as testimonies as to how people should behave toward one another (Underhill 1953:255). In his trickster guise, his misadventures often led to the creation of various specific landforms in the territories of these cultures.

Grinnell makes this specific for the Blackfoot:

> (Old Man)…made the Milk River (the Teton) and crossed it and being tired, went up on a little hill and lay down to rest. As he lay on his back, stretched out on the ground, with arms extended, he marked himself out with stones, - the shape of his body, head, legs, arms, and everything. There you can see those rocks today (Grinnell 1962b:137).

Human Effigy Discussion

The rectangular human effigy body forms have been identified by others to certify Algonkian depictions (Dewdney 1964; Habgood 1967). The difference is that some Algonkian human figures have pointed shoulders and a 'V' neck appearance on the upper torso, whereas the Saskatchewan human effigy outlines have only square shoulder portrayals.

Clandening's 1863 observation of the Wild Man Butte effigy holding a bow and arrow in one hand (1928:260) presents an unconformity among northern Great Plains human boulder effigies. Only the Cabri Lake and Dewdney Avenue effigies have definite sex depictions. The sex of the Wild Man Butte was not discussed by Clandening (1928) and only speculated upon by Dyck (1981), while the sex of the Kayville effigy is suggested only by the possible comparison to an Ojibwa pictograph. Perhaps the best observation is:

> Sometimes we walk a tightrope between scientific anthropology and lewd sexology…while such sentiments accurately reflect the prejudicial notions of propriety valid in our own culture, they should, nevertheless have no place in the dispassionate examination of the cultural manifestations of other peoples who follow their own rules of etiquette… (Wellman 1974:2).

Geometrics Analogies (Class IV)

A variety of geometrics are found in Saskatchewan and from the published accounts are dispersed across the northern Great Plains. While some concentrations of vision quest geometrics appear to be in southern Montana and in northern and eastern Wyoming, their presence elsewhere, both peripherally and across the study area (see Table 9), prohibits any speculation concerning diffusion of particular ceremonial and religious practises. Included in geometrics are a number of monuments described by their possible functions which seem to relate to ethnographic accounts.

Geometric Subclass IVA

The information qualifying DkOj-2 as a visioning site is that such a site "Is commonly "U" shaped or oval, at the discretion of the individual or his Elder instructor, and may consist of a single rock tier or several tiers up to 3 feet in height" (Fredlund 1969:15). The 'U' shape commonly had an accompanying alignment which reflected some aspect of the experienced vision, but there weren't any definite regulations (Cooper 1956).

Also, DkOj-2 is assumed to represent a vision quest site based on its similarity to a recorded Atsina site built and reported by Little Man during his vision quest:

> He was lying face down and he heard something, just like something puffing, coming towards him. He said he knew right away what it was because from what he had heard old people say, the bear when it travels puffs a whole lot as if it were out of breath. So he knew it was a bear. The bear went in a circle right around him. Pretty soon the bear came over. *Little Man had a little oblong nest outlined with rocks…and open toward his feet. This is called his 'call-for-power' lodge* [my emphasis]. After the bear had come around several times it must have sat down because Little Man didn't hear him anymore. He wasn't supposed to look up and see what it was that came to him…You just have to take whatever it is and just think hard about the power you want.
>
> So when the bear came over he put his paw right on Little Man's head. He went away again and soon after he came back again and put his paw on Little Man's back just at the level where his heart was. The bear went off again and Little Man noticed that he went straight back from his head. The third time when he came back he touched the soles of Little Man's feet. He went off again the same way and not so very long after he came back and this time he sat down towards the opening of the nest about 10 to 12 feet away from it (Cooper 1956:285-286).

This description of this nest closely resembles the DkOj-2 structure. The circle that the bear walked could be the oblong nest ('U') periphery; the three walks away might be represented by the three boulder lines, and the location where the bear sat down could be represented by the dolomite boulder. While DkOj-2 is probably not Little Man's site, there are a sufficient number of similarities to qualify this figure as a vision quest site. The isolated and exposed location was suitable for a "denial [of the vision seeker's wish] until a vision was received" (Wildschut 1960:7). Often the denial was accompanied by the "sacrifice of strips of flesh or the dismembering of a finger joint" (Cooper 1956:285,290). This self-torture was sought:

> …on continually recurring occasions – for mourning, for warpaths,

for revenge, for curing disease, or in consequence for vowing during
disease, for a name for a child, for a design for entrance into a
society; and on all these occasions the seeker ordinarily receives
his power or commands directly without specifically acquiring a
guardian spirit (Benedict 1923:29).

DkOj-2 might be attributed to the Atsina because of the close construction
resemblances to the Little Man story. Cree, Saulteaux, and Sarcee vision quests, restricted to
boys who had not indulged in sexual relations, usually occurred on an elevated wooden
platform, in a den, or on a raft anchored off-shore (Mandelbaum 1979:159-160). Blackfoot
quest lodges were more commonly constructed from brush (Corbett 1934:24), while the Crow
built a boulder platform upon which to recline (Wildschut 1960:7).

The fire-cracked rock located near this vision quest monument possibly indicates
that the vision-seeker underwent a sweat lodge cleansing. Sweat lodge structures were
constructed from willow shafts stuck in the ground in a small circle, the uprights fastened
across the circle to make a conical hut which was covered with robes or brush to constrict the
steam. Rocks were heated outside the lodge and passed in by helpers (Hilger 1952:129) and
water was trickled over the rocks to produce steam (Lowie 1922:429).

The Blackfoot and Cheyenne restrict the use of a sweat lodge to ceremonial purposes
although the Crow and Flathead tribes use the sweat lodge for pleasure as well as for personal
hygiene. To the Cree, the sweat lodge is a vital element of their lives not restricted to ceremony
or mere pleasure (Dusenberry 1962:120).

Nineteen other vision quest sites with 34 'U' shaped nests or ovals have been identified
on the northern Great Plains. Specifically, there are 15 sites with 29 features in Montana;
three sites with four features in North Dakota, and a single feature site in South Dakota (see
Table 9). Additionally, circular stone-lined pits (Fig. 2) may have had a similar function.

Geometric Subclass IVB

The feature at DgNf-5 (Figs. 113, 159) is interpreted as a war lodge after the description
and illustration of a Blackfoot structure (Ewers 1944: plate, 184,185). The structures were
made primarily of logs overlain with brush. The bases of the logs were supported by a breastwork
of logs or stones (Ewers 1968:126). The resultant boulder outline should confirm the location
of a boulder-supported war lodge.

This assumed war lodge is the only one located, to date, in Saskatchewan. Though
the interpretation is conjectural, it might have been constructed by the Piegan, as they often
erected a war lodge within striking distance of an enemy camp (Schultz 1980). The location
of this lodge among eight habitation circles may suggest that the raiders intended to intimidate
their foe through a realization that the raiders were so certain of their success that they camped
on their foe's doorstep. Alternatively, some tribes believed that such enclosures were possessed
by malevolent enemy powers (Schultz 1980:326). War lodges were not destroyed after use, as
they were sometimes repaired by whatever war party that came upon the structure during a
raid (Malouf 1963:4).

The majority of the known war lodges, attributed to the Blackfoot, are recorded in Montana and Wyoming (Christensen 1963; Ewers 1944; Kidwell 1969; Schultz 1978, 1980). It seems that pits and lodges were commonly used in the western half of Montana while war lodges, but not pits, characterized the native uses in the eastern half of the state (Malouf 1963:10). DgNf-5 is located about one kilometer north of the Canadian – American border above the eastern side of Montana, qualifying Malouf's observations.

Figure 159: The Marj Giles Circle

The location of at least one site in Saskatchewan may not be peculiar, as the Blackfoot were reputed to have occupied this area until they were forced out by the Cree and Assiniboine. Or, the location of this site might suggest an excursion by Blackfoot into enemy territory after their eviction time.

Geometric Subclass IVC

The boulder configuration at DkOe-2 also does not have a comparable outline on the Great Plains. Since it was first published (Watson 1975:20), various observers have speculated that the outline possibly represents a bird or a locomotive or a dog (Fig. 114). As the outline is unique, its construction of only iron-stained quartzite cobbles may have been to alert adept observers to a workable lithic material. None of the boulders in the adjacent 45 habitation circles were of this stone type. The floodplain and creek banks to the west of the site were devoid of any quartzite boulders; however, the upper beach ridge with the monument contained these boulders in the soil matrix. The majority of the lithic tools located within the two (prehistoric ?) excavations were constructed from the quartzite cobbles.

A similar patterned site was located south of DgNf-5 in Montana (Davis 1975:30). It is not known whether the two sites are related, as Davis did not mention a common rock type used for the construction; however, the similarity in monument depiction (Figs. 113 and 143) may suggest some relationship.

As a test to the validity of this figure representing an indication of a workable lithic material, two other known Saskatchewan quarry sites and their environs were surveyed. While neither revealed any possible boulder configurations within a two kilometer radius, the concentrations of spalled lithic materials (a fused shale and a cryptocrystalline quartzite) were in sufficient surface quantities, so that a boulder monument might not have been required to locate either of the quarries.

Other Examined Geometric Sites

The ManitobaThunderbird nests listed by Carmichael (1979) at EgKx-15 may have served as vision-quest features (Fig. 139); however, in this research they are treated as defensive or lookout shelters, based on descriptions noted by J. J. Bigsby in the Lake and Cook Counties of Minnesota during his 1823 survey of the British – American boundary:

> ...a hollow pile of stone at the lower end of one of the rapids between Bois Blanc Lake and Lake Croche, where the Chippewa or Wood Indians in former days used to watch for their invaders, the Sioux of the plains, a race of horsemen and warriors. He also says that until lately the arrows of the Sioux, shot during a conflict on Lake Croche, might be seen sticking in the clefts of the rocks there. In Lake Lacroix, a few miles from the Pewabic (or Bottle) portage on an island near the south main, are the remains of a round tower, or defensive building of some sort, 27 feet in diameter. It was erected by the Indians and commands a wide view of expanse and woody isles (in: Winchell 1911:379).

The recovery of "arrows" may suggest an offensive action; however, other tools might suggest an assemblage necessary to maintain a person during an extensive sojourn in the "nest". The physical discomfort experienced by Carmichael while testing the "Thunderbird's Nest" (1979:102) may have been partially due to boulder settling in the years since it was constructed. The hordes of mosquitoes which afflicted Carmichael (1979:102) in conjunction with the presence of ceramics at EgKx-15 (1979:38) might suggest that containers were used for the transportation of "...the oil (of which it [the bear] yields several gallons) is useful to anoint their hair and to rub on their bodies, in order to defend them from musketoes...it is an excellent substitute for butter and makes even the poorest meat palatable"(Grant 1960:344).

Vision questing sites were located in isolated or dangerous situations (Benedict 1923:2; Schultz 1980:144-154) away from campsites. Persons seeking visions fast (Conner 1982:85), thereby dismissing the need for foodstuff containers. The proximity of EgKx-15 to a campsite should rule out its use as a visioning site. Thus EgKx-15 and the three similar constructions at Wanipigow Lake (Carmichael 1979:97-98) may have been built for other uses. Three of the Manitoba sites discussed are within the immediate vicinity of water, and all four have a commanding view of the immediate waterways (Carmichael 1979:107-121); therefore, their use as defense/lookout shelters may be a more persuasive analysis. Similar shelters were noted in Montana as defense-observation lookouts (Schultz 1980:213,326; Lamb 1970:109).

Sixteen other geometrics are listed in Table 9 (Figs. 115-118, 135-138 and 140-147). An additional 31 boulder mosaics were listed by the University of South Dakota (Table 9); however, as they were not illustrated they have been referenced on Fig. 3 showing only their general locations. While the three Ontario geometrics (Figs. 140 to 142) are not located on or near the Great Plains environs, they are included to illustrate the differences between Plains and Woodland boulder monuments. While some boulder monuments have been noted near North Bay in Ontario (Tyyska and Burns 1973), the geographical distance and dearth of these depictions between these and at the Whiteshell locality in Manitoba may indicate a disconformity of cultures or interests in using boulders to create figures and designs. The human and animal rock outlines in southern California (Setzler 1952) should represent a similar disconformity as there are no reported effigy monuments between that area and the central or Northwestern Plains.

Specific Tribal Associations with Specific Monument Types

Considering the possible access routes and associated cultural sources, the possible impetus for boulder monument origins on the northwestern Great Plains might be postulated. While the Hopewell people had established trade networks that spanned the Great Plains, their effigies were constructed of different materials, were larger than most Plains configurations, and were mainly fashioned for burial functions. At the same time, if the Middle Missouri Cultures, which may have originated from the Middle Mississippian tradition (Willey 1966:320), were the responsible agency, boulder monuments should have been encountered throughout the entire expanse of their Missouri River occupations.

It is noteworthy that the major occurrences of boulder monuments appear to be along major and minor rivers. The distribution possibly suggests that river valleys were some of the exploration/exploitation routes during the term of recording some ceremonial practice or other event with a boulder monument.

Medicine wheels and ceremonial circles are more abundant on the western side of the Canadian Plains. As the Blackfoot are the only tribe recorded to continue medicine wheel constructions into the twentieth century, it is tempting to credit them with the origin of these features. While other tribes have used medicine wheels for vision quests and other uses (Wilson 1981:337-358), these uses would appear to pertain to employing existing features rather than creating them.

   The majority of the 37 medicine wheels defined by this research for the northwestern Great Plains occur on lands which are, or have been, occupied by the Blackfoot during the past 400 years. If these features were representative of the Athapaskans who passed through this area, one should also expect to find other concentrations of medicine wheels from the Boreal Forest to the Yellowstone geysers and the Black Hills through to the Platte River in southern Nebraska. If, as others have stated, medicine wheels were a Cheyenne or other recent migrant Algonkian tradition, these features should be concentrated in Wisconsin and Minnesota through to the Dakotas and western Montana. However, as the known concentrations are in Saskatchewan and Alberta, it seems more plausible to suppose that the greater possibility supports a Blackfoot tradition. It is possible that the ceremony(s) responsible for medicine wheel construction may have been adopted by other tribes, denoting dispersal occurrences in southern Montana, western South Dakota, and northern Wyoming. Since it is also possible that the Ojibwa, Cree and Assiniboine may have built medicine wheels, not all of the Saskatchewan and Alberta medicine wheels can be conclusively attributed to the Blackfoot.

   Ceremonial circles were subdivided into four varieties. While Matoki lodges seem to pertain specifically to Blackfoot women, the other ceremonial circles possibly represent universal northern Plains traditions, because of the variety of tribes that use them and the variety of functions which they may represent.

   While ceremonial circles are not numerous nor showing area concentrations, they do seem to illustrate a line pattern extending from the west side of Lake Manitoba through Saskatchewan into central Alberta. Although a concentration doesn't seem to exist for the 12 ceremonial circles in Alberta (see Figure 3), the occurrence of the majority of them on traditional Blackfoot territory (extending south into northern Montana) seems to suggest that they could have been of Blackfoot origin. Their use by other tribes (Watetch 1959:22; Thomas and Ronnefeldt 1976:101) in Saskatchewan and Montana suggests that other tribes may have created them for ceremonies and other uses.

   The two human effigy concentration areas seem to suggest the possible inauguration of a tradition at two separate centres. The centres are speculated to represent the division of the Middle Dakota into the Assiniboine and the Yankton proper during their western migrations. Winter counts, as studied by Howard (1976) for the Yankton-Yanktonai, indicate that these types of history records began at least as early as A.D. 1682 (1976:20). Through his discussions of these early histories he states that the Dakota originally employed the use of pictographs to represent "the most important or unusual event of the past twelve months" (Howard 1976:1-2). It is possible that boulder monuments depict such "noteworthy events", outlined on the ground surface using boulders as the permanent marking device.

   During the early nineteenth century, the Dakota insisted that their original homeland was northwest of their Minnesota location (Winchell 1911:XII). Additionally, in 1804 Lewis and Clark recorded that various Dakota bands claimed a territory from the Mississippi through to the Montana Rockies and back to the confluence of the Des Moines River with the Mississippi (Thwaites 1969:98-99). While portions of this area were probably disputed with other tribes, the territory suggests the Dakota's exploitation range.

The Wiciyela or Middle Dakota (Nakota) were associated with the Minnesota district (Howard 1966:11). Originally, all Dakota probably shared a common language and culture. While separation from "the original seven council fires" may have induced linguistic differences and the adoption of other people's cultures (Howard 1966:3), their own cultures and ceremonies should have maintained certain basic elements.

From 1660 to 1731 the Assiniboine occupied an area from Lake Superior in Ontario to the Touchwood Hills in Saskatchewan (Ray 1974:6-12). During most of this time Lake of the Woods was referred to as "Lac des Assiniboils" (Ray 1974:11), possibly indicating continuous occupation of that region. At the same time the Middle Dakota moved west out of Minnesota to the east side of the Missouri River:

Human and animal effigies along the eastern and southeastern portions of the northwestern Great Plains seem to occur mainly in the regions adopted by the Assiniboine and the Yankton-Yanktonai, in the vicinity of Lake of the Woods, Ontario, at Whiteshell in Manitoba, along the Missouri River in southern North Dakota and northern South Dakota, and the adjoining portions of Minnesota and Iowa. The sparsity of effigies in northern North Dakota presents a problem of boulder monument route dispersal. The complete absence of reports of these features between the Garrison Dam in North Dakota and southern Saskatchewan may attest a discontinuity of Yankton-Yanktonai exploitation range, destruction or submergence through construction of the Garrison Dam and early agriculture activities, or boulder monument constructions in Saskatchewan by different cultures. If the Yankton-effigy association is correct, the presence of a turtle effigy (Gilmore 1932) in Nebraska might be viewed as evidence of Yankton southern expansion.

The geometric boulder monument types cannot be assigned completely to any specific tribal entity, either by type or variety. While the vision quest site at DkOj-2 seems to mirror an Atsina recorded event, the possibility that this was Little Bear's actual vision quest nest is too remote to be considered. The war lodge structure, possibly attributed to the Piegan, was located in an area frequented by these people when they waged war. The uniqueness of the assumed quarry site prohibits any possible tribal association. Since these structures occur in areas frequented by many proto-historic tribes, they may have been constructed by any of those tribes. The same holds true for the suspected war lodge remnant and proposed quarry indicator. The major difficulty with each of these sites is establishing an ethnic relationship to individual type sites. Without the advantage of numerous sites within each subclass to illustrate variation, these interpretations must be viewed as extremely tenuous.

The inclusion of the Manitoba Thunderbird nests illustrates that a definition other than a vision quest assessment is possible. As for tribal association, one can only assume that they were constructed by Archaic (Middle Period - pre-0A.D.) peoples (Carmichael 1979:85) who were commonly harassed by others.

Comparisons with Other Symbolic Systems

Pictographs (rock paintings) and petroglyphs (rock carvings) are common in the areas peripheral to the Plains region; however, petroglyphs are the major depiction found in southern Saskatchewan, where rock outcroppings or glacial erratics are located. The only boulder features sometimes found in conjunction with Plains petroglyphs are habitation circles; boulder monuments seem to be non-existent in the immediate vicinities. One exception is the location of a vision quest site (a boulder monument construction) together with petroglyphs and drive line cairns (economic, rather than ceremonial boulder configurations) at DkPj-1, the Head-Smashed-In Buffalo Jump in Alberta (Brink et al. 1985:262). The other known exception is from Uyttenhager's observation of a "…large white boulder…[with]…a face and numerous other marks incised in it (McCorquodale 1961) at the Minton Effigy. These examples may be anomalies rather than common site occurrences.

Steinbring's thesis of boulder monument occurrence at sites away from pictograph sites as representing a continuation of style in a different medium (1980:245) is a reasonable one. However, his thesis of boulder monument figures and designs (located along the Whiteshell River in the Canadian Shield of eastern Manitoba), being repeated at various Plains sites (1980:327) is not completely acceptable as there are no medicine wheels, Matoki lodges, bisected circles, vision quest structures, bison effigies, or salamander effigies in Manitoba, either in the Shield or in the province's grasslands further west. Granted, there are animal effigies along the Whiteshell River; however, aside from turtles alone, there are differences in the animals depicted. The occurrence of different figures at the Plains sites should indicate either later initiation of ceremonies adapted to a new environment, the invention of new symbols as a result of cultural amalgamation, lack of identification and destruction, or other forces.

The Minnesota and Iowa boulder monument concentrations also occur away from pictograph and petroglyph sites. The lack of recorded sites along the rivers in North Dakota may be due to their destruction by various modern activities, (at least one recorded site being drowned by the Garrison Dam; see Libby 1910), or a lack of interested recorders during the early settlement years.

A review of pictographs and petroglyphs both in the areas peripheral to the Plains and on the Plains proper revealed some Minnesota figures with designs similar to medicine wheels (Winchell 1911:Pl. V No. 4, Pl. VI No. 10, Pl.VIII Nos. 1-4[3], Pl. IX No. 2) which have been attributed to "western branches of the Dakota" (1911:560). Although one other pictograph, near Rocky Dell in Oklahoma, seems reminiscent of the Big Horn Medicine Wheel (Conrad 1963:61, Figure 7, upper left plate), the absence of medicine wheels reported south of South Dakota should dispel any possibility of similar purpose or meaning between these rock art and boulder monument depictions.

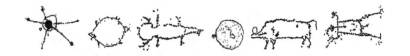

6 - CONCLUSIONS

Consideration of the Initial Propositions

A review of ethnohistoric accounts and the archaeological record provided an inventory of ethnic polities which may have occupied the Saskatchewan plains or entered onto the northern Great Plains since the twelfth century. Historical explorers' documents recorded early migrations and tribal explorations onto the Plains from surrounding environments; however, they presented very scant mention of boulder monuments.

This examination of boulder monuments, and the variety of cultures associated with the northwestern Great Plains, identified four tribes (Blackfoot, Ojibwa, Cree, and Dakota) that can be linked directly with some of these features. Other tribes (Mandan, Crow, Sarsi, Assiniboine, Atsina, etc.) may be linked to boulder monuments through their associations with the preceding tribes, characteristics of some of their cultural activities (as speculative comparisons), or by motif designs peculiar to their specific cultures. The possible Ojibwa-Mandan components at the Wild Man Butte Human Effigy (DgNc-1) and the possible Ojibwa-Dakota components at the Minton Effigy (DhNe-2) seem to reflect some aspects of separate cultures amalgamating at isolated sites. As such these components may reflect an economic transfer of ceremony or a cultural exchange of ideology.

The concentration of medicine wheels and ceremonial circles in Saskatchewan and Alberta seems to support a Blackfoot or more general Algonkian origin; however, the more southerly and easterly concentrations of animal and human effigies seem analogous with Ojibwa or Siouan origins. If some of the speculations are correct, particularly those directly analogous to the customs of specific tribes, then it is likely that boulder monuments do reflect a variety of cultural traditions.

Another proposition involves the situation in space of boulder monuments and their specific landscape elevations as purposeful indicators — perhaps memorials — of perception, achievement, or group occupation. Ceremonial circles, animal effigies, geometrics and most human effigies and medicine wheels occur on local secondary heights of land. In Saskatchewan the exceptions are the Moose Mountain Medicine Wheel (DkMq-2) on a local height of land, and the Dewdney Avenue Human Effigy (EcNh-1) and Dick Giles Circle (DgNg-2) in valley complexes. Individually, most boulder monument classes have been shown to exhibit certain site peculiarities which could have represented distinct signing mechanisms to the constructor's tribesmen or allies.

The possibility of using animal effigies to illustrate environmental attributes, the use of some medicine wheels to define specific campsite identifications, the possible quarry alignment and the symbolism of the human female effigies' association with campsites, suggests that a trained (prehistoric) observer could ascertain territorial ownership and local resource amenities.

The depiction of a major spiritual being, "Old Man", is suggested at the two major Saskatchewan sites of male human effigies. The presence of a stone ring at each site may indicate that one individual created the effigy, or the ring may have other symbolic import, directly related to that of the figurative effigy itself.

The isolation of the vision quest site, completely removed from any stone circles, denotes an individual achievement. The associated fire-cracked rock in this case may suggest the presence of an assistant; however, the absence of stone circles supports the near-complete seclusion of the petitioner.

Other problems remain unresolved. Some sites possess numerous stone circles and the presence of cairns within the boulder monument should place both the cairns and the circles within the same time span. The increased numbers of stone circles at some monument sites seems suggestive of repeated usage of a favourite place. The association of certain cairns at some sites presents an enigma which could not be positively identified through analogy with any of the ethnographic or historic references. One possible explanation is that the boulders within some cairns may have been used to support perishable items (brush with feathers, hair, hide, cloth, etc.) either as an identity element or to present a barrier, as has been hypothesized for the use of the deadmen/cairns in the funnel markers of bison drive sites. When the perishable items fell into disrepair, and the site abandoned, only the monument and cairns would be left as visible markers.

Where stone circles lie between, or are transected by, medicine wheel spokes, contemporaneity of occurrence may be implied. As has been mentioned, all boulders available were probably used to construct the central feature to make it distinct on the prairie. Therefore, the presence of stone circles may imply concurrent or later occupation; the presence of a monument's boulders should have presented a comfort/discomfort to the purposeful residents of a habitation circle (comfort by the knowledge of being on a known sacred site and willful discomfort from respecting a family/ancestor's feature within the living area).

There remains a need for an encompassing and universal classification system for all Great Plains boulder monuments. Whether the model presented herein is accepted or replaced with a different format is irrelevant – a foundation for boulder monument classification will have been established.

Hopefully, we may be better able to discern various functions if we have a larger sample, and one from different regions on the northern Plains. In some instances there was only a single monument within a particular subclass used in the present analysis; therefore, greater variety was generated in the subclass by including boulder monuments from outside Saskatchewan. This selection of comparative analogies does not mean that these comparisons are the only ones available or that they are absolutely correct; rather, this has been an exercise to examine the possibilities that exist.

Insofar as lichenometry is concerned, it appears that there are too many biological and human-induced variables to permit a successful application of this dating mechanism on the Saskatchewan Plains, at least at this time. The technique clearly requires some refinements in understanding lichen fire ecology and in the sphere of defining thalli establishment, favourable encroachment/dominance factors, and succession rates. The growth rates need to be identified for the appropriate species over a greater period of time (40 to 60 years [establishment and survival under the current greenhouse effects]). That identification/ examination time also will permit investigations into other potentially suitable species with radial growth patterns.

The eight proto-historic dates achieved by artifact associations for the older boulder monuments (see Table 10), seem to substantiate the recent lichenometry dates. Consequently, the close grouping of lichenometry dates may mirror reality with respect to the final site usage at some locations. However, the questionable confidence levels for the lichenometry-calculated dates, and the recognized lack of control for environment comparisons, yield a problematic dating method which currently cannot be considered practical or applicable. While the designed application failed in providing absolute dates, the study was included as a stepping stone for future archaeologically-related lichenometric research. This point of view justifies the old proverb that recorded negative information is as valid as positive information because it provides an aid toward directing future endeavours.

While problematic for precision dating, lichenometry as a relative dating tool may be of some benefit toward defining different boulder components on individual sites. The radiate lichens should grow at a constant rate on all boulders. All establishment and succession rates, which are dependant on immediate environmental conditions, should be constant at most boulder monument sites. Therefore, it should be possible to identify early from more recent boulder structures on the basis of thallus sizes on the different boulder structures in any given site.

Discussion and Conclusion

A major perplexity exists when attempting to conjoin ethnographic analogies to boulder monument sites, mainly due to our inability to assign definite dates to these features. Only Payepot's May 1908 burial monument construction date (Watetch 1959:22) and the 1940 construction date for the Steel Medicine Wheel (Dempsey 1956:181; Quigg 1984:12) are precisely known. The Many Spotted Horses Medicine Wheel (Quigg 1984:37) dates probably to 1884, but subsequent disturbances and reconstructions make it uncertain that the surviving wheel is in fact the one erected after Many Spotted Horses died.

The two radiocarbon dates available for other medicine wheels date buried horizons, whereas the features which define the site's classifications are either surface or semi-surface configurations. Better analogies and site classifications may be possible when many more features within each of the monument classes have been excavated and dated with contemporaneous associated materials.

The classification presented herein separates medicine wheels from ceremonial circles. Specifically, this approach has permitted the designation of the assumed Matoki Lodge remnants as configurations denoting separate ceremonial celebrations, rather than including ceremonial circles under the previous, too broad rubric of "medicine wheel". This ability to ascribe specific ethnographic analogies to the four medicine wheel subclasses, and to the subclasses for each of the other classes, should increase the possibility that sufficient information is available to qualify some analysis beyond pure speculation.

Regarding the underlying question: "Who constructed or originated the boulder monument tradition on the Great Plains?", I believe that while the majority of the features are of Algonkian invention, others have vestiges of Siouan origin. More specifically, the Blackfoot probably constructed the earliest medicine wheel and ceremonial circle prototypes, whose forms were borrowed by Blackfoot-associated Algonkians, and the outlines possibly were redefined or realigned to fit the contemporary mythologies of later ethnic groups using the sites.

The more southerly occurrence of human and animal effigies in Saskatchewan, coupled with the southern Manitoba, Minnesota, and North Dakota effigies, seems to indicate a south-eastern to north-western progression, when compared to ethnohistoric tribal movements. The location of a turtle effigy in central Alberta, where turtles don't exist in the natural environment, should aid toward the north-western progression analysis. As the primary tribe which expanded in that direction was the Assiniboine, a probable Assiniboine origin is the most plausible analysis. Additionally, the cut-sod outline which accompanied the Wild Man Butte Human Effigy in 1863 is similar in nature to a Mandan expression of noteworthy events. A possible Algonkian (Ojibwa)–Siouan(Mandan) amalgamation of cultural traditions may have been reflected at the site.

As the majority of human effigies occur on territories well within recorded Assiniboine exploited districts, they might be inferred to be Siouan in origin, with the possibility of tradition borrowing or exchange by Algonkian tribes. While it may be possible to assume that the medicine wheels encountered in Saskatchewan and Alberta are probably of Blackfoot origin, it would be incorrect to state the same supposition for all northern Great Plains medicine wheel sites. The twentieth century continuation of medicine wheel construction definitely represents a Blackfoot cultural awareness of an ancient tradition. Additionally, the near universality of the ceremonial uses for features like the war lodge and vision quest structures together with the fluctuating tribal territories suggests that many tribes may have been responsible for these types of monuments.

This study is one archaeologist's attempt at understanding and telling others about a complex and fascinating array of prehistoric North American phenomena. More questions than answers have resulted. While the research needs have been put forth, hopefully to bear fruit with future work, an equally important need must be met. Boulder monument sites are fragile, and continue to be harmed by modern human activities that take place on the Great

Plains landscape (Figs. 120, 160).

Effective legislation needs to be in place in each jurisdiction where the monuments occur, and it needs to be enforced. Equally, we should not allow ignorance of either the existence of known monuments by land-users, or of the significance of these features, to result in the damage to or loss of these remnant sites.

This book has been in part an attempt to help educate all who need such information and education – essentially, all of us – that we need to cherish and protect these "wonderful things" (with apologies to Howard Carter).

Figure 160: The Ted Douglas Human Effigy in the Cabri Lake Hills, quite clearly a (disturbed) "copy" of the Cabri Lake Human Effigy, 10 km distant from this to the south as the crow flies

156

ILLUSTRATION CREDITS

Chapter 1: Fig.1, Ted Douglas; 2, George Tosh; 3, Ian Brace; 4, RSM; 5, 6, 7, Ian Brace after Richards and Fung.

Chapter 2: Fig. 8, 9,Ian Brace; 10, RSM; 11, Kehoe 1973; 12, RSM; 13, Kehoe 1973; 14, Quigg/ASA; 15, ASA; 16, 17, RSM; 18, 19, 20, 21, 22, 23, Quigg/ASA; 24, Kehoe 1973; 25, Over 1941; 26, 27, Kehoe 1973; 28, 29, RSM; 30, Dempsey 1956; 31, 32, ASA; 33, Brown 1963; 34, 35, 36, 37, Quigg/ASA; 38, Rood and Rood 1983; 39, ASA; 40, Calder 1977; 41, Grinnell 1922; 42, 43, RSM; 44, Kehoe 1973; 45, Begg 1915; 46, Graspointer 1980; 47, 48, 49, 50, 51, Quigg/ASA; 52, ASA; 53, 54, RSM; 55, 56, RSM; 57, Tamplin n.d.; 58, Jerde 1959; 59, Rutkowski and Westcott 1979; 60, Nicholson 1980; 61, 62, RSM; 63, 64, 65, 66, Quigg/ASA; 67, ASA; 68, 69,RSM; 70, George Tosh; 71, Tim Jones; 72, RSM; 73, Bayrock 1965; 74, 75, Sutton 1965; 76, Steinbring 1980; 77, 78, 79, 80, Over 1941; 81, Libby 1910; 82, 83, 84, RSM; 85, Sutton 1965; 86, Buchner 1976a; 87, Buchner 1976b; 88, Sutton 1965; 89, 90, Steinbring 1980; 91, Over 1941; 92, Steinbring 1970; 93, George Tosh; 94, 95a, Gill and Hymers; 95b, V. Vigfusson; 95c, 96, 97, RSM; 98, Wormington and Forbis; 99, 100, ASA; 101, Kehoe and Kehoe 1957; 102, Bryan 1968; 103, 104, Steinbring 1970; 105, Simms 1903b; 106, Malouf 1975; 107, Kehoe and Kehoe 1957; 108, Lewis and Lewis 1891; 109, Lewis 1889; 110, Hudak 1972; 111, RSM; 112, Carpenter 1975; 113, RSM; 114, Watson 1975; 115, 116, 117, Buchner 1976b; 118, Buchner and Callaghan 1980; 119, George Tosh; 120, George Tosh and Ted Douglas; 121, Tim Jones; 122, George Tosh; 123, RSM; 124, George Tosh; 125, Ian Brace and Ken Reischke; 126, RSM; 127, Ian Brace and Ken Reischke; 128, George Tosh; 129 (both), Zenon Pohorecky; 130, Clifford Crickett; 131, 132, George Tosh; 133, RSM; 134, Ian Brace; 135, 136, 137, Buchner 1976a; 138, Buchner 1976b; 139, Carmichael 1979; 140, 141, 142, Tyyska and Burns 1973; 143, Davis 1975; 144, Rea 1966; 145, 146, 147, Over 1941.

Chapter 3: Fig. 148, Swanton 1952, Ewers 1955, 1979, Lewis 1942, Kerr 1966, Thomas and Ronnefeldt 1976.

Chapter 4: Fig. 149, Brodo 1981; 150, 151, Ian Brace.

Chapter 5: Fig. 152, Watson 1975; 153, John Duerkop; 154, W. A. Marjerrison; 155, George Tosh; 156, 157, 158, James 1830; 159, RSM.

Chapter 6: Fig. 160, Saskatchewan Archaeological Society.

RSM - Royal Saskatchewan Museum (formerly Saskatchewan Museum of Natural History)
ASA - Archaeological Survey of Alberta - unpublished records

REFERENCES CITED

Adams, Gary
  1978 The Alkali Creek sites. In: *Tipi Rings in Southern Alberta*, Occasional Papers Nos. 8 & 9. Archaeological Survey of Alberta, Edmonton.

Allen, Joel A.
  1876 The American bisons, living and extinct. *Memoirs of the Geological Survey of Kentucky*, I (Pt. II). Welch, Bigelo & Co., University Press, Cambridge.

Andrews, J. T. and P. J. Webber
  1969 Lichenometry to evaluate changes in glacial mass budgets: as illustrated in north-central Baffin Island, N.W.T. *Arctic and Alpine Research* 1(3):181-194.

Angier, Bradford
  1972 *Feasting Free on Wild Edibles*. Stackpole Books, Harrisburg, Pa.

Anonymous
  1950 *North Dakota: A Guide to the Prairie State* (1ˢᵗ ed., 1938). Compiled by workers of the Federal Writers Project of the Works Progress Administration for the State of North Dakota, Bismarck.

Armstrong, R. A.
  1976 Studies on the growth rates of lichens. In: *Lichenology: Progress and Problems*, ed. by D.H. Brown, D.L. Hawksworth and R.H. Bailey, pp. 309-322. Academic Press, London and New York.

Arthur George W.
  1975 *An Introduction to the Ecology of Early Historic Communal Bison Hunting among the Northern Plains Indians*. National Museum of Man, Mercury Series, Archaeological Survey of Canada, Paper No. 37. Ottawa.

Aveni, A. F.
  1977 *Native American Astronomy*. University of Texas Press, Austin.

Barbeau, Marius
  1974 *Indian Days on the Western Prairies*. Bulletin No. 163. Anthropological Series No. 46. Department of Secretary of State, National Museum of Canada, Ottawa.

Basso, Keith H. (editor)
  1971 *Western Apache Raiding and Warfare: From the Notes of Grenville Goodwin*. The University of Arizona Press, Tucson.

Bayrock, L. A.
  1963 The Consort Site: A preliminary report for the 1963 field season. *Archaeological Society of Alberta Newsletter* (1):1-4. Edmonton.

Beardy, Jackson
  1969 Wesakachak and the geese. In: *I Am An Indian*, ed. by Kent Gooderham, pp. 62-64. J.M. Dent & Sons (Canada) Limited, Toronto.

Begg, W. A.
  1915 Personal letter of the Saskatchewan Township Inspector, Surveys Branch, to the Deputy Minister of the Saskatchewan Department of Agriculture. Letter on file with the Aboriginal History Unit of the Royal Saskatchewan Museum in Regina.

Behler, John L. and F. Wayne King
   1979 *Field Guide to North American Reptiles and Amphibians.* The Audubon Society and
        Alfred A. Knopf, Inc., New York.
Benedict, James B.
   1967 Recent glacial history of an alpine area in the Colorado Front Range, U.S.A.; I.
        Establishing a lichen-growth curve. *Journal of Glaciology* 6(48):817-832.
Benedict, Ruth Fulton
   1923 *The Concept of the Guardian Spirit in North America.* Memoirs of the American
        Anthropological Association Number 29. Reprint, 1964. Kraus Reprint Corporation,
        New York.
Berthrong, Donald J.
   1972 *The Southern Cheyennes.* University of Oklahoma Press, Norman.
Beschel, Roland
   1950 Lichens as a measure of the age of recent moraines (Flechten als Altersmaszstab
        rezenter Moranen). Zeitschrift für Gletscherkunde and Glazialgeologie, Bd. 1:152-161.
        (Translated by William Barr, University of Saskatchewan, May, 1967).
   1957 Lichenometry in glacial forelands (Lichenometrie im Gletschervorfeld). *Jahrbuch des*
        Vereins zum Schutze der Alpenpflazen und-tiere (München). (Translated by William Barr,
        University of Saskatchewan, May, 1968).
   1961 Dating rock surfaces by lichen growth and its application to glaciology and
        physiography (lichenometry). In: *Geology of the Arctic, ed. by* G. O. Raasch, 2:1044-
        1062. University of Toronto Press, Toronto.
   1973 Lichens as a measure of the age of recent moraines. *Arctic and Alpine Research*
        5(4):303-309.
Bland, John H.
   1971 *Forests of Lilliput: The Realm of Mosses and Lichens.* Prentice-Hall, Inc., Englewood
        Cliffs, New Jersey.
Bowers, Alfred W.
   1965 *Hidatsa Social and Ceremonial Organization.* Smithsonian Institution, Bureau of
        American Ethnology, Bulletin 194, Washington, D. C.
Braithwaite, Max
   1975 *The Western Plains.* The Illustrated Natural History of Canada. Natural Science of
        Canada Limited, Toronto.
Brink, Jack, Milt Wright, Bob Dawe and Doug Glaum
   1985 *Final Report of the 1983 Season at Head-Smashed-In Buffalo Jump, Alberta.* Manuscript
        Series No. 1, Archaeological Survey of Alberta, Edmonton.
Brodo, Irwin M.
   1964 Field studies of the effects of ionizing radiation on lichens. *Bryologist* 67:76-87.
   1981 Lichens of the Ottawa region. *Syllogeus* 29:60. National Museum of Natural Sciences,
        National Museums of Canada, Ottawa.
Brown, Lionel A.
   1963 The Fort Smith medicine wheel, Montana. *Plains Anthropologist* 8(22):255-330.
Brumley, John H.
   1988 *Medicine Wheels on the Northern Plains: A Summary and Appraisal.* Archaeological

Survey of Alberta Manuscript Series No. 12. Alberta Culture and Multiculturalism, Edmonton.

Bryan, Alan
1968 The first people. In: *Alberta: A Natural History, ed. by* W. C. Hardy, pp. 277-293. M. G. Hurtig Ltd., Edmonton.

Bryson, Reid A. and Wayne M. Wendland
1967 Tentative climatic patterns for some late glacial and post glacial episodes in central North America. In: *Life, Land and Water,* ed. by William J. Mayer-Oakes , pp. 271-298. University of Manitoba Press, Winnipeg.

Budd, Archibald C. and Keith F. Best
1964 *Wild Plants of the Canadian Prairies.* Swift Current Experimental Farm, Canada Department of Agriculture, Ottawa.

Buchner, Anthony P.
1976a The 1973 rock art studies at the Tie Creek site: A preliminary report. In: Papers in Manitoba Archaeology, *Miscellaneous Papers #2: Studies in Manitoba Rock Art* I:10-22, Petroforms; Department of Tourism, Recreation and Cultural Affairs. Historic Resources Branch, Winnipeg.
1976b A survey of eastern Manitoba petroforms – 1974. In: Papers in Manitoba Archaeology, *Miscellaneous Papers #2: Studies in Manitoba Rock Art* I, I:23-35, Petroforms; Department of Tourism, Recreation and Cultural Affairs. Historic Resources Branch, Winnipeg.

Buchner, A. P. and R. Callaghan
1980 The Astwood site. In: Papers in Manitoba Archaeology, *Miscellaneous Papers #10, Studies in Eastern Manitoba Archaeology,* pp. 71-108. Department of Cultural Affairs and Historic Resources, Historic Resources Branch, Winnipeg.

Buikstra, Jane
1979 Contributions of physical anthropologists to the concept of Hopewell: A historic perspective. In: *Hopewell Archaeology, ed. by* David S. Brose and N'omi Greber , pp. 220-233. The Kent State University Press, Kent, Ohio.

Burpee, Lawrence J. (editor)
1907 *York Factory to the Blackfoot Country, the Journal of Anthony Hendry [Henday]:1754-1755.* Proceedings and Transactions of the Royal Society of Canada, Third Series 1(2):307-360.
1927 *Journals and Letters of Pierre Gaultier de Varennes de la Vérendrye and His Sons.* The Champlain Society, Toronto.

Bushnell, D. I.
1905 An Ojibway ceremony. *American Anthropologist* 7(1):69-73.
1922 *Villages of the Algonkian, Siouan, and Caddoan Tribes West of the Mississippi.* Smithsonian Institution, Bureau of American Ethnology, Bulletin 77. Washington, D.C.

Byrne, William J.
1973 *The Archaeology and Prehistory of Southern Alberta as Reflected by Ceramics.* National Museum of Man Mercury Series, Archaeological Survey of Canada, Paper 14 (3 volumes). Ottawa.

Calder, James M.
    1977 *The Majorville Cairn and Medicine Wheel Site, Alberta.* National Museum of Man
        Mercury Series, Archaeological Survey of Canada, Paper No. 62. Ottawa.
Campbell, Walter Stanley
    1927 The tipis of the Crow Indians. *American Anthropologist* 29(1):87-104.
Capes, Katherine H.
    1963 *The W. B. Nickerson Survey and Excavations, 1912-15, of the Southern Manitoba Mounds
        Region.* Anthropology Papers, National Museum of Canada, No. 4. Department of
        Northern Affairs and National Resources, Ottawa.
Capron, Louis
    1953 *The Medicine Bundles of the Florida Seminole and the Green Corn Dance.* Smithsonian
        Institution, Bureau of American Ethnology, Bulletin 151, Anthropological Papers No.
        35:155-210. Washington, D.C.
Carmichael, Patrick H.
    1979 *The Thunderbird Site, EgKx-15: A Prehistoric Petroform and Habitation Site in Manitoba.*
        Papers in Manitoba Archaeology, Final Report No. 6. Department of Tourism and
        Cultural Affairs, Historic Resources Branch, Winnipeg.
Carpenter, Edmund
    1978 Silent music and invisible art. *Natural History* 87(5):90-99.
Carpenter, Jim (editor)
    1975 The Burmis Boulder Paving Site, Project 14. Archaeological Society of Alberta, pp. 36-
        40. Lethbridge Centre, Alberta.
Carter, William "Moah Mefkewe"
    1973 *Medical Practices and Burial Customs of the North American Indians.* Namid Printers and
        Publishers, London, Ontario.
Christensen, T. N.
    1963 Pentagons of the northwestern plains. *The Trowel & Screen* 4(6):2-4. Billings
        Archaeological Society, Billings, Montana.
Clandening, William H.
    1928 Across the Plains in 1863-1865; by William Clandening of Walkerton, Upper Canada,
        now Ontario, Canada. *North Dakota Historical Quarterly* II(4):246-272. (Part 8 of
        Volume VIII of the Collections of the State Historical Society of North Dakota, July,
        1928).
Clark, Ella Elizabeth
    1969 Coyote and the monster of the Columbia. In: *I Am An Indian,* ed. *by* Kent Gooderham,
        pp. 26-29. J. M. Dent & Sons (Canada) Limited, Toronto.
Clements, Forrest
    1931 Plains Indian tribal correlations with Sun Dance data. *American Anthropologist*
        33(2):216-227.
Cocking, Matthew
    1909 *An Adventurer from Hudson Bay, Journal of Matthew Cocking from York Factory to the
        Blackfeet Country, 1772-1773,* L. J. Burpee (editor). Transactions and Proceedings,
        Royal Society of Canada, 2 (Section 2). Toronto.

Cohen, Yehudi A.
  1968 Beginnings in cultural adaptation: archaeological explorations. In: *Man in Adaptation: The Biosocial Background*, ed. by Yehudi A. Cohen, pp. 281-290. Aldine Publishing Company, Chicago.

Conner, Stuart W.
  1982 Archaeology of the Crow Indian vision quest. *Archaeology In Montana* 23(3):85-128.

Conrad, David E.
  1963 The Whipple expedition on the Great Plains. *Great Plains Journal* 2(2):42-66.

Cooper, John M.
  1956 *The Gros Ventres of Montana: Part II, Religion and Ritual.* Catholic University of American Anthropology Series, No. 16. The Catholic University of America Press, Washington, D.C.

Corbett, E. A.
  1934 *Blackfoot Trails.* The Macmillan Company of Canada Limited, St. Martin's House, Toronto.

Coues, Elliott (editor)
  1897 *New Light on the Early History of the Greater Northwest. The Manuscript Journals of Alexander Henry and of David Thompson*, Volume II. New York.

Davis, Leslie B.
  1975 *The Prehistory of the Whitewater-Frenchman Creek/Milk River Locality, Northeastern Montana: An Introduction.* Montana State University, Bozeman.
  1988 *Avonlea Yesterday and Today: Archaeology and Prehistory.* Saskatchewan Archaeological Society, Saskatoon.

Deaver, Ken
  1980 U.S. Department of the Interior, Bureau of Land Management, Cultural Resource Inventory Records. Unpublished records from the Fresno Reservoir Survey Project for the Montana Water and Power Resource Service. Records on file with Professional Analysts, 1015 Broadwater, Billings, Montana.

DeMallie, Raymond J. (editor)
  2001 *Handbook of North American Indians, Vol. 13: Plains (Part 1).* Smithsonian Institution, Washington.

Dempsey, Hugh A.
  1956 Stone "medicine wheels" – memorials to Blackfoot war chiefs. *Journal of the Washington Academy of Sciences* 46 (6):177-182.

Denig, Edwin Thompson
  1953 *Of the Crow Nation.* Bureau of American Ethnology, Bulletin 151. Anthropological Papers, No. 33:1-74. Smithsonian Institution, Washington, D.C.

Dewdney, Selwyn
  1964 Writings on stone along the Milk River. *The Beaver* Winter:22-29.
  1978 Aboriginal rock paintings in Manitoba: A preliminary description of 27 sites east and northeast of Lake Winnipeg. In: *Papers in Manitoba Archaeology, Miscellaneous Papers #8, Studies in Manitoba Rock Art* II:105-134. Department of Tourism and Cultural Affairs, Historic Resources Branch, Winnipeg.

Dickson, Gary
  1977 *Prehistoric Northern Manitoba*. Manitoba Museum of Man and Nature, Winnipeg.
Dusenberry, Verne
  1962 *The Montana Cree: a Study in Religious Persistence*. Stockholm Studies in Comparative
        Religion. Almquist & Wiksell, Stockholm, Sweden.
Dyck, Ian G.
  1981 New light on the Wild Man Butte boulder configuration. *Saskatchewan Archaeology*
        2(1):54-72. Regina.
  1983 The prehistory of southern Saskatchewan. In: *Tracking Ancient Hunters*, ed. by Henry T.
        Epp and Ian Dyck, pp. 63-140. Saskatchewan Archaeological Society, Regina.
Dyck, Ian and Richard E. Morlan
  2001 Hunting and gathering tradition: Canadian Plains. In: *Handbook of North American
        Indians, Vol. 13: Plains (Part 1)*, ed. by Raymond J. DeMallie, pp. 115-130. Smithsonian
        Institution, Washington.
Eddy, John A.
  1974 Astronomical alignments of the Big Horn medicine wheel. *Science* 184(4141):1035-
        1043.
  1975 Medicine Wheels and Plains Indian Astronomy. Paper presented at a seminar on
        Native American astronomy, Colgate University, Hamilton, New York, Sept. 23, 1975.
  1976 Archaeoastronomy of North America: cliffs, mounds, and medicine wheels. In: *In
        Search of Ancient Astronomies*, ed. by E.C. Krupp, pp. 133-136. Doubleday & Company
        Inc., Garden City.
  1977 Probing the mystery of the medicine wheels. *National Geographic* 151(1):140-146.
  1979 Medicine wheels and Plains Indian astronomy. In: *Native American Astronomy*, ed. by
        A. F. Aveni, pp. 147-169. University of Texas Press, Austin.
Ewers, John C.
  1944 The Blackfoot war lodge: its construction and use. *American Anthropologist* 46(2), part
        1:182-192.
  1955 *The Horse in Blackfoot Culture*. Smithsonian Institution Bureau of American Ethnology,
        Bulletin 159. Washington, D.C.
  1958 *The Blackfoot: Raiders on The Northwestern Plains*. University of Oklahoma Press,
        Norman.
  1968 *Indian Life on the Upper Missouri*. University of Oklahoma Press, Norman.
  1973 *Ethnological Report on the Blackfeet and Gros Ventre Tribes of Indian Lands in Northern
        Montana, Docket No. 279-A, Indian Claims Commission*. Clearwater Publishing
        Company Inc., New York.
  1979 *Plains Indian Painting*. Stanford University Press. Stanford University, California.
  1981 Water monsters in plains Indian art. *American Indian Art Magazine*, Autumn:38-45.
Ferry, B. W., M. S. Baddeley, and D. L. Hawksworth (editors)
  1973 *Air Pollution and Lichens*. Athlone Press, London.
Finnigan, James T.
  1980 Interpreting tipi ring structures. *Napao* 10(1&2):1-6. Department of Anthropology and
        Archaeology, University of Saskatchewan, Saskatoon.
  1982 *Tipi Rings and Plains Prehistory: A Reassessment of Their Archaeological Potential*. National

Museum of Man Mercury Series, Archaeological Survey of Canada, Paper No. 108. Ottawa.

Fletcher, Alice C.
  1902 Star cult among the Pawnee – a preliminary report. *American Anthropologist* 4(4):730-736.

Follman, G.
  1961 Lichen based age determination of encrusted monuments of Polynesian Easter Island. *Natural Science* 48:627-628.

Forbis, Richard G.
  1963 The direct historical approach in the prairie provinces of Canada. *Great Plains Journal* (1):1-8.

Fox, Richard A., Jr.
  1980 Cultural Resource Inventory of The Saskatchewan Intertie Transmission Line Right-of-Way, Northwestern North Dakota, Volume I. Prepared in fulfillment of Basic Electric Power Cooperative, Bismarck, North Dakota, Contract 61201. University of North Dakota Archaeological Research, Department of Anthropology and Archaeology, University of North Dakota.

Franklin, John
  1970 *Narrative Of A Journey To The Shores Of The Polar Sea In The Years 1819, 1820, 1821, and 1822.* Charles E. Tuttle Company, Publishers, Tokyo. Reprint by M. G. Hurtig Ltd., Edmonton.

Fredlund, Dale
  1969 Vision quest sites and structures. *Archaeology in Montana* 10(1):14-20.

Frison, G. C.
  1978 *Prehistoric Hunters of the High Plains.* Academic Press, New York.

Gerson, Uri and Mark R. D. Seaward
  1977 Lichen-invertebrate associations. In: *Lichen Ecology*, ed. by Mark R. D. Seaward, pp. 69-120. Academic Press, New York.

Gilbert, O. L.
  1971 The effect of airborne fluorides on lichens. *Lichenologist* 5:26-32.

Gill, Judith and Merna Hymers
  1968 Indian Boulder Effigies on the Northern Plains. Unpublished research report prepared for Z.S. Pohorecky's Archaeology 404 class, University of Saskatchewan, Saskatoon, Saskatchewan. March 15.

Gilmore, G. H.
  1932 Turtle mound, in Cass County, Nebraska. *Nebraska History Magazine* 13(3):166-169.

Gilmore, Melvin R.
  1929 A Mandan monument to a national hero. *Indian Notes* 6(2):147-151. Museum of the American Indian, Heye Foundation, New York.

Glover, Richard
  1962 *David Thompson's Narrative, 1784-1812.* The Champlain Society, Toronto.

Grant, Peter
  1960 "The Saulteaux Indians" vers 1804. In: *Les Bourgeois de la Compagnie du Nord-Ouest*, ed. by L. R. Masson, II:306-366, Antiquarian Press Ltd., New York.

Graspointner, Andreas
    1980 *Archaeology and Ethno-History of the Milk River in Southern Alberta*. Western Publishers,
          Calgary.
Grey, Donald C.
    1963 Big Horn medicine wheel site 48BH302. *Plains Anthropologist* 8(19):27-40.
Grinnell, George Bird
    1922 The medicine wheel. *American Anthropologist* 24(3):299-310.
    1962 *Blackfoot Lodge Tales*. University of Nebraska Press, Lincoln.
    1969 The race. In: *I Am An Indian*, ed. by Kent Gooderham, pp.47-48. J.M. Dent & Sons
          (Canada) Limited, Toronto.
Griswold, Gillett
    1970 Aboriginal patterns of trade between the Columbia Basin and the northern plains.
          Archaeology In Montana 11(2-3):1-96.
Habgood, Thelma
    1967 Petroglyphs and pictographs in Alberta. *Archaeological Society of Alberta Newsletter* 13
          & 14:1-40. Edmonton.
Hale, M. E.
    1952 Studies on the lichen *Rinodina oreina* in North America. *Bulletin of the Torry Botanical
          Club* 79:251-259.
    1974 *The Biology of Lichens*. William Clowes & Sons Limited, London.
    1979 *How to Know the Lichens*. Wm. C. Brown Co., Dubuque, Iowa.
Hall, Edward T.
    1944 Recent clues to Athapascan prehistory. *American Anthropologist* 46:98-105.
Hall, Robert L.
    1976 Ghosts, water barriers, corn, and sacred enclosures in the eastern woodlands. *American
          Antiquity* 41(3):360-364.
Hallowell, A. Irving
    1936 The passing of the Midewiwin in the Lake Winnipeg region. *American Anthropologist*
          38(1):32-51.
Hamilton, Basil G.
    1896 The Diary of Basil G. Hamilton, Assistant Land Inspector for the C.P.R. Unpublished
          manuscript, Glenbow-Alberta Institute, Calgary.
Hassrick, Royal B.
    1964 *The Sioux*. University of Oklahoma Press, Norman.
Hedlin, R. A.
    1978 Land and agriculture in the Canadian Prairie Provinces. *Manitoba Nature* 19(4):16-25.
Heizer, Robert F.
    1942 Ancient grooved clubs and modern rabbit-sticks. *American Antiquity* 8(1):41-56.
Hickerson, Harold
    1962 *The Southwestern Chippewa: An Ethnohistorical Study*. American Anthropologist 64(3)
          Pt. 2, Memoir 92.
Hilger, Sister M. Inez
    1952 *Arapaho Child Life and Its Culture Background*. Smithsonian Institution. Bureau of
          American Ethnology, Bulletin 148. Washington, D.C.

Hind, Henry Youle
　1971 *Narrative of the Canadian Red River Exploration Expedition of 1857 and of the Assiniboine and Saskatchewan Exploring Expedition of 1858* (2 volumes). Reprinted by M. G. Hurtig, Ltd., Edmonton.

Hodge, Frederick Webb (editor)
　1907 *Handbook of American Indians North of Mexico.* Smithsonian Institution, Bureau of American Ethnology, Bulletin 30, Part 1. Washington, D.C.

Howard, James H.
　1966 *The Dakota or Sioux Indians, a Study in Human Ecology.* Reprints in Anthropology, 20. J. & L. Reprint Company, Lincoln, Nebraska. Reprinted from: University of South Dakota, Anthropological Papers, No. 2, pp. 1-86. Vermillion, South Dakota.
　1972 Notes on the ethnogeography of the Yankton Dakota. *Plains Anthropologist* 17(58, Pt. 1):281-307.
　1976 Yanktonai ethnohistory and the John K. Bear winter count. *Plains Anthropologist* 21(73, Pt. 2):1-78.
　1977 *The Plains-Ojibwa or Bungi, Hunters and Warriors of the Northern Prairies with Special Reference to the Turtle Mountain Band.* Reprints in Anthropology, 7. J. & L. Reprint Company, Lincoln, Nebraska. Reprinted from: University of South Dakota, W. H. Over Museum, Anthropological Papers, pp. 1-244. Vermillion, South Dakota.

Hudak, Joseph G.
　1972 Boulder outlines in Southwestern Minnesota. *Plains Anthropologist* 17(58):345-346.

James, Edwin (documenter)
　1830 *A Narrative of the Captivity and Adventures of John Tanner during Thirty Years Residence among the Indians in the Interior of North America.* Ross Haines, Inc., Minneapolis, 1956 Edition.

Jenness, Diamond
　1938 The *Sarcee Indians of Alberta.* National Museum of Canada, Bulletin 90, Anthropological Series No. 23. Canada Department of Mines and Resources, Ottawa.

Jerde, Tom
　1979 The Morstad site. *Saskatchewan Archaeology Newsletter* 54(3 & 4):21-23.

Jochimsen, Maren
　1966 Does the size of lichen thalli really constitute a valid measure for dating relict glacio-morphological features? *Geografiska Annaler* 48A(3):157-164. (Translated by William Barr, University of Saskatchewan, March, 1967).

Johnson, Alice M. (editor)
　1967 *Saskatchewan Journals and Correspondence.* Hudson's Bay Record Society 26. London.

Johnson, Elden
　1969 *The Prehistoric Peoples of Minnesota.* Minnesota Historical Society, St. Paul.

Jones, T. E. H.
　1981 *The Aboriginal Rock Paintings of the Churchill River.* Anthropological Series 4, Saskatchewan Museum of Natural History, Regina.

Kehoe, Alice B. and Thomas F. Kehoe
　1979 *Solstice-aligned Boulder Configurations in Saskatchewan.* National Museum of Man, Mercury Series, Canadian Ethnology Service, Paper No. 48. Ottawa.

Kehoe, Thomas F.
  1954 Stone "medicine wheels" in southern Alberta and the adjacent portions of Montana:
       Were they designed as grave markers? *Journal of the Washington Academy of Sciences*
       44(5):133-137.
  1958 Three dry-laid masonry structures in the northern Rocky Mountains. *American
       Antiquity* 23(4):430-432.
  1960 *Stone Tipi Rings in North-central Montana and the Adjacent Portion of Alberta, Canada:
       Their Historical, Ethnological, and Archaeological Aspects.* Smithsonian Institution
       Bureau of American Ethnology, Anthropology Paper 62, Bulletin 173:417-473.
  1965 *Indian Boulder Effigies.* Saskatchewan Museum of Natural History, Regina. Popular
       Series No. 12.
  1973 Stone "medicine wheel" monuments in the northern plains of North America.
       Proceedings of the XIth International Congress of Americanists 11, Symposium III-V:183-
       189, Rome.
Kehoe, Thomas F. and Alice B. Kehoe
  1957 Boulder effigy monuments in the northern plains. *Journal of American Folklore*
       72(284):115-127.
  1976 Solstice-aligned boulder configurations in Saskatchewan. *Calgary Archaeologist* (4):
       41-44.
Kennedy, Michael Stephen (editor)
  1961 *The Assiniboines.* University of Oklahoma Press, Norman.
Kerr, D. G. G.
  1966 *An Historical Atlas of Canada* (2nd ed.). Thomas Nelson & Sons Ltd., Don Mills,
       Ontario.
Keyser, James D.
  1979 Late prehistoric period bison procurement on the Milk River in north-central
       Montana. *Archaeology In Montana* 20(1):1-241.
Kidd, Kenneth E.
  1937 *Blackfoot Ethnography.* Archaeological Survey of Alberta, Manuscript Series, No. 8
       (reprinted 1986). Alberta Culture, Edmonton.
Kidwell, Arthur S. Jr.
  1969 The conical timbered lodge on the Northwestern Plains: historical, ethnological, and
       archaeological evidence. *Archaeology In Montana* 10(4):1-49.
Kroeber, A. L.
  1902 *The Arapaho.* American Museum of Natural History, Anthropological Papers I:1-454.
       New York.
  1908 *Ethnology of the Gros Ventre.* American Museum of Natural History, Anthropological
       Papers I (Pt. IV):141-281. New York.
  1939 *Cultural and Natural Areas of North America.* University of California Publications in
       Archaeology and Ethnology, 38.
  1952 *The Nature of Culture.* The University of Chicago Press, Chicago.
Lamb, W. K. (editor)
  1970 *The Journals and Letters of Sir Alexander Mackenzie.* Macmillan of Canada, Toronto.

Lehmer, Donald J.
1971 *Introduction to Middle Missouri Archaeology*. National Park Service. U. S. Department of the Interior, Washington, D.C.

Lewis, Oscar
1942 *The Effects of White Contact upon Blackfoot Culture*. American Ethnological Society, Monograph 6. University of Washington Press, Seattle and London.

Lewis, T. H.
1889 Stone monuments in southern Dakota. *American Anthropologist* 2(2):159-164.
1890 Stone monuments in northwestern Iowa and southwestern Minnesota. *American Anthropologist* 3:269-274.
1891 Boulder outline figures in the Dakotas, surveyed in the summer of 1890. *American Anthropologist* 4(1):19-24.

Libby, O. G. (editor)
1910 A boulder outline on the upper Missouri. *Collections of the State Historical Society of North Dakota*, III:685-687. Bismarck.

Loendorf, Lawrence L.
1969 Pryor Mountain archaeology. *Archaeology in Montana* 10(2):21-53.
1970 Prehistoric patterns of campsite selection in the Pryor Mountains, Montana. *Archaeology in Montana* 11(1):17-44.

Lowie, Robert H.
1909 *The Northern Shoshone*. American Museum of Natural History Anthropological Papers (Pt. II): 169-306. New York. (Reprinted in 1975).
1912 *Social Life of the Crow Indians*. American Museum of Natural History, Anthropological Papers 9(Pt. II):179-248. New York.
1915 *Societies of the Arikara Indians*. American Museum of Natural History Anthropological Papers 11 (Pt. VIII):645-678. New York.
1922 *The Religion of the Crow Indians*. American Museum of Natural History Anthropological Papers 25, Part II: 309-444. New York.
1956 *The Crow Indians*. Holt, Rinehart, and Winston, New York.
1963 *Indians of the Plains*. The Natural History Press, Garden City, NJ.

Maher, W. J.
1969 Mammals in Saskatchewan. In: *Atlas of Saskatchewan,* ed. by J. Howard Richards and K. I. Fung, pp. 80-82. University of Saskatchewan, Saskatoon.

Malouf, Carling
1962 Stone piles. *Archaeology in Montana* 3(4):1-4.
1963 Battle pits and war lodges. *Archaeology in Montana* 5(2):1-11.
1967 Historic tribes and archaeology. *Archaeology in Montana* 8(1):1-16.
1975 Missouri River headwaters archaeology. *Archaeology in Montana* 16(1):1-42.

Mandelbaum, David G.
1979 *The Plains Cree: An Ethnographic, Historical, and Comparative Study*. Canadian Plains Studies, 9. Reprint of 1940 work, with additional portions of original dissertation included. Canadian Plains Research Center, Regina.

Masson, L. R. (editor)
1960 *Les Bourgeois de la Compagnie du Nord-Ouest, Volume I*. Antiquarian Press Ltd., New

York.

McClintock, Walter
  1923 *Old Indian Trails.* Houghton Mifflin Company, Boston and New York.

McCorquodale, Bruce A.
  1961 1961 diary, on file with the Aboriginal History Unit, Royal Saskatchewan Museum,
       Regina.

McCracken, Harold
  1959 *George Catlin and the Old Frontier.* Bonanza Books, New York.

McGee, D.
  1897 *The Siouan Indians.* Smithsonian Institution. Bureau of American Ethnology Annual
       Reports 15. Washington, D.C.

Montgomery, Henry W.
  1908 Prehistoric man in Manitoba and Saskatchewan. *American Anthropologist* 10(1):33-40.

Mooney, James
  1907 *The Cheyenne Indians.* Memoirs of the American Anthropological Association 1(Pt.
       6):357-442. Reprint (1964), Kraus Reprint Corporation, New York.

Morgan, Lewis Henry
  1959 *The Indian Journals, 1859-1862.* Leslie A. White (editor). The University of Michigan
       Press.

Morton, A. S.
  1939 *The Journal of Duncan M'Gillivary of the North West Company at Fort George on the
       Saskatchewan, 1794-5.* With introduction, notes, and appendix by Arthur S. Morton.
       Macmillan, Toronto.

Newcomb, Thomas P.
  1967 Some fact and much conjecture concerning the Sun River medicine wheel, Teton
       County, Montana. *Archaeology in Montana* 8(1):17-23.

Nicholson, B. A.
  1980 Delta Head. Seasonal report written for Manitoba Historic Resources. Manuscript on
       file with the author, Brandon, Manitoba.

Nye, Wilbur Sturtevant
  1962 *Tales of the Kiowa.* University of Oklahoma Press, Norman.

Oliver, Symmes C.
  1962 *Ecology and Cultural Continuity as Contributing Factors in the Social Organization of the
       Plains Indians.* University of California Press, Berkley and Los Angeles.

Ossenburg, N. S.
  1974 Origins and relationships of Woodland peoples: The evidence of cranial morphology.
       In: *Aspects of Upper Great Lakes Anthropology*, ed. by E. Johnson, pp. 15-39. Minnesota
       Historical Society, St. Paul.

Over, W. H.
  1941 Indian picture writing in South Dakota. University of South Dakota Museum,
       Archaeological Studies, Circular IV:44-54.

Paget, Amelia M.
  1909 *The People of The Plains.* Ryerson Press, Toronto.

Parsons, Elsie Clews
   1939 *Pueblo Indian Religion, Volume I*. University of Chicago Press, Chicago.

Peck, Trevor
   2002 Archaeologically recovered ammonites: evidence for continuity in Nitsitapii ritual. *Plains Anthropologist* 47(181):147-164.

Peske, G. R.
   1966 Oneota settlement patterns and agricultural patterns in Winnebago County. *Wisconsin Archaeologist* 47:188-195.

Pohorecky, Zenon
   1979 Faces Carved on Boulders in Southern Saskatchewan. Unpublished paper presented at 23rd International Congress of Americanists, Vancouver, BC, August 16. Copy on file in library of Saskatchewan Archaeological Society, Saskatoon

Powell, Peter J.
   1969 *Sweet Medicine*. University of Oklahoma Press, Norman.

Prufer, Olaf
   1965 *The McGraw Site, a Study of Hopewellian Dynamics*. Scientific Publications of the Cleveland Museum of Natural History 4(1):1-144.

Quaife, M. M.
   1926 *Yellowstone Kelly, The Memoirs of Luther S. Kelly*. Yale University Press, New Haven.

Quigg, Michael J.
   1984 *Medicine Wheel Descriptions for the Northwestern Plains*. Alberta Culture, Archaeological Survey of Alberta. Edmonton, Alberta.

Quimby, George I.
   1968 Habitat, culture, and archaeology. In: *Man in Adaptation, The Biosocial Background*, ed. by Yehudi A. Cohen, pp. 291-296. Aldine Publishing Company, Chicago.

Ray, Arthur J.
   1974 *Indians in the Fur Trade: Their Role as Trappers, Hunters, and Middlemen in the Lands Southwest of Hudson Bay 1660-1870*. University of Toronto Press, Toronto.

Rea, Bayard D.
   1966 Rock alignments in central Wyoming – an introduction. *The Wyoming Archaeologist* 9(3):15-53.

Reeves, Brian O. K.
   1983 *Culture Change in The Northern Plains: 1000 B.C. – 1000 A.D.* Occasional Paper No. 20, Archaeological Survey of Alberta, Edmonton.

Richards, J. Howard
   1969 Physical features of Saskatchewan. In: *Atlas of Saskatchewan*, ed. by J. H. Richards and K. I. Fung, pp. 41-43. University of Saskatchewan, Saskatoon.

Richards, J. H. and K. I. Fung (editors)
   1969 *Atlas of Saskatchewan*. University of Saskatchewan, Saskatoon, Saskatchewan

Richardson, David H. S.
   1975 *The Vanishing Lichens*. Douglas, David and Charles Ltd., Newton Abbot, London, Vancouver.

Richardson, David H. S. and Colin M. Young
   1977 Lichens and vertebrates. In: *Lichen Ecology*, ed. by Mark R.D. Seaward, pp. 121-144.

Academic Press, New York.

Riley, Thomas J., Charles R. Moffat and Glen Freimuth
  1961 Prehistoric raised fields in the upper Midwestern United States, an innovation in response to marginal growing conditions. *North American Archaeologist* 2(2):101-116.

Ritzenthaler, Robert E.
  1963 The effigy mound builders in Wisconsin. *Lore Leaves* No. 9. Reprinted February, 1976. Milwaukee Public Museum.

Rodnick, David
  1937 Political structure and status among the Assiniboine Indians. *American Anthropologist* 39(3), part 1:408-416.

Romer, Alfred Sherwood
  1970 *The Vertebrate Body* (4th ed.). W. B. Saunders Company, Toronto.

Rood, Ronald J. and Vicki Overholser Rood
  1983 Report of the Class I and II Cultural Resources Investigations of a Portion of the Cendak Water Project Area, Eastern South Dakota. Volume II. Report on file with the South Dakota Archaeological Resource Center.

Russell, Dale R.
  1991 *Eighteenth-Century Western Cree and Their Neighbours.* Archaeological Survey of Canada Mercury Series Paper 143. Canadian Museum of Civilization, Ottawa.

Rutkowski, Chris and Guy Westcott
  1979 The Alonsa petroform. *Winnicentrics* 18(9):4-7. Royal Astronomical Society of Canada, Winnipeg.

Schlesier, Karl
  1987 *The Wolves of Heaven: Cheyenne Shamanism, Ceremonies, and Prehistoric Origins.* University of Oklahoma Press, Norman.
  2002 On the Big Horn Medicine Wheel: a comment on Matthew Liebmann, *Plains Anthropologist* 47-180:61-71. *Plains Anthropologist* 47-183:387-392.

Schultz, James Willard
  1978 *Why Gone Those Times?* Edited and with an introduction by Eugene Lee Silliman. University of Oklahoma Press, Norman.
  1980 *Blackfeet and Buffalo.* Edited with an introduction by Keith C. Seele. University of Oklahoma Press, Norman.

Setzler, Frank M.
  1952 Seeking the secret of the giants. *National Geographic* (3):390-404.

Sewell, J. H.
  1944 The Vigfusson Collection and Field Notes. Unpublished manuscript on file, Royal Saskatchewan Museum, Regina, Saskatchewan.

Sheard, J. W.
  1974 The genus *Dimelaena* in North America north of Mexico. *The Bryologist* 77(2):128-141.
  1977 Paleogeography, chemistry and taxonomy of the lichenized ascomycetes *Dimelaena* and *Thamnolia. The Bryologist* 80(1):100-118.

Simms, S. C.
  1903a A wheel-shaped stone monument in Wyoming. *American Anthropologist* 5(1):107-110.
  1903b A Crow monument to shame. *American Anthropologist* 5:374.

Skeels, L. L. M.
  1967 Location of the Indian Tribes at First White Contact. Unpublished Master's thesis, University of Calgary, Calgary, Alberta.
Skinner, Alanson
  1914 *Political Organization, Cults and Ceremonies of the Plains Cree.* American Museum of Natural History Anthropological Papers 11(Pt. 6). New York.
Spencer, Robert F., Jesse D. Jennings, Charles E. Dibble, Elden Johnson, Arden R. King, Theodore Stern, Kenneth M. Stewart, Omer C. Stewart, William J. Wallace
  1965 *The Native Americans.* Harper & Row, Publishers, New York.
Squier, E. G. and E. H. Davis
  1973 *Ancient Monuments of The Mississippi Valley* (Comprising the results of extensive original surveys and explorations with a new introduction by James B. Griffin). American Museum Society Press, Inc., New York.
Stands In Timber, John and Margot Liberty
  1967 *Cheyenne Memories.* Yale University Press, New Haven.
Stebbins, Robert C.
  1951 *Amphibians of Western North America.* University of California Press, Berkeley.
Steinbring, Jack
  1970 The Tie Creek boulder site of southeastern Manitoba. In: *Ten Thousand Years: Archaeology in Manitoba,* ed. by W. Hlady, pp. 223-268. Manitoba Archaeological Society, Winnipeg.
  1980 *An Introduction to Archaeology on the Winnipeg River.* Papers in Manitoba Archaeology, Miscellaneous Paper No. 9, Department of Cultural Affairs and Historic Resources, Winnipeg.
Steward, Julian H.
  1955 *Theory of Culture Change.* University of Illinois Press, Urbana.
Stoltman, James B.
  1979 Middle woodland stage communities of southwestern Wisconsin. In: *Hopewell Archaeology,* ed. by David S. Brose and N'omi Greber, pp. 122-139. The Kent State University Press. Kent, Ohio.
Sutton, Richard W.
  1965 The Whiteshell boulder mosaics. *Manitoba Archaeological Newsletter* 2(1):3-10.
Swanton, John R.
  1952 *The Indian Tribes of North America.* Smithsonian Institution, Bureau of American Ethnology, Bulletin 185.
Syms, E. Leigh
  1970 Unpublished field notes. On file with the author.
  1977 *Cultural Ecology and Ecological Dynamics of the Ceramic Period in Southwestern Manitoba.* Plains Anthropologist 22(76) Part 2, Memoir 12.
  1982 Identifying prehistoric western Algonkians: a holistic approach. In: *Approaches to Algonkian Archaeology,* ed. by Margaret G. Hanna and Brian Kooyman, pp. 1-34. Chacmool, The Archaeological Association of the University of Calgary, Calgary, Alberta.

172 REFERENCES

Tamplin, Morgan J.
  n.d. An Investigation of Stone Features Near Dand, Manitoba. Unpublished manuscript on
    file with the author.
Tarasoff, Koozma J.
  1980 *Persistent Ceremonialism: The Plains Cree and Saulteaux.* National Museum of Man
    Mercury Series, Canadian Ethnology Service, Paper No. 69, Ottawa.
Terrell, John Upton
  1975 *The Plains Apache.* Thomas Y. Crowell Company, New York.
Thomas, David Hurst
  1976 *Figuring Anthropology.* Holt, Rinehart, and Winston, New York.
Thomas, Davis and Karin Ronnefeldt (editors)
  1976 *People of the First Man: Life among the Plains Indians in Their Final Days of Glory, The
    Firsthand Account of Prince Maximilian's Expedition up the Missouri River, 1833-34.* Clarke,
    Irwin & Co. Ltd., Toronto and Vancouver. 2nd Edition.
Thompson, David
  1916 *David Thompson's Narrative of His Explorations in Western America, 1784-1812.* J. B.
    Tyrrell (editor). Champlain Society Publication No. 12, Toronto.
Thwaites, R. G. (editor)
  1959 *The Jesuit Relations and Allied Documents, Volume 18.* Reprinted edition. Greenwood
    Press, New York.
  1969 *Original Journals of the Lewis and Clark Expedition, 1804-1806, Volume 6.* Arno Press,
    New York.
Todd, J. E.
  1886 Boulder mosaics in Dakota. *The American Naturalist* 20(1):1-4.
Turney-High, Harry Holbert
  1941 *Ethnography of the Kutenai.* American Anthropological Association Memoir 56.
Tyyska, Allen Edwin and James A. Burns
  1973 *Archaeology From North Bay to Mattawa.* Ontario Ministry of Natural Resources,
    Research Report 2. Historic Sites Branch, Toronto.
Umfreville, Edward
  1954 *The Present State of Hudson's Bay.* Edited with an introduction by W. Stewart Wallace.
    Ryerson Press, Toronto.
Underhill, Ruth Murray
  1953 *Red Man's America.* The University of Chicago Press, Chicago.
Vickers, J. Rod
  2003 Napi figures: Boulder outline effigies on the Plains. In: *Archaeology in Alberta: A View
    from the New Millenium,* ed. by Jack W. Brink and John F. Dormaar, pp. 242-254.
    Archaeological Society of Alberta, Medicine Hat.
Walker, Ernest G.
  1988 The archaeological resources of the Wanuskewin Heritage Park. In: *Out of the Past:
    Sites, Digs and Artifacts in the Saskatoon Area,* ed. by Urve Linnamae and Tim E. H.
    Jones, pp. 75-89. Saskatoon Archaeological Society, Saskatoon.
Watetch, Abel
  1959 *Payepot and His People.* Modern Press, Saskatoon, Saskatchewan.

Watson, Gilbert C.

   1972 Jelly Ranch medicine wheel EeNg-1. *Saskatchewan Archaeological Newsletter* 37:18.

   1974 Medicine wheel near Canuck, Saskatchewan. *Saskatchewan Archaeological Newsletter* 45:6.

   1975 Research report 1974. *Saskatchewan Archaeological Newsletter* 49:16-24.

   1976 Cabri Lake human effigy. *Saskatchewan Archaeological Newsletter* 52(1):17.

Webber, Alika Podolinsky

   1964 Divination rites. *The Beaver*, Summer:40-41.

Webber, P. J. and J. T. Andrews

   1973 Lichenometry: a commentary. *Arctic and Alpine Research* 5(4):295-302.

Wedel, Mildred Mott and Raymond J. DeMallie

   1980 The ethnohistorical approach in Plains area studies. In: *Anthropology on the Great Plains*, ed. by W. Raymond Wood and Margot Liberty, pp. 110-128. University of Nebraska Press, Lincoln.

Wedel, Waldo R.

   1959 *An Introduction to Kansas Archaeology*. Smithsonian Institution. Bureau of American Ethnology, Bulletin 174. Washington, D.C.

   1961 *Prehistoric Man on the Great Plains*. University of Oklahoma Press, Norman.

Weist, Tom

   1977 *A History of the Cheyenne People*. Montana Council for Indian Education, Billings.

Wellman, Klaus F.

   1974 Some observations on human sexuality in North American Indian rock art. *Southwestern Lore* 40(1):1-12. Colorado Archaeological Society, Boulder.

Welsch, Peter H., Steven A. LeBlanc, Patrick T. Houlihan, and Paul E. Faulstich

   1984 People of the southwest. *Masterkey* 58(2):3-64.

Wildschut, William

   1960 Crow Indian medicine bundles. In: *Contributions from the Museum of the American Indian, Volume 17*, ed. by John C. Ewers. Heye Foundation, New York.

Will, George F.

   1921 An unusual group of mounds in North Dakota. *American Anthropologist* 23(2):175-179.

Willey, Gordon R.

   1966 *An Introduction to American Archaeology, Volume One: North and Middle America*. Prentice-Hall, Inc., New York.

Wilson, Michael

   1981 Sun Dances, Thirst Dances, and medicine wheels: A Search for Alternative Hypotheses. In: *Megaliths to Medicine Wheels, ed. by* M. Wilson, Kathie L. Road, and Kenneth J. Hardy, pp. 333-370. Chacmool, The Archaeological Association of the University of Calgary, Calgary.

Winchell, N. H.

   1911 *Aborigines of Minnesota, Based on the Collections of Jacob V. Brower, and on the Field Surveys and Notes of Alfred J. Hill and Theodore H. Lewis, 1909-1911*. The Minnesota Historical Society, St. Paul.

Wissler, Clark

   1913 *Societies and Dance Associations of the Blackfoot Indians*. Anthropological Papers of the

American Museum of Natural History 11 (Pt. IV):359-460.

1927 *North American Indians of the Plains*. American Museum of Natural History, Handbook Series No. 21 (Third Edition). New York.

1947 *Star Legends among the American Indians*. American Museum of Natural History, Guide Leaflet Series, No. 91. New York.

Woolhouse, H. W.

1968 The measurement of growth rates in lichens. *Lichenologist* 4:32-33.

Wormington, H. M. and R. G. Forbis

1965 *An Introduction to the Archaeology of Alberta, Canada*. Denver Museum of Natural History Proceedings, 11. Denver.

Wreschner, Ernst E.

1980 Red ochre and human evolution: a case for discussion. *Current Anthropology* 21(5):631-644.